Jacob

Kathmandu, Nov '96

The Islamic State

By the Same Author

The Bohras

The Islamic State

Asghar Ali Engineer

VIKAS PAPERBACKS
a division of
VIKAS PUBLISHING HOUSE PVT LTD

VIKAS PUBLISHING HOUSE PVT LTD
576, Masjid Road, Jangpura, New Delhi-110 014

First Paperback Edition, 1994

Printed at Kay Kay Printers, Delhi - 110006.

Preface

The nature and scope of the Islamic State has been brought into sharp focus by the current developments in the Islamic world. The rulers of the Islamic countries very loosely use the term Islamic State or Islamic Revolution and no doubt, more than anything else, they are motivated by their own political considerations in using these terms specially as the religion of Islam has a powerful appeal to the peoples of these countries. In my opinion the holy Quran which is the source book of all the Islamic teachings does not spell out any fixed form of state; instead it strongly urges on the establishment of a just and egalitarian society.

I have attempted in this book to trace out the origin and growth of Islamic State tthrough various historical periods so as to demonstrate that even among the highest authorities on Islam there has never been any fixed or universally acceptable form of Islamic State. As for the nature of the Islamic polity the Quran lays due emphasis on Shura' (consultation) thus clearly indicating that the nature of Islamic policy is democratic in spirit. For Shura' too Quran does not specify any concrete institutional form leaving it to the Muslim peoples of different ages and countries to evolve according to their historical conditions. I maintain that the concrete form of State—whether Islamic or otherwise—depends more on the class forces and property relations in a particular historical epoch than on anything else. The changes which the concept of Islamic State underwent, the changes in historical conditions and property relations clearly demonstrate this. I have also tried to analyse in this book the causes of a current Islamic upsurge sweeping through the countries of the Middle East. It is for the readers to decide whether I have been able to present my thesis forcefully and convincingly or not.

Contents

Introduction

Almost all the Muslim countries belong to what is called the third world. Located in Asia and Africa, most of these countries are poor and backward. Today few Arab countries have, on account of their oil wealth, comparatively better resources to develop. The oil weapon, increasingly used by the Arab countries since the Arab-Israel war of 1973, has brought more political awareness among the Arab masses. The political developments during late seventies and eighties in Iran too, fall into this pattern. This heightened political awareness among the Muslim peoples is bound to create certain problems and new areas of tension.

The ruling classes in these countries are not interested in any radical change in the society, much less in the redistribution of national wealth. They are, on the contrary, quite keen to preserve the status-quo which, in case of these Muslim countries, mean, more often than not, preserving the medieval social order. The oil revolution, therefore, in the form of increased political awareness has posed new challenges before the ruling classes in these Muslim countries. As the traditional Islam, with all its medieval trappings, hold great appeal for the Muslim peoples of these countries, the ruling classes are trying to meet the new challenges by reinvigorating some of the medieval practices of the traditional Islamic societies. A section of Muslims, especially in countries like Algeria are lending support to the fundamentalist movements.

Some of these countries have declared themselves as the Islamic states not by reactivating the core-values of early Islam but by proclaiming imposition of certain punishments prescribed by Islam like cutting off hands of thieves or stoning adulterers or adulteresses to death. In these self-proclaimed Islamic states women are also subjected to more restrictions like wearing veil or *chador* compulsorily, confining themselves to the domestic chores, etc. Thus we see that by declaring such peripheral measures (these punishments called *uqubāt* are, after all, not central to the teachings of Islam; punishments, mild or strong, certainly cannot be a substitute for the central vision of a society), countries governed by military dictatorship, on the one hand, and, those ruled by monarchs on the other, consider themselves to be the Islamic countries.

Recently some Muslim countries did proclaim themselves to be Islamic countries by imposing the Islamic criminal code. These countries had varied socio-political system. Can they be considered as having the Islamic state simply by virtue of having imposed the Islamic criminal code? This question is fundamental and cannot be answered right away without taking the complete socio-economic and political situation into consideration. Yet, most of the people are treating this question superficially, the developments in Iran aroused unusual interest in the Western countries and articles with banner headlines like "Militant Islam on the March," or "The Soldiers of Allah Advance" appeared in the leading papers of these countries. These articles, needless to say, were written with journalistic flavour lacking proper understanding or in-depth analysis. Some articles were no better than an information package.

Thus in an article published in *The Economist*, on this subject entitled "Soldiers of Allah Advance" the author observes :

> 'Another reason for the aliveness of Islam today is that, as a religion and a society, it has never been allowed to relax or to become hidebound or fossilised. From its earliest years Islam has been under challenge, political spiritual and cultural, from the Christian west. The political and cultural challenge has been at its most intense, and inescapable, in the past hundred years.' 'How very different the history of Islam would have been', the author raises the question, 'how much more like the history of Buddhism, if its original home had been, say, Indonesia. On its home ground at the cross-roads of three continents, hard up against an expanding Europe, Islam has had to be vigilant in self-defence.[1]

Further on the author of the above article feels that :

The most serious challenge to all Islamic countries today is on the plane of culture, the world-wide 'culture' of the materialistic affluent society

[1]Militant Islam, *Soliders of Allah Advance*, *Business Standard*, 4 February 1979, reproduced from *The Economist*.

> drugs and pop music and pornography, the corroding acids of modernity. In this sense Islam rejects the west as a source of decadence and muddled values. And the more so when the local political allies of the west tend to be unrepresentative, dissolute or repressive rulers, and the local economic partners of western multi-national companies are grasping and corrupt. Against them Islam seems to provide certainty of belief and correctitude of behaviour.[2]

Many western observers were baffled by the fact that the younger generation of some Islamic countries were enthusiastically taking to the traditional ways, some young women even taking to wearing *chador* (veil) which their mothers once had given up in favour of mini-skirts. But these observers, as is quite clear from the extracts of the article quoted above lack understanding of the socio-economic forces and forces of human faith moulding various events in the society of temporary or permanent nature. They jump to hurried conclusions from the superficial observation of socio- political phenomenon. The talk of Islamic revivalism or militant Islam on the march is a result of such a superficial understanding. Or, what is more probable, it is a deliberate move on the part of certain Western powers to encourage revivalist forces in the Arab world (the countries of the middle- east are both economically and politically very important and sensitive) in order to preserve the present social order which is being increasingly threatened by radical and revolutionary forces.

In view of its world-wide significance and use and abuse of the concept of Islamic state, it is necessary to clearly understand as to what it is all about. Theoretically speaking no two *'ulamā* (traditional scholars of Islam) agree on the interpretation of this concept, even in broad outline, much less in details. The Prophet himself did not leave behind any comprehensive theory of the Islamic state; certain of his practices and sayings provided guidelines to the Caliphs who followed him. But the four pious Caliphs over a period of 30 years faced vastly different and much more complex situation on account of rapid victories the Muslim armies won over the territories of the Roman and Sassanid empires. The Islamic rule during the Prophet's time was confined to the Arabian peninsula which was mostly inhabited by nomadic tribes and hence he did not have to face very complex problems as the later Caliphs did.

The Caliphs themselves had to resort to innovations (*bid'ah*) to run the

[2] *Ibid.*

government in the changing situation as it was possible to find precedence for many things in the Prophet's practice. They also resorted to the practice of *ijtihad* (literally exertion or creative interpretation) while facing new situations and problems as per the Prophet's advice to M'adh bin Jabal whom he had deputed to Yemen. It would, therefore, be necessary to examine the historical developments during and immediately after the death of the Prophet to understand the early character of the Islamic state. There have been widely different interpretations of various events and bloody episodes which took place after the death of the second Caliph 'Umar as the civil war broke out and near chaotic situation developed. These episodes, although involving doctrinal differences and disputes, have important bearings over the development of the theory of Islamic state and hence will be dealt with in the first two chapters of this book. Needless to say, we will not be interested in doctrinal or sectarian differences; we will be dealing with those aspects which have important bearings on the theory and practice of an Islamic state.

The period of glorious caliphate lasted only for 30 years. With the passing of the reigns of government in the hands of Mu'awiyah, the basic character of the Islamic state underwent fundamental transformation. Now it became a dynastic rule and caliph became a monarch. Moreover, with more conquests and consequently more recruitments the weight of armed forces gradually increased. This brought about a fundamental change in the structure of the government. The composition of the ruling classes also changed with mercantile class losing influence and bureaucracy, landed aristocracy and military officers gaining the upper hand. Despite the Abbasid caliphs' religious pretensions, the nature of the caliphate no longer remained theocratic. However, it was no new development as the Umayyad rule itself was more of Arab national rule (with many pagan Arab customs having been revived) than Islamic rule. For all practical purposes the Islamic rule had come to an end after the initial 30-year period.

All these developments naturally caused embarrassment and unrest among the *'ulamā*, the theoreticians of Islamic ideology. Some of them considered the Umayyad and Abbasid regimes as un-Islamic and kept away from them. But such *'ulamā* were far and few in between. A large number of them reconciled themselves with the contemporary realities and tried to modify the theory of Islamic state to suit the exigencies of the situation. Among them were Abu Yusuf (he wrote his famous book *Kitāb al-Kharaj*) and Al-Ghazali (we find his views on the nature of Islamic rule scattered in many of his books specially hīs *al-iqtisad fī-al-I'tiqad*). Nizam al-Mulk, who rose from secretarial rank to be the Prime Minister of the Abbasid caliph and is an example of neo-Sassanid extremism in his political views. After disintegration of the Abbasid empire various independent Muslim states came into existence. The rulers of these states were secular monarchs and hardly had any pretensions of holding power by virtue of religious sanction. These rulers called themselves as *Zill-e-ilahi* (shadow of God) unlike Abbasid caliphs who insisted on being addressed as Amir al-Mu'minin (commander of the faithfuls). There was nothing Islamic about these states except the selective enforcement of the Islamic shari'ah. It would be interesting to throw light on the theories of Islamic state or simply "state" of the Muslim thinkers of the medieval period. This will help us in understanding the nature of transformation which took place in the structure and functioning of state in the Islamic world.

The Muslim states, hardly different from other states in structure and functioning, continued in a state of decadence till many of them came under the sway of colonial powers during the 19th century. The impact of western colonial rule had an unsettling effect on these traditional Muslim societies. Different classes of people responded differently to the shattering challenges. The Pan-Islamic movement of Jamaluddin Afghani was a reaction to this humiliating situation. However, Afghani's movement was not totally past-oriented; it was an attempt by him to unite the Muslim countries smarting under the colonial rule to fight against it. He stood for the progressive interpretation of Islam and fought against medieval sloth. His political disciple, Muhammad 'Abduh, the grand mufti of Egypt, launched a powerful reform movement and fought against the British colonialism in Egypt. The resistance to the colonial rule also took the form of revivalist movements in these Islamic countries. The Mahdist uprising of the Sudan, the Fara'idi movement of Bengal in India, etc. fall into this category. These movements cannot just be disposed of as religious aberrations but need to be properly analysed in terms of socio-economic forces and political situation.

The First World War brought about a total disintegration of the Uthmani Sultanate and created national awareness among the Arabs who were under its domination. In fact this was the beginning of formation of nation states in the Muslim world. The Khilafat movement which was aimed at the establishment of Uthmani rule over the Muslim world proved a mere aberration and was soon abandoned by its enthusiasts when the Young Turks themselves abolished caliphate and established a modern nation state. Thus it will be seen that despite international moorings of Islamic ideology, nation states came to be established as the new productive forces and production relations made this development inevitable. Today, despite the talk of Islamic brotherhood, the Muslim world stands divided into nation states. It is necessary to understand various forces which have brought this compelling reality into being despite strong ideological opposition to it.

Today, most of the Muslim countries belong to the third world and are poor and backward. Till the late sixties there was not much development in these countries. Nasser took a bold stand against the black-mail by American imperialism and nationalized the Suez canal. His political philosophy which was basically inspired by the ideal of Arab nationalism, gave new inpetus to the radical forces in the Arab world. Though a devout Muslim, he preferred Arab nationalism to the concept of Islamic brotherhood as he well understood the realities of the modern world. The Arab Ba'ath party also lays emphasis on the Arab unity and not on the unity of the Muslim world. The Ba'ath Party which stands for socialism (not necessarily for Marxian variety of socialism) and anti-imperialism is ruling in Iraq and Syria. The Ikhwan al-Muslimin (the Muslim Brotherhood), a revivalist movement, on the other hand, has so far remained peripherial in the Arab politics.

Nasser's open confrontation with imperialism and Zionism gave a sense of pride and self-assurance to the Arabs. The Muslim Brotherhood, on the other hand, advocating Islamic revivalism, always remained a tool in the hands of status-quoists who wanted to preserve feudal order with the help of imperialist powers. When the young Nasser overthrew the decrepit rule of King Farooq in 1952, the Muslim Brotherhood went on the rampage. Mr Anwar Abdel-Malek, an Egyptian intellectual, says in his book *Egypt—Military Society*:

> On the morrow of Friday, January 25, 1952--when British armour took its heavy toll of Egyptian lives in Ismailia—Cairo was set on fire by select activist groups, which were later identified in the (unpublished) trial proceedings as belonging to the extreme right in league with various forces intent on blocking the path of the rising United National Front...[3]

The Saudi monarch who prides himself with enforcement of Islamic

[3]Anouar Abdel-Malek, *Egypt—Military Society*, Vintage Books, New York, 1968, see the preface.

* But present as an extra parliamentary force, usually ruthlessly suppressed. cf: Egypt, Syria (HAMA 1982)

shari'ah in his regime (and by implication claims it to be an Islamic state) has always been very close to the USA and in the forefront to curb the movements aimed at radical socio-economic transformation in the Arab world. The Saudi monarch tried to prop up the Imam Badr of Yemen when the people's revolt broke out against him in the early sixties. King Saud wanted to sustain the theocracy of Imam Badr in order to stem the tide of change both political as well as social. Saudi Arabia sought the American support though it knew very well that the Zionist state of Israel was the outpost of American imperialism. Saudi Arabia was similarly backing up North Yemen in its fight against the Marxist regime of South Yemen. While the Arab left stands for the Arab unity, Saudi Arabia and the Muslim Brotherhood talk of Islamic unity. Nasser, although a devout Muslim himself, never took the talk of Islamic unity seriously and brusquely brushed it aside when suggested by the Saudi monarch late 'Abd al-'Aziz.

Thus we see that the concept of Islamic state is not mere theocratic one but involves basic questions of political alignments and socio-economic transformation in the modern industrial era. We propose to deal with these fundamental questions while examining the claims of those advocating Islamic theocracy in the modern world. It can be pointed out here, before we undertake detailed analysis in the subsequent chapters, that not the countries championing the cause of Islamic state but modern and left oriented countries have drawn up plans to effect basic transformation in their social structures. No Muslim country as yet has produced strong bourgeois class to undertake the task of industrialization and modernization. Despite certain changes in the superstructure (as a result of graft and not organic growth), most of these countries still live in the middle ages. It is, therefore, all the more necessary to concretely define the concept of Islamic state whether it is embodiment and continuation of these medieval practices or is it capable of interpretation conducive to re-structuring of society in keeping with the principles of social justice in an industrial society. The conservative forces in the Islamic world, it must be admitted, have a definite edge over those advocating radical socio-economic changes so far as the sanctified religious beliefs and practices are concerned. Maxime Rodinson observes :

> Already we can see that the ruling strata will make use of Islam to give religious endorsement to their conservative attitudes. They have plenty of facilities for doing that. It is open to them, as it is not to the 'progres-

> sives,' to appeal to tradition. True, the archaic traditions that prevail in ways of life and social relations have, historically, nothing specifically Muslim about them. But they have been sanctified by Islam, and it is easy to mobilize religious fanaticism, however lacking in justification this may be, against those who would interfere with them. The ruling classes have ways of influencing ministers of religion, to whom independence and economic progress make it possible to give a place among the privileged, rescuing them from the poverty (and closeness to the masses) to which the colonial regimes often confined many of them.[4]

And then Rodinson concludes :

> In this event, Islam will be a barrier against the rise of the forces of change, and this barrier will not hold. It will suffer a crisis like that of Christianity in the nineteenth century, and this despite the extra strength it will draw from its role as a national religion.[5]

What is happening in the Islamic world today is much more complex than predicted by Maxime Rodinson. The struggle between conservative forces and progressive ones goes on what the progressives seem to be loosing out for the present at least. In Iran the Muslim clergy had captured power and though earlier extremism is not to be seen, but still they seem to be retaining it. Rafsanjani, the President of Iran, is not a theologian himself, but needs the support of prominent Ayatullahs to rule. Rafsanjani is a moderate person and seems to be inclining towards west. We no longer hear the epithet "great Satan" for America anymore from Iran. Iran cannot do without western aid for its industrial development. It had to temper its extremism. In South Yemen too the revolution has petered out and it has merged with conservative North. Algeria is in trouble from the Islamic militants. Syria there seems to be no change and Iraq is being pounded and had to emphasise its Islamic identity and compromise its left of the centre policy. In Afghanistan the left revolution has petered out and right wing Islamic parties have captured power. The course of history is proving to be too complex and cannot be determined by any ideological frame-work, whether of the right or of the left. Both Iran as well as Afghanistan on two opposite poles, illustrate it best.

[4]Maxime Rodinson, *Islam and Capitalism*, Allen Lane, 1974, pp. 232-33.
[5]*Ibid.*, p. 233.

In Islamic countries undoubtedly there is great pull of Islam and Islamic culture. There is anti-west mood among the people. The rise of Islamic militancy in number of countries like Egypt and Algeria will bear this out. But it is also difficult to say that the Islamic militancy will finally triumph. Islamic militancy attracts people when not in power. But it runs into serious problems once it assumes power. It too is unable to solve complex socio-economic problems. Iran, as pointed out above, had to moderate its policies after a few years of extremism. In Pakistan too Zia apparently resorted to Islam but soon after his death Islamic parties found themselves seriously weakened. Moderate leaders like Benazir Bhutto and Nawaz Sharif came to power. In the recently held elections (October, 1993) Islamic parties were nearly rejected by the electorate. They could manage to get only a couple of seats. But, on the other hand, in Egypt, Algeria etc., Islamic militancy being in opposition seems to be in ascendency as it does not have to share any responsibility of power. However in the prevailing situation in the Islamic countries, one cannot ignore, or even trifle with, the force that religion is. Islam, specially for the Arabs, is coterminous with nationalism.

Constantine Zurayk, a liberal Christian Arab nationalist feels that,

> The Arabs need a sense of collective responsibility, a feeling of belonging to a nation, but one of a special sort: a nation which draws its inspiration from a religion. For the Arabs this religion can only be Islam.[6]

Similarly Michel Aflaq, another Christian Arab and the founding leader of the Ba'ath Party says in one of his speeches,

> Where there is Islam, there is Arabism and its brilliance, since it is not possible to separate one from the other. Islam is the spirit of Arabism and forms the personality of the Arab nation. With the advent of Islam, the Arab nationalism entered a new matured and decisive stage. It could even be said that it was created with this great historic event....The strength of Islam is derived from the power of the Arab nation, and vise [vice] versa.[7]

The Arab-Israel conflict has further accentuated the feelings of Arab

[6] Tareq Y. Ismael, *The Arab Left*, Syracuse University Press, 1976, p.4
[7] See Mr Michel Aflaq's speech in *Iraq Today*, nos. 86 and 87, vol. iv, April 1-30, 1979, p.5.

nationalism. The humiliating defeat of the Arabs more than once at the hands of the Zionists has created an acture situation. According to Constantine Zurayk the need for fundamental modernization of Arab modes of thought, action and life was made urgent by the threat of Zionist expansion. Nothing, he asserted, was more dangerous to the Arabs than this threat. The basic danger did not lie in the innate superiority of one people over another. The Zionists, he maintained, live in the present and for the future, while the Arabs continue to dream the dreams of the past and to stupefy themselves with their fading glory.[8]

The problem of resurgence of Islam has to be understood from this angle also. The oil was used as a weapon by the Arabs in their struggle against imperialism and Zionism for the first time after the Arab-Israel war of 1973. The oil revolution gave the Arabs a new sense of pride vis-a- vis the western countries who had subjugated them and strengthened the hands of Israel. The initiative for using oil as a weapon against imperialism and Zionism, it must be remembered, came from the countries ruled by the left parties. The conservative Arab countries like Saudi Arabia were pro-America and were reluctantly dragged along. Nevertheless, it brought about a new awakening among the Arab peoples and one of its corollaries was resurgence of Islam, it being, as pointed out above, coterminous with the Arab nationalism. However, it has produced a highly complex situation in the Arab world today with contradictory pulls and pressures. This also needs to be analyzed in the context of the forces generated by the new developments after the 1973 Arab-Israel and 1991 Gulf war in order to understand this phenomenon which is so loosely talked about in the press today. This book is an attempt in that direction.

[8] Tareq Y. Ismael, op. cit., p.5. Mr Ismael has given Zurayk's quotation from his book *The Meaning of Disaster*, translated by R. Bayly Winder, Beirut, Khayyat's College Book Cooperative, 1956, p.34.

Khayyat's, Rue Bliss nr. AUB Ras Beirouth ?

1. Islamic State--Its Origin and Evolution

In and around Mecca, the birthplace of Islam, the institution of State, before and immediately after the birth of Islam, was unknown. Mecca, on the eve of the birth of Islam, was emerging as a centre of international commerce and complex financial operations. Thus, Professor W. Montgomery Watt, a noted Islamist, says:

> Mecca was more than a mere trading centre, it was a financial centre....But it is clear that financial operations of considerable complexity were carried on at Mecca. The leading men of Mecca in Muhammad's time were, above all, financiers, skilful in the manipulation of credit, shrewd in their speculations, and interested in any potentialities of lucrative investment from Aden to Gaza or Damuscus. In the financial net that they had woven not merely were all the inhabitants of Mecca caught, but many notables of the surrounding also. The Quran appeared not in the atmosphere of the desert, but in that of high finance.[1]

However, the emerging urban conglomeration that was Mecca was surrounded by a vast desert called al-Rub'a al-Khāli. It was sparsely populated by the Bedouin Arabs who were nomads. Some of these nomads occasionally settled down in Mecca. Mecca, thus, lived in the shadow of tribal morality and traditions before the rise of Islam. Although commercial operations were taking place on ever growing scale in this mercantile town situated on an important international trade route, the new morality, concomitant to the new mercantile culture had not struck deep roots and was, as yet, in transitional phase. But, of course, the conflict between old and new moralities was already emerging on the surface and was causing considerable tension. The Prophet Muhammad, a perceptible observer of

[1] W. Montgomery Watt, *Mohommad at Mecca*, Oxford University Press, 1953, p.3.

* The Empty Quarter — a bit to the E & SE of Mecca.

the Meccan social scene, soon sensed the social malaise and spent long years in the cave of Hira in meditation. However, unlike other religious preachers, Muhammad's meditation in an isolated cave did not result in his renouncing the world or leading passive life.

The Prophet, after the revelation, as he sincerely believed, of God's message to him came back from the cave of Hira not only to preach but also to transform the old social structure. Muhammad, it must be remembered, was not, unlike many other preachers, interested in teaching individual morality within the old structure of society. His problematic was not innate individual morality alone; for him the moral problem was at the same time a social problem and hence his new morality could take shape only by transforming the old social structure. But the Meccan merchants would not listen to him as they thought, quite naturally, that he threatened their supremacy.

As pointed out above, Mecca—an important city on the international trade-route—had not developed an institution of State. Unlike the city states of Greece, there was neither an elected head nor the elected senators to run the administration of the city. No taxes were collected and neither the army nor the police existed as no repressive machinery was needed. It is little strange but true that although a powerful mercantile class had developed, state machinery to protect its interests was yet to evolve. The super-structure does not mechanically change with the change in the base. Yet it can be said that the conditions were ripe due to changes occurring in the economic base (from nomadism to mercantile capitalism) of the society for a state machinery to evolve. These socio-economic conditions led the Prophet, as we will see further, to establish in Arabia the hitherto unknown institution of State.

Until the rise of Islam tribal morality reigned supreme even in Mecca. Montgomery Watt says:

> The Meccans had retained the attitudes and social institutions appropriate to the life of the nomad in the desert, such as blood feuds and clan solidarity. Even if they had not been pure nomads for some time, they had remained sufficiently close to the desert to have preserved much of its outlook. The essential situation out of which Islam emerged was the contrast and conflict between the Maccans' nomadic outlook and attitudes and the new material (of economic) environment in which they found themselves.[2]

[2]W. Montgomery Watt, *Muhammad—Prophet and Statesman*, Oxford University Press, 1961, pp. 48-49.

The question then arises, in the absence of any governmental control, how social stability was ensured in the Meccan society? A decision making body called mala'a (senate) looked after these functions. However, it does not mean that the members of the senate were elected or that the majority decisions were implemented. Mala'a, in fact, comprised tribal chiefs called sheikhs. These sheikhs sat on the mala'a in Mecca and took unanimous decisions. Since the responsibility of enforcing the decision was on respective tribal chiefs, majority decision did not mean anything. Any tribal chief dissenting would mean non-implementation of decision within that tribe and hence it would have no universal validity. Therefore, all the decisions of the mala'a were unanimous and were implemented through the authority of their respective tribal chiefs. In Mecca, due to transformation of nomadic economy into mercantile economy, these sheikhs also happended to be wealthy merchants. Thus the mala'a, in a way, had become an instrument of oligopolists.

These tribal chiefs and other powerful individuals who had accumulated a great deal of wealth wanted to retain control over the mala'a. They deeply resented any one individual assuming preponderance either by himself or in league with a foreign power like the Byzantine or Sassanid empire. The early historians of Islam tell us how the Arab leaders of Mecca frustrated the attempt of a rich merchant to acquire the status of a ruler of Mecca. This incident described below throws interesting light on the political ethos of the upper strata of the Meccan society :

> 'Uthman b. Huwayrith, a merchant, entertained some ambitions of his own to achieve pre-eminent position with the help of a foreign power, in this case Byzantium. He adopted Christianity and received some measure of support. This was, perhaps, part of the Byzantine reaction to the Persian conquest of the south. But soon the wealthy merchants of Mecca became suspicious. The overt act which, it appears, led to the wreck of 'Uthman's scheme was his denunciation, as inspiring to kingship, by the person of his own clan of Asad, al-Aswad b. al-Muttalib. 'Uthman ultimately failed in his design.[3]

There are two aspects of this event which have important bearings. Firstly, the Arabs were quite conscious of their strong position as the suppliers of

[3]Asghar Ali Engineer, *The Origin and Development of Islam*, Orient Longman, 1979.

goods which were in great demand in Byzantium. The Byzantine rulers had their eye on the strategic trade route as well as the sources of supply. The Arabs, therefore, wanted to guard their political independence and looked upon with suspicion anyone who tried to establish contacts with foreign powers. Secondly, as pointed out earlier, the Meccan Arabs till then had strong tribal ethos and were, therefore, averse to the very idea of being ruled by any single individual. The institution of kingship cannot develop in such a society. It would be worthwhile to throw some light on the nature of Bedouin tribes which inhabited the desert around Mecca and Medina, the two important urban conglomerations.

Ibn Khaldun, the famous Arab historian observes about the Bedouins: "...that the Bedouins are a savage nation, fully accustomed to savgery and the things that cause it. Savagery has become their character and nature. They enjoy it, because it means freedom from authoriy and *no subservience* to leadership..."[4] (italics mine). The Meccan Arabs, in keeping with their tribal attitudes, resented subservience to any authority. The institution of mala'a was in keeping with their national genius. Even their vocabularly had no word for king. Ibn-Khurdadbeh, a Muslim historian, under the title, *Epithets of the Rulers of the World* gives the titles of different rulers of the world including Persia, Rome, Turk, China, India, Abbysinia etc. But there is no mention of Arabia (of course, in this we do not include South Arabia and northern buffer states on the borders of Byzantium and Persia) as no ruler existed there. The word *malik* was used for foreign kings.

Muhammad, the Prophet of Islam met with stiff resistance from the leaders of Mecca as they thought that if his claim as the Prophet of Allah was accepted then he would acquire preponderant position among them and such a status they were not prepared to acceed to any individual from amongst them, much less to a poor orphan boy who, by the prevailing notions of social status, did not measure upto them. Muhammad, as even his worst enemy realized, was a man of determination and future vision. He well understood the fact that the status quo cannot prevail for long in view of the changing economic relations. There was economic prosperity at the top but the poor and the weak were not being cared for and such a situation had created social tensions. The tribal practice required that the material possessions be distributed and not accumulated whereas mercantile logic pressed for accumulation of wealth and reinvestment of the surplus after consumption.

[4]Ibn Khaldun, *The Muqaddimah*, tr. by Rosenthal and abridged by N.J. Dawood, Princeton University Press, 1970, p.118.

H.A.R. Gibb observes:

> But there was darker side to the prosperity of Mecca. It displayed the familiar evils of a wealthy commercial society, extremes of wealth and poverty, an underworld of slaves and hirelings, and social class- barriers. It is clear from Muhammad's fervent denunciations of social injustice and fraud that this was one of the deep inner causes of his unsettlement. But the ferment within him did not break out in the preaching of social revolution; it was thrust instead into a religious channel and issued in a deep and unshakable conviction that he was called by God to proclaim to his fellow citizens the old warning of the Semitic prophets: Repent, for the judgment of God is at hand.[5]

Muhammad was deeply concerned with remedying the social malaise at Mecca. He had spent his childhood in a Bedouin tribe and he knew that the Bedouins did not accumulate wealth. He had also taken part in business operations and had accompanied trade caravans to Syria. He, therefore, knew the importance of this international commerce for the economy of Mecca. His spiritual experiences in the cave of Hira convinced him that the rich should spend part of their wealth for the welfare of the poor and weak if the social malaise had to be removed and peace ensured. Thus the early verses of the Quran, crisp and vigorous, exhort the Meccan rich and warn them: "Let no misers who hoard the gifts of Allah think that their avarice is good for them; it is nothing but evil. The riches which they have piled shall become their fetters on the Day of Resurrection. It is Allah who will inherit the heavens and the earth. He is cognizant of all your actions."[6]
Again in another verse the Quran warns :

> As for the unbelievers, neither their riches nor their children shall in the least protect them from His scourge. They are the heirs of Hell, and there they shall remain for ever. The wealth they spend in this world is like a freezing wind that smites the cornfields of men who have wronged themselves, laying them waste. Allah is not unjust to them; they are unjust to their own souls.[7]

[5]H.A.R. Gibb, *Muhammedanism*, Oxford University Press, 1969, p.17.
[6]The *Quran*, tr. by N.J. Dawood, *The Imrans*, Penguin Books, 1966, p.412.
[7]The *Quran*, *op. cit.*, p.406.

These Quranic verses clearly and unmistakably show that the unequal distribution of wealth in defiance of the tribal morality had created deep resentment among the poor and unprotected in the Meccan society. In the absence of any state machinery or law and order enforcing agency, the situation had become all the more delicate. An attempt was also made by some people in Mecca to form an association to protect the interests of the weak. Thus, to some extent, class solidarity was replacing the tribal solidarity. As the powerful merchants formed inter-tribal corporations, the deprived individuals also tried to form their own associations cutting across tribal boundaries. One such association was called Hilf al-Fudul (The League of the Virtuous). "Az-Zubair," says Muhammad Hamidullah, "the eldest uncle and head of the family of the Prophet, took the initiative of convening a public meeting, in the house of a venerated old rich man, 'Abdullah bin Jud'an, where it was decided to found an Order of Chivalry, the famous Ḫilf al-Fuḏūl, whose members swore to come to the help of any of every person oppressed in the town. The young Muhammad also participated enthusiastically in the ceremony of oath taking. Later, when he was recognized as a messenger of Gofficial, he used to say: I have attended the meeting to inaugurate Ḫilf al-Fuḏūl; I am not prepared to forgo this [honour] even against the whole herd of red camels, and even today if anybody calls me for help in the name of this order, I shall run to his help.'"[8]

Other scholars like Prof. Watt give a little different version of the formation of the League; but nevertheless, all of them agree that the league was formed to ensure justice to the weaker sections. From this it is not difficult to draw the conclusion that in view of the developing commercial economy in Mecca, an acute need was being felt for an agency (although there was no clear conception of state) which could, on the one hand, ensure some sort of social justice to the poor and weak and, on the other hand, maintain order in the society. Also, the expanding commercial operations with other countries created pressure for some kind of security system to ensure safe conduct of the goods involved in these transactions. Prof. Mohammad Habib observes :

> Maulana Shibli, the greatest biographer of the Prophet in our country, does not estimate the Prophet primarily as 'a man of affairs' on the ground

[8]Muhammad Hamidullah, *Muhammad Rasulullah*, Centre Culturel Islamique, Paris series no. 4, Hyderabad Deccan, 1974, p.7.

that he was essentially a spiritual and moral teacher. This is correct and no biography of the Prophet, however brief, can ignore a reference to his religious teachings. Still from the viewpoint of the growth of political institutions, the main work of the Prophet was the establishment of a '*security system*' for the whole of Arabia except the regions subordinate to Byzantine and Persia. It was rock on which his successors built.[9] (Italics mine.)

Prof. Mohammad Habib has pointed out two things: firstly, agreeing with Maulana Shibli, the great Indian biographer of the Prophet, he says that the Prophet was a spiritual and moral teacher; secondly—and this is what is most important from our point of view—that from the viewpoint of the growth of politcal institutions, his *main work* (emphasis supplied) was to have established a security system for the whole of Arabia. In other words the Prophet was the founder of the institution of state around Medina and Mecca to begin with which, later on, embraced whole of Arabia. However, it does not mean that the institution of state was totally unknown to the Arabs of Mecca, it was *non-existent* in that region as material conditions were not ripe until the middle of sixth century to give birth to it.

In the south of the Arabian peninsula was the region called Yemen which had known one of the oldest civilizations of the world. A few centuries before the rise of Islam, Yemen was highly prosperous and was ruled by the Himyarite kings. However, around four hundred years before Islam, according to Al-Isfahani, a tenth century historian, the dam of al-Ma'rib burst destroying forever the prosperity of that region. But it appears this breach was restored and according to Yaqut, another historian, the final catastrophe occurred after 542 A.D. and before 570. In his correspondence with Marx, Engels has also taken note of this fact :

This artificial fertilization of the land which immediately ceased when the irrigation system fell into decay, explains the otherwise curious fact that whole stretches which were once brilliantly cultivated are now waste and bare (Palmyra, Petra, the ruins in the Yemen, districts in Egypt, Persia and Hindustan); it explains the fact that one single devastating war could depopulate a country for centuries and strip it of whole civilization. Here too, I think, comes in the destruction of the South Arabian trade, before

[9] *A Comprehensive History of India*, Vol. V. *The Delhi Sultanate*, ed, by Mohammad Habib and Khaliq Ahmed Nizami, Delhi, 1970, p.4.

Mohammad, which you very rightly regard as one of the chief factors in the Mohammedan revolution.[10]

Thus we see that Yemen, on account of its agricultural base and sedentary population, had already developed the institution of state. The agricultural operations needed an irrigation system and that could be provided only by a strong central government and hence the institution of kingship in Yemen.

Similarly, along the fertile crescent in the north, two Arab states i.e. Ghassanids in the north-west and Lakhmidians in the north-east had come into existence. They were essentially buffer states for the Byzantine and Sassanid empires. Many legends about these two Arab states and their rulers were popular in and around Mecca. The Meccan merchants had to deal with the rulers of these states in connection with their trade caravans. It can thus be seen that in those parts of Arabia where agriculture was possible on a large scale and where it was the mainstay of economy supporting a large sedentary population, either an independent state ruled by some native dynasty as in Yemen or a client state as in the north-east or north-west Arabia had come into existence. Moreover, these states were on the periphery of the Arabian desert, not in its midst.

Mecca, the cradle of Islam, was, on the other hand, in the midst of the Arabian desert and no agriculture was possible there. Thus there was no scope for developing the institution of kingship or dynastic rule. Only lately the people settled around the sanctuary of Mecca built near a well (water is a rare commodity in a desert) had taken to commerce. On the eve of the emergence of Islam, Mecca had, as pointed out above, grown into a large centre of international commerce and there were quite a few rich merchants belonging to different tribes, especially to the tribe of Quraysh. However, the tribal traditions and commercial set-up were not congenial to the development of monarchy. The rich traders of Mecca jealously guarded their freedom and their right to have a say in the decision making process. Mala'a (a sort of senate), although a product of tribal type of democracy, was acceptable to these rich merchants as many of them being tribal chiefs themselves, had representation in it.

However, this institution was proving itself inadequate in the face of fast expanding commercial activities and the resulting complex situation

[10]Marx and Engels, *On Religion* Schocker Book, New York, 1967, pp.124-125.

wherein the lower sections of the society felt highly aggrieved as the earlier Meccan verses of the Quran quoted above clearly show. Moreover, in this complex situation, simple tribal traditions which did not admit of private property, could not have sufficed. More sophisticated laws governing property relations, inheritance, commercial contracts, and various other socio-juridical aspects were needed. Islam, during the course of its development in Mecca and Medina, precisely fulfilled this role. It laid down a broad framework of the laws governing personal and property relations. In fact, once the preponderant position of the Prophet was established, he became, in the vacuum that existed in the then Arabian society, the only source of guidance for his followers even in strictly personal and private matters. Any problem that arose between two individuals or an individual and the society, he was consulted and in all these matters his sayings and doings were meticulously recorded and followed. Thus grew the main corpus of the Islamic jurisprudence which forms the core of Islamic laws followed by the Muslims all over the world.

In Mecca the Prophet, after the proclamation of his divine mission, had no smooth sailing. The rich merchants of Mecca, as pointed out above, deeply resented emergence of any individual with preponderant position. Moreover, what irked them further was Muhammad's humbler social origin. Though born in the tribe of Quraysh, he belonged to a comparatively poorer clan of Hashim. What is more, he was an orphan under the protection of his grandfather. The Meccan rich did not reconcile to the idea of accepting the divine mission of an orphan of such a humble origin. In the commercial milieu of Mecca wealth had become a status symbol. Muhammad and his devoted followers were faced with severe persecution which gradually increased in intensity. We are not concerned with these details here. Suffice it may to say that when the Prophet could no longer tolerate the inhuman persecution of his followers, he decided to migrate to Medina--an oasis some 300 miles north of Mecca.

Medina, unlike Mecca, was not principally a commercial town although commercial operations were carried on mainly by the Jews on a limited scale as compared to Mecca. The principal inhabitants of this town were the tribes of Aws and Khazraj who, it appears, originally came from Yemen and the Jews belonging to the tribes of Banu-Nadir and Banu-Qurayzah.[11] The inter-tribal war between Aws and Khazraj had shattered the peace of

[11] Asghar Ali Engineer, *Islam-Muslims-India*, Lok Vangmaya Griha Ltd, Bombay, 1975, pp. 17-18.

this embattled town. Like Mecca, Medina was also without any state authority to enforce peace. The Jews who owned large tracts of date-palms in this oasis sometimes acted as the arbiters in this bitter dispute but, judging from the unhappy situation then prevailing in Medina it appears that they did not acquit themselves in an honourable way in discharge of their duty and acted in a partisan way. The people of Medina were, therefore, looking for someone who could bring relief to this war-torn town. Muhammad came to fulfil this role. However, it was not an easy task and the Prophet had to move very cautiously. As already pointed out, there was no legitimately constituted authority in the town. He, therefore, took steps to set-up such an authority with due sanction of the various constituents of the Medinese population. He drew up a constituion.

The constitution, federal in nature, had multiple clauses in order to accommodate various groups and their interests. Ibn Hisham has this to say about the constitution :

> Ibn Ishaq said that the Messenger of God drew up an agreement between the immigrants and the helpers (and) in which the Jews were also included. They (i.e. the Jews) were allowed to follow their religion and retain their properties. Some conditions were laid down on them and they were allowed some conditions. (The document began) In the name of God, the Merciful, the Compassionate. This is a writing of Muhammad the prophet between the believers and Muslims of Quraysh and Yathrib (i.e. Medina) and those who follow them and are attached to them and who crusade along with them. They are a single community distinct from other people. The Jews would share the expenses with the Muslims so long as they fight. The Jews of Bani 'Auf would constitute one *ummah* with the Muslims. For Jews is their religion and for Muslims theirs (persons themselves along with their slaves are included).[12]

Some of the clauses of this important agreement were: Those Jews who follow us are entitled to our aid and support so long as they shall not have wronged us or lent assistance (to any enemies against us) (paragraph 16). They (i.e. Jews and Muslims) shall help one another in the event of any attack on the people covered by this document. There shall be sincere friendship, exchange of good counsel, fair conduct and no treachery between them (paragraph 37). The Prophet included even pagans in this

[12]Sirah Ibn Hisham, Vol. 1, p. 2780 n.d., private collection.

agreement. "No pagan is to give protection to any person of Quraysh, either his goods or his person, or take his part against any believer" (paragraph 20). The agreement also spelled out a variety of obligations by which all the believers were bound (with the exception of the Jews and pagans). They were to help anyone of their members who was crushed by burden of debt (paragraph 11). They were not to take side of an unbeliever against a believer, or kill a believer on account of their connections with an unbeliever (paragraph 14). All believers, even the humblest, were assured of the protection of Allah and so owed one another exclusive aid and "protection" (paragraph 15). In the event of war, believers were not to make peace individually with the enemy (paragraph 17). If one of their number were killed, they were to make common cause against the murderer and those who helped him, and either fight them together or accept the blood-price together (paragraph 19 and 21). They were not to give aid or shelter to any evil-doer (muhdith, literally "innovator," in other words anyone infringing the moral code) (paragraph 22). They were to maintain their own internal law and order, themselves punishing any wrong-doers amongst them (paragraph 13).[13]

It can thus be seen that the above agreement brought into existence not only a community but also became a foundational document of a state. The close scrutiny of the clauses of this agreement shows that until after this agreement was drawn up, the Prophet had not acquired the status of an unchallenged ruler. This agreement was very cautious and tactful reform on the part of Muhammad. Thus R.A. Nicholson remarks: ..."no one can study it without being impressed by the political genius of its author. Ostensibly a cautious and tactful reform, it was in reality a revolution. Muhammad durst not strike openly at the independence of the tribes but he destroyed it, in effect, by shifting the centre of power from the tribe to the community; and although the community included Jews and pagans as well as Moslems, he fully recognized, what his opponents failed to foresee, that the Moslems were the active, and must soon be the predominant partners in the newly founded state."[14]

Montgomery Watt's comments on this document are equally important:

Muhammad was by no means the ruler of this community. The Emigrants

[13]Maxime Rodinson, *Mohammed,* Allen Lane, The Penguin Press, 1971, pp. 153-54.

[14]R.A. Nicholson, *A Literary History of the Arbs*, Cambridge University Press, 1969, p.173.

were treated as a clan, and he was their chief, but there were eight other clans with their chiefs. If the Constitution is good evidence at this point, he was only marked off from other clan chiefs by two things. Firstly, the people primarily concerned in this agreement which we are calling the Constitution are *believers*, and that implies that they accept Muhammad as prophet. That should mean accepting as a binding rule whatever comes as revelation, and attributing to Muhammad, a certain prestige as the recipient of revelation and perhaps a wisdom beyond that of ordinary men, at least in religious matters. It does not mean the acceptance of his opinion in matters not covered by revelations. Secondly, however, the Constitution states that 'wherever there is anything about which you differ, it is to be referred to God and to Muhammad.' ...In these early months, then, Muhammad can have been no more than the religious leader of the Medinan community. In strictly political matters he was only the head of the 'clan' of Emigrants, and probably less powerful than several other chiefs.[15]

So far, as pointed out earlier, there was no state machinery or any similar repressive organ, neither in Mecca, nor in Medina. The people were used to living a free life uncontrolled by any external authority except, of course, the tribal traditions. The repressive organs of a state like the police and army were also unknown. There was no law except the tribal traditions. The tribal chief too was, at best, a first among the equals. The chieftainship, moreover, was not treated as hereditary. After the death of the chief, his successor used to be elected by the tribal assembly the chance being usually given to the ablest among them. The tribal chief could be subjected to severe criticism for his failures although he normally held the office till his death. The Arabs guarded this freedom jealously.

However, as discussed earlier, the socio-economic scene at Mecca had radically changed and the new developments created pressure for the establishment of a state authority. But it could not get translated into practical shape due to strong influence of tribal traditions and the rich merchants' resistance to subordinate themselves to any authority. But in Medina the meaningless blood-feud for a long period between its two principal tribes made the necessity of such an authority urgently felt. But, even to them, the tribal autonomy was so important that the Prophet had

[15]W. Montgomery Watt, *Muhammad—Prophet and Statesman, op. cit.*, pp. 95-96.

to move very cautiously in getting the legitimacy of the new institution accepted. In fact, as can be seen from the clauses of the agreement given above, he had to leave most of the matters to the tribes themselves. Only those matters which could not be resolved or which pertained to inter-tribal disputes could be referred to him for arbitration.

Thus this cautious reform or revolution as Prof. Nicholson chooses to call it, became the first effective step towards the formation of a state in Medina. Through his statesman like conduct the Prophet established peace by bringing an end to the longstanding blood-feud between the tribes of Aws and Khazraj. It enhanced his prestige and won him more adherents from among these tribes. Maxime Rodinson observes:

> On the whole, the people of Medina accepted Muhammade's role as arbiter. The movement began with the weakest clans, who had suffered from the activities of the more warlike chiefs. They wanted peace in the oasis and the cost was very small. They recognized Allah as the One God but they already knew him as the most powerful. The difference was not so very great....They acknowledged that the words uttered by Muhammad were transmitted to him by the voice of Allah; this too was not hard to accept. The Messenger's sincerity was obvious, and the words of Allah were good and accorded with the aspirations of the community as a whole. There was no reason why they should not be accepted as authentic. The man was intelligent, good-natured and likeable—in short, a valuable addition to the community of Medina. It was their good luck that his Qurayshite neighbours had been stupid enough to deprive themselves of such a remarkable character."[16]

Thus we see that the state apparatus so created by the Prophet was quite primitive. All the services were performed voluntarily and, as far as his Muslim followers were concerned, in a spirit of cooperation. There was no bureaucracy, police or army. As yet, the character of the newly founded state was not repressive. In the conditions prevailing in Medina at that time such a character of the state was out of question. Unlike Mecca, Medina had not, until then, developed new socio-economic formations. Tribal mode of life was predominant and being an oasis collective cultivation of date-palms provided means of subsistence. There were no rich merchants and the land was collectively owned either by clans or tribes. The

[16]Maxime Rodinson, *op. cit.*, pp. 155-56

institution of private property was, by and large, absent and, therefore, the question of propertied class did not arise. The state develops and acquires repressive character only in a society dominated by the propertied classes. Adam Smith, in the early draft of his *The Wealth of Nations* says:

> In a Civilized Society the poor provide for themselves and for the enormous luxury of their Superiors. The rent, which goes to support the vanity of the slothful Landlord, is all earned by the industry of the peasant....Among savages, on the contrary, every individual enjoys the whole produce of his own industry. There are among them, no Landlords, no userers, no tax gatherers.[17]

The Medinese Arabs had not yet entered into the "civilized society" and belonged to the "savage stage" wherein the fruits of their industry were not appropriated by their superiors. So a repressive state apparatus was not needed to ensure collection of rent or taxes. What had, in fact, necessitated a supra-tribal authority like the one established by the Prophet was the inter-tribal war which resulted in meaningless blood-shed without any let or hindrance. And hence, the Prophet, at the most, could claim the position of an arbiter and not of an unchallenged ruler, to begin with. It was only much later that he acquired a unique position.

Hence to begin with there was no theocratic state in Medina. All the Prophet did was to recognize the existing reality and accord complete autonomy to the Medinese tribes. He also allowed the non-Muslims in Medina to follow their religion and co-exist with his followers provided they honoured the terms of the agreement and did not endanger the security of Medina by conspiring with the opponents of the Prophet from Mecca. Various laws which became the integral part of Islamic jurisprudence were revealed much later through different verses over a period of time. At that time these laws, which were revealed later, could not have become the basis of that state. The penal code which prescribed punishments like chopping off hands for stealing or inflicting hundred lashes for adultery (the punishment of stoning to death is not mentioned in the Quran for adultery or fornication) was also prescribed later. The personal laws

[17] Adam Smith, "An Early Draft of The Wealth of Nations (c. 1763)," in William Robert Scott, *Adam Smith as Student and Professor,* Glasgow, 1937, pp. 326-28. Quoted by Lucio Colletti, *From Rousseau to Lenin*, Oxford University Press, Bombay, 1978, p. 156.

(Ahwāl al- Shakhsiyah) regarding marriage, divorce, inheritance, etc. came into operation only after the relevant verses were revealed in Medina at later dates. It will thus be seen that the theocratic state did not come into existence all of a sudden; neither was it a pre-conceived idea. It was a gradual evolution depending on the situation as it developed from time to time.

To begin with, the Prophet, as we have seen, conceded complete autonomy to the tribes in Medina whether they accepted the new faith or not. The Pagans of Medina were also given the same status. As the situation demanded the tribes were allowed to take care of the law and order situation according to their own light. What was most important at that time for the Prophet was to obtain their consent for creating a sort of confederation of various units (tribal or otherwise) as existing in Medina. In the prevailing circumstances creating of a community (ummah) was more important than creation of state. In fact the social conditions in Medina did not warrant such a development. But the Prophet and his principal followers hailed from Mecca and they were well aware of the situation prevailing there. The Muslims from Mecca had experienced commercial way of life and some of them had been successful traders also. They took to buying and selling as a way of life in Medina too. Thus soon the social situation developed working in favour of change and set new forces into motion.

In these circumstances conflict with Mecca was inevitable as it was a big trading centre and without throttling the rich merchants of Mecca, Medina could not acquire the position it was aspiring for. And soon a series of battles ensued with Mecca. Naturally, the Prophet became the supreme leader and commander and as such battles could not be fought without a shrewd and an able leader. Muhammad, despite occasional set- backs, led them to victory. This undoubtedly enhanced his prestige among the people of Medina and chastened the "mighty" Meccans. The Prophet was no longer merely the chief of his Meccan followers as originally provided for in the agreement he drew up; he was now the supreme leader of the entire community in Medina. Although the Prophet was emerging as the unquestioned leader, the community created by the "social contract" was not free of internal tensions. The Jews and hypocrites like 'Abdallah ibn Ubayy who, in fact, had never taken kindly to the Prophet's leadership, started violating the agreement in various ways. The Prophet, in addition to the Meccan unbelievers, had to deal with these internal enemies. He now possessed necessary resources to teach these traitors to the Allah's cause a befitting lesson. Banu Nadir, a Jewish tribe, even tried to kill him. One of the most critical biographer of Muhammad, Maxime Rodinson has to say this about the incident :

> Among those in Medina he approached (i.e. Muhammad) for contributions was the Jewish tribe of Banu n-Nadir, who lived on the extreme south- east corner of the oasis. He appeared at the council of the Banu n-Nadir on the Sabbath, accompanied by a number of the more important men of his community, among them Abu Bakr, 'Umar and the Medinan chief Usayd ibn Hudayr. The council, having declared its willingness to contribute to the expenses, went on with its business, requesting the noble visitors to sit down outside and wait for the outcome. While they thus waited sitting against a wall, the council, it is alleged, discussed whether this was not the longed--for moment for getting rid of Islam and its founder. Suddenly Muhammad got to his feet. Allah had warned him, he explained afterwards, that some such conspiracy was being hatched at that very moment. In fact it was not altogether unlikely assumption and one which, given a minimum of political intuition, anyone less intelligent than the Prophet might have suspected. However that may be, Muslim accounts claimed to know who at the council had proposed dropping a large boulder, a millstone, from the rooftop on to the Prophet's head, who had agreed to do it and who had opposed it.[18]

Muhammad, as a head of a state now, acted strongly wherever the situation called for. Banu Nadir "got the punishment they deserved." They were besieged by the Prophet's followers and the settlement was arrived with them only on the condition that they agreed to leave Medina leaving behind their arms. "They went," Rodinson says, "defiantly proud and perhaps glad to escape so *lightly* (emphasis mine) from such a perilous situation. They had friends and relatives and some of them, land at Khayber, the great Jewish centre in the north of the Hejaz....One more counterweight to the power of Muhammad was vanishing with it."[19]

One after the other the Jewish tribes were brought under control and the Prophet's authority in Medina became undisputed. But Mecca still continued to be recalcitrant although in the new situation, it had realized that it was losing out to the Prophet. The Meccan's earlier unsuccessful siege

[18] Maxime Rodinson, *Ibid.*, pp. 191-92
[19] *Ibid*, p. 193.

had convinced them it was no longer possible to destroy Muhammad. He was too powerful to be defeated. His victories over the Jewish colonies, his expeditions to the north, his treaties with the Bedouin had all increased his power still further. Moreover, the Muslims in Medina were seriously interfering with the trading activities of the Meccans which was of serious concern to them. Gradually the Meccans had realized the futility of fighting against Muhammad who was a growing power in the region. Still the tribal loyalties were very strong in shaping the course of events.

Behind the Prophet's conquest of Mecca also lay one such event. In Rajab, 8 A.H. (November 629), in pursuance of the vendetta going on for several years, some persons of the Banu Bakr, Beduin allies of Quraysh, attacked Banu Khuza'a, Muslims' allies who lived not far from Mecca. In all twenty of the Banu Khuza'a were slain. Muhammad was bound to help his harassed allies. The Meccans feared reprisal from the Prophet and his followers. They sent Abu Sufyan, an astute diplomat, as their emissary to Medina and waited anxiously for the outcome. The Prophet was in no mood to oblige his Meccan adversaries. He started preparations for the crucial expedition to Mecca. After making careful preparations, he set out to conquer Mecca on the head of a 10,000 strong army—a massive force by the standards of Arabia at that time. It was on 10th of Ramadan of the year 8 A.H. i.e. 1 January 630 A.D.

The Meccans soon realized that resistance was vain. They again despatched Abu Sufyan to settle terms with the Prophet. He formally embraced Islam and returned to Mecca to announce the Prophet's terms. If the Prophet and his followers were allowed to enter the city peacefully, no harm will come to anyone. The life and property of all those who did not resist would be safe. They were required to stay indoor and lay down their arms. Muhammad and his followers entered the city on 20th Ramadan, year 8 (11 January 630) in four columns. The streets were deserted. Only a handful of fanatics resisted not more than twenty of whom were killed as against two or three on the Muslim side.

Muhammad's behaviour with his Meccan detractors was statesman like. He declared general amnesty for the past offences. But the few propagandists who had composed verses ridiculing the Prophet were put to death. The Meccans swore obedience to him in the precincts of the holy sanctuary. He did not compel anyone to embrace Islam but the awed Meccans now vied with each other in adopting the new faith. After all the history and strength were on the side of Islam. Thus we see that Muhammad emerged as the supreme ruler of Arabia. Now most of the Bedouin tribes also started falling in line by swearing allegiance to him. The year after the conquest of Mecca is known as the Year of Deputations in the Islamic history. In this year various Bedouin tribes sent their deputations to the Prophet to accept them into his fold. When the hosts of Arabia came flocking to join his faith, the Pophet felt that his work was accomplished. He was now accepted as the Messenger of God as well as the ruler of Arabia (a few Christian Arabs and the Jews, of course, had not accepted him in the former capacity).

This state, naturally, came to be known as the first Islamic state. However, it can be seen from its evolution that it was not, contrary to the general notion about it, a pre-conceived theocratic state. It evolved following a zigzag historical course. The Prophet was no day dreamer or a mere ideologue. He was tactful, shrewd and pragmatic and firmly dealt with concrete situations, even ruthlessly, if necessary. In this respect he was unlike Buddha or Christ. It would be wrong to see him as a stereotype prophet. The state founded by him was not a theocratic state in the sense that it was not based on any pre-conceived comprehensive ideology. The Quran was not revealed to him in one stroke, neither were all its verses ready at hand to guide him in founding the state although he deferred certain decisions until the relevant verses were revealed.

The very foundational document of this first ever Islamic state—the agreement drawn by the Prophet as discussed above—was not based on revelation. It was a tactful document drawn by the Prophet to shift the centre of power from the tribal unit to the newly created confederation which was referred to as *ummah*. Moreover, he allowed various groups to follow their traditional laws and each group was made responsible to enforce order within the group by observing these traditional laws. He was in no hurry to enforce *Islamic laws*; these laws were not even revealed to him until much later. The Meccan verses, revealed to him before migration to Medina, were mostly vigorous condemnation of the Meccan rich for accumulation of wealth, their arrogance and neglect of the life hereafter or they pertained to the stories of the earlier prophets. Some verses drew vivid picture of heaven and hell and the day of resurrection when everyone will have to account for his or her deeds.

"Woe to all back biting slanderers," one of the Meccan verses declare, "who amass riches and sedulously hoard them, thinking that their treasures will render them immortal! By no means! They shall be flung to the Destroying Flame. Would that you knew what the Destroying Flame is like! It is Allah's own kindled fire, which will rise up to the hearts of men.

It will close upon them from every side, in towering columns."[20] In yet another Meccan verse it is said, "Have you thought of him that denies the Last Judgement? It is he who turns away the orphan and does not urge others to feed the poor. Woe to those who pray but are heedless in their prayer; who make a show of piety and give no alms to the destitute."[21]

The other long *surahs* revealed in Mecca, as pointed out earlier, contain the stories of earlier Biblical prophets from Adam to Christ or exhortations for prayer, alms or invitation to contemplate over the signs of nature. There are no verses, in this early Meccan period of juristic nature which could lay the foundation of a theocratic state. Even the concept of *zakat,* during this period, was of purificatory nature, rather than a levy. It was much later in Medina that it became a compulsory state- levy. The verses prescribing various laws like those of marriage, divorce, inheritance, certain commercial transactions as well as those prescribing punishments for various crimes like theft, adultery, fornication, murder etc. were all revealed in Medina over a period of time. Initially, when the Prophet drew up the agreement to set-up the confederation in Medina, he had allowed the various constituents to follow their respective traditions for maintaining law and order. It was only when the number of Muslims gradually swelled and Muhammad faced various problems among his own followers that he looked for the divine guidance and the relevant verses were revealed.

The Muslims approached the Prophet whenever they faced any new situation about which they had no knowledge. The Prophet either expressed his personal opinion about the matter (which were recorded or memorized as his traditions) or he waited till Allah sent His revelation. The Prophet's followers also recorded minutely the various aspects of his behaviour which later came to be known as his *sunna.* Of course, some orientalists like D.S. Margoliouth, challenge, with some justification, the fact that *sunna* meant the practices of the prophet. He maintains that "(1) the Prophet had left no precepts of religious decisions--i.e. had left no *Sunna* or Hadith outside the Qur'an; (2) the *Sunna* as practiced by the early Muslim community after Muhammad was not at all the *Sunna* of the Prophet but was the pre-Islamic Arabian usage as it stood modified through the Qur'an; and; (3) later generations, in the 2nd/3rd century, in order to give authority and normativity to this usage, developed the concept of the *Sunna* of the Prophet and forged the mechanism of the Hadith to realize

[20] The *Quran, op. cit.,* p. 28.
[21] *Ibid.*

this concept. H. Lammens, in his *Islam: Beliefs and Institutions* expresses the same view and declares tersely that the practice (*Sunna*) must have preceded its formulation in the Hadith."[22]

Whatever the truth the fact remains that the later generations of Muslims considered it as the Prophet's *Sunna* and emulated it meticulously. However, later on many problems arose for which there were no precedents in the Prophet's sayings or *Sunna*. The companions of Muhammad or thte later *'ulama* had to resort to *ijtihad* (interpretation) or *qiyas* (analogy) to resolve these problems. Even the Prophet himself was aware of such possibility and he is said to have advised his followers to resort to *ijtihad* whenever confronted with new situation. "When Ma'ad was appointed ruler of Yemen," says Iqbal, "the Prophet is reported to have asked him as to how he would decide matters coming up before him. 'I will judge matters according to the Book of God,' said Ma'ad. But if the Book of God contains nothing to guide you?' 'Then I will act on the precedents of the prophet of God.' 'But if the precedents fail?' 'Then I will exert to form my own judgement.'"[23]

Iqbal also further observes, "The student of the history of Islam, however, is well aware that with the political expansion of Islam systematic legal thought became an absolute necessity, and our early doctors of law, both of Arabian and non-Arabian descent, worked ceaselessly until all the accumulated wealth of legal thought found a final expression in our recognized schools of law."[24]

The important question then arises: what was the character of the state evolved during life-time of Muhammad? Could it be described as a theocratic state? I think the question cannot be answered straight away in yes or no. As we have seen above the origin of this state was not pre-conceived or preceded by divinely ordained laws. Its origin was in concrete history and to begin with it was based on the mutual agreement between various tribes and groups residing in Medina. Moreover, even after Muhammad achieved pre- eminent position and the number of his followers increased, all his decisions were not derived from the revelations from Allah. No doubt some of his decisions were later confirmed by the divine revelations but it did not apply to all his act. Many of his decisions

[22]Quoted from D.s. Margoliouth's book *Early Development of Islam* by Fazlur-Rehman in his *Islam*, Islamic Research Institute, n.d. Karachi, P. 45.

[23]Dr Sir Muhammad Iqbal, *The Reconstruction of Religious Thought in Islam*, Ashraf Press, Lahore, 1960 p. 148

[24]*Ibid.*

and opinions were based on the age-old traditions of the Arabs and some on the concrete situations as he faced; in other words many of his decisions were based on the exigencies of situations.

However, as pointed out by Margoliouth, whatever Prophet Muhammad did by way of accepting, rejecting or modifying the pre-Islamic Arabian traditions, was passed on to the posterity as the *Sunna* of the Prophet and it also became part of the socio-religious complex which emerged later. It was quite natural in a way. Prophet Muhammad had achieved--it can be said without exaggeration--the almost impossible. Though for the mercantile society of Mecca some sort of state authority which could mediate between conflicting interests of the emerging classes (these classes were, of course, in the process of formation and still had strong tribal associations, a highly complex and confused situation, no doubt) had become necessary, the tribal ethos and its structural pattern were till then too strong to allow that to happen. It required the genius of Muhammad to bring about this much needed social revolution. Yes, emergence of Islam was a great revolution for the Arabia of early seventh century and Prophet Muhammad was its supreme architect. With his religious formula—there are no gods but one God—he delivered a strong blow to the tribal structure which was, at least in the Meccan mercantile milieu, going through the process of disintegration.

Emergence of Islam was a turning point in the history of Arabia. Prophet Muhammad had perceived the new forces taking shape within the womb of the old tribal society. He not only perceived these forces, he also had the ability to mould them so as to create the society of his vision. It was therefore, not surprising if he acquired such a unique position. His companions and followers and those belonging to later generations looked towards him, his revealed book, his traditions or practices for guidance in every matter and, if they failed to find in them what they sought, they resorted to *ijtihad* and *qiyas* (analogy) so that they could conform to the Prophet's teachings indirectly, if not directly. In this sense the state founded by Muhammad can be construed as a theocratic state. The Quranic revelations on which many of the Prophet's state policies were based had universal elements which transcended immediate spatio-temporal limits, the Islamic state in this sense can be said to be based on ideology and hence to that extent can be described as an ideological state.

If we say that the Islamic state emerged in a concrete historical situation and was based on the new historical forces as they were shaping in the womb of old society the question then arises how far was it representative of certain social classes? This is an important question in the context in which we are dealing with this subject. As we have seen a new mercantiele class was emerging in Mecca breaking the old tribal barriers. But this class still maintained close connection with its tribal past and was not conscious of the role of an institution like that of the state. Such an imbroglio usually prevails when the new forces are shaping within the womb of an old society. But, nevertheless, the rich merchants of Mecca were certainly conscious of their commercial interests and had formed business corporations transcending the tribal limits. Those who were less successful and felt deprived of, also formed an association called Ḥilf al- Fuḍul, as discussed above, to defend their interests. Thus it can be seen that new classes were emerging in Mecca.

Prophet Muhammad, with his vision of a new society, was not allowed to preach as the merchants of Mecca, unaware of the potentialities of the new religion, felt that a poor orphan was claiming precedence over them by declaring himself as the messenger of God. He was forced to migrate and lay foundation of the new state in a town which needed it but for different reasons. Thus we see that the class which needed the Prophet's vision and dynamism most drove him out of the town. The state founded in Medina, therefore, instead of getting support from the Meccan merchants, came in direct clash with them. However, one should not confuse the clash with the Meccan merchants with that of their interests.

The Prophet, who was determined to preach the new faith in the face of heavy odds and founded a federal community, therefore, acquired a unique position in it. Moreover, its superstructural form was religious and expressed through revelational commands, it added to the uniqueness of the Prophet's position in the state structure established by him. While this imparted theocratic character to the state founded by him, it did not necessarily pre-empt the role of group, class or tribal interests. After all an ideology or a system of ideas, in the broadest sense, is accepted by a people only if it is, in the ultimate analysis (although apparently or in its immediate expression it may give contrary impression), in its well- defined interests. This conformity with the terrestrial interests is not (and as far as Islam is concerned is certainly not) necessarily contrary to the religious spirit. The very fact that a large number of Arabs ultimately accepted the new faith--and the Arabs due to the hard conditions they lived in, were very practical people and not mere abstract idealists--shows that it was in keeping with their broad aspirations.

Islam, although aware of the evils of the accumulation of wealth (this is what had happened in Meccan society and hence strong condemnation of it in the Quranic verses revealed in Mecca), did not altogether disapprove of private property. Any such position would have meant its total rejection by the influential mercantile class of Mecca. Not only that, historically speaking, it would have meant going back to the tribal way of life, had the private property been disapproved of. Islam played, as pointed out earlier, a progressive historical role by fusing tribes into an *ummah* i.e. a nation. The divisions into tribes and nations, it was emphasized, was only for the purpose of identification. Trading was not only approved of, it was positively encouraged. According to one tradition of the Prophet, "A truthful and honest trader will be in the company of prophets, scrupulous persons and martyrs."[25]

It can thus be seen that the Islamic state founded by Prophet Muhammad, although not dominated by the traders as a class, did portect their interests. Further developments after the death of the Prophet, as we shall see in the subsequent chapters of the book, brought about profound changes in the character of the Islamic state as its class composition changed over a period of time. So from the development of the state founded by the Prophet traced out above it can be seen that it was not theocratic in character to begin with and gradually it acquired that character as more and more laws were prescribed by the divine commands. However, all the acts of the Prophet were not commanded by the divine will in the form of revelations; many of them were based on his personal judgements and the Arab traditions. However, for the later generations of Muslims all such acts—termed as *Sunna*—had to be followed as meticulously as the divine commands thus, by and large, ignoring the spatio-temporal character of these acts. This injected an element of dogmatim and reduced the scope of historical dynamics. But the tide of event played its own part. We will examine this in more detail in the next chapter.

[25] 'Allama Yusuf Qardawi, *Al Ḥalāl wa al-Harām fi-al-Islam*, Urdu tr. by Shams Pirzada, Al-Darus Salfiyah, Bombay, 1977, p.184.

2. The Theory and Practice of Islamic State after the Prophet

Prophet Muhammad as the founder and theoretician of the Islamic state had a unique position as its executive head. In fact he was a legislator (through divine revelation as well as his personal pronouncements and practices all of which acquired a sacred character for the Muslims), executive as well as a jurist. He was not answerable to anyone as far as the revealed commands were concerned. But, in the absence of divine revelations, it was his wont to consult his companions. In fact he was commanded by God to do so. The Quran commands the Prophet "And consult them (i.e. those around you) in (important) matters."

Taha Husain, a noted writer and scholar of Islam from Egypt quotes the above verse of the Quran to show that the state founded by Muhammad was not a theocratic state. He maintains that nothing can be more misleading than the concept that the state founded by the Prophet of Islam was a theocratic state. For, Islam, after all, is a religion which lays emphasis on the unity of God, prophethood (of Muhammad) and then on righteous living. It also drew attention towards this and the other-worldly life but it did not deprive human beings of their freedom and it (Islam) did not become an absolute master of man nor did it suspend his initiative to act; it, on the other hand, made him the master within certain limits. It showed what was desirable and what was repulsive and, of course, it laid emphasis on reason and gave freedom (with the help of reason) to think what was good and in the interest of common people and to take part in the common good to the extent possible. The God commanded the Prophet to consult the faithfuls in (their) affairs. If everything had to be decided in the heavens, there was no need to consult anyone.[1]

[1]Dr Taha Husain, *Al-Fitnat al-Kubra*, Vol. 1 *'Uthman*, Urdu tr. by Abdul Hamid Nomani, Ajmal Press, Bombay (year not mentioned), pp. 28-29.

Any serious student of the Islamic history would agree with what Dr Taha Husain says for, as we have seen in the first chapter, all the decisions taken by Muhammad were not based on the divine commands. The Prophet, in many important matters, was guided by the Arab customs and the pressure of public opinion in finally deciding the issues. From the close scrutiny of the early sources of Islamic history it is not wide off the mark to maintain that the Prophet could only carry out the legal decisions with the endorsement and consent of public opinion and under its pressure. As we have seen, the Prophet was the great arbiter of the community in all disputes. But he seems to have been called upon only in the last resort, or in matters of great importance. Here, again, it was the old Arab system which worked in the normal way, with its absence of written law or any supreme authority and its consideration of ethnic groups and individuals as autonomous powers.[2]

It is, therefore, evident that the Islamic state cannot be construed as purely Islamic state. What the Prophet left behind him was an extremely primitive state-structure based more on local traditions and the Arab ethos as, during his life time, the religion of Islam as well as his temporal power had remained confined to the Arabian peninsula. Ustadh Ahmad Muhammad Jamal of Egypt rightly maintains that Islam did not evolve any definite form of government...nor did it lay down details for it. It only lay-down some foundational principles of generalized nature which do not vary with space and time and on which it is possible to build (a state) for the welfare of the people.[3]

Qamaruddin Khan, Professor of Islamic history, Karachi University, is of the opinion that "the Quran does not aim to create a state but to create a society."[4] Prof. Khan considers the absence of any definite form of government in Islam as a blessing. "Hence whatever the form and shape of the state," says Khan, "If the Quranic society is realised in it, it may bear the designation of the Islamic state. The omission of the details is therefore a great blessing to the Muslim community, because it makes it possible for Islam to march with the progress of time and adjust itself to new conditions and new environments."[5] But the absence of any definite form had its

[2] Maxime Rodinson, *Mohammed*, Allen Lane The Penguin Press, 1971, p. 224.

[3] See Ustadh Ahmed Muhammad Jamal's paper on *Fikrah al-Dawlah fi al-Islam,* International Islamic Colloquium Papers, Punjab University Press, Lahore, 1960.

[4] Qamaruddin Khan, *Al-Mawardi's Theory of the State,* Bazm-i-Iqbal, Lahore, (year not given), p. 4.

[5] *Ibid.*

disadvantage also; some opportunist *'ulama* supported and justified even oppressive states which in content, if not in form, were contrary to the spirit of Islam. We will examine this little more in detail later.

The first important question which arose after the death of the Prophet was that of finding his successor as a head of the Islamic state. This question created a permanent schism in the Muslim community. Those who were later known as shi'ahs maintained that the Prophet had nominated his cousin and son-in-law 'Ali as his successor. They cite, in support of this claim, among other things, the Prophet's famous tradition (hadith) that "Of those whose master I am, 'Ali is their master." But, according to the Sunnites, this pronouncement is not the categorical statement in favour of 'Ali's succession. Keeping in view the Arab ethos, this appears to carry more conviction. In many respects the Prophet, as already pointed out, had followed the Arab traditions which did not conflict with the new religion.

As yet, there was no radical break with the tribal ethos although in Mecca and Medina socio-econoomic transformation was taking place. Many Bedouin tribes also had embraced Islam as it symbolized a new emerging power although these tribes had not undergone any social transformation. There was dialectical interaction between these desert tribes and those who had taken to the sedentary way of life in the urban conglomerations at Mecca and Medina. In such circumstances it was very difficult for nomination to be accepted. Whenever a tribal chief had to be elected, the important members of the tribe collected together to elect the most competent among them. After the death of the Prophet, and before he was buried, everyone who mattered thought of finding a new head of the community. The prominent people of Medina gathered at a place called Saqifa Banu Sa'idah and after bitter controversy, elected Abu Bakr, the father- in-law of the Prophet as his temporal successor.

Abu Bakr, the first successor of Prophet Muhammad, thus assumed power as a result of some sort of consensus among the important people of Medina. It was, of course, not an election on the basis of adult franchise as it happens in the parliamentary form of government in our own time. Also, there was no question of any party seeking people's mandate on the basis of some programme. Neither any term of office was fixed. It was an "election" for life and with undefined powers. But what Abu Bakr said on assuming charge as caliph shows that there was sense of being responsible to the people. He is reported to have said, "O people! Behold me—charged with the cares of Government. I am not the best among you; I need all your advice and all your help. If I do well, support me; if I mistake, counsel me.

To tell the truth to a person commissioned to rule is faithful allegiance; to conceal it, is treason. In my sight, the powerful and the weak are alike; and to both I wish to render justice. As I obey God and His Prophet obey me; if I neglect the laws of God and the Prophet, I have no more right to your obedience."[6]

What Abu Bakr said was more democratic in spirit than the present day pronouncements of the political leaders as, until much later, the Islamic state had not developed the repressive machinery. There was no paid army, police or bureaucracy to carry out the repressive functions of the state. It is for this reason that during the reign of the first four caliphs we find many instances of fearless criticism of the government voiced in public. This was in keeping with the traditions of the Bedouin tribes. But later on as the repressive machinery developed and caliphate changed into dynastic rule, no such public criticism was possible.

As pointed out earlier, most of the nomadic tribes had accepted Islam as it was the rising power in that area and not out of deeper conviction or on account of pressures generated, as in Mecca (and to a lesser extent in Medina), due to socio-economic transformation taking place in the base of the society. To the nomadic tribes the institution of state did not make any sense, whatsoever. On the contrary it means curtailment of their much valued freedom they enjoyed in the desert. Islam also had made *zakat* (poll tax) obligatory on every Muslim. After the establishment of state it had to be paid to the state treasury every year. Abu Bakr, on being elected as caliph, took measures to collect *zakat* from all the Muslims including the nomadic tribes. This move was resisted by the Bedouin tribes who, on the death of the Prophet, had again shown the signs of turbulence.

According to Suyuti, "When the news about the death of the Prophet spread around Medina, many Arab tribes renounced Islam and refused to pay *zakat.* Abu Bakr ordered troops to march (against the rebel tribes). 'Umar advised against such measure but he (Abu Bakr) said that I will fight against them even if they refuse to pay one year's *zakat* or a young one of a goat which they used to pay to the Prophet."[7] (tr. mine.) It was the first rebellion against the Islamic state in Medina and was crushed by the Islamic troops. This is known as the war of *ridda* (apostasy) in the history of Islam. The importance of crushing this rebellion by the Bedouin tribes

[6]Sayed Athar Husain, *The Glorius Caliphate*, Academy of Islamic Research and Publications, Lucknow, 1974, p. 19.

[7]Suyuti, *Tarikh al-Khulafa*, Urdu tr. Maulavi Hakim Shabbir Ahmed, Kitab Khana Ashrafiyah, Delhi (year not mentioned), p. 73.

cannot be overemphasized here. It gave new life to the nascent state. Baladhuri, quoting a prominent companion of the Prophet 'Abdullah bin Mas'ud, says, "After the death of the Messenger of God, we were standing on cross roads where, if Allah had not obliged us in the person of Abu Bakr, it was likely that we would have been destroyed."[8] (tr. mine.) Sir William Muir also feels, "But for him (i.e. Abu Bakr), Islam would have melted away in compromise with the Bedouin tribes, or, might have perished in the throes of its birth."[9]

It can thus be seen that for the people of Medina (as well as of Mecca) the institution of state had come to stay as it was a socio-economic necessity for them whereas for the nomadic tribes of desert it did not fulfil any such function. Hence their revolt against it. In fact, throughout the history of Islam these nomadic tribes remained turbulent and never completely surrendered to any central authority. These tribes, being non-sedentary, always remained on the periphery of political power which was wielded by the town people. While choosing successor to the Prophet, everyone present was unanimous on the question of electing caliph either from amongst the Immigrants (from Mecca) or from Ansars (i.e. helpers from Medina). Although theoretically all Muslims were equal, the caliphate was thought to be the monopoly of the Quraysh (a leading tribe of Mecca to which the Prophet belonged). However, later on the Khwarij (Seceders, a sect of Islam mainly comprised of the desert tribes) strongly advocated that any Muslim could become caliph provided he fulfilled certain qualifications.

The main cry of the seceders was *la hukma illa lillahi* (i.e. God alone can rule). Prof. Nicholson says about the seceders, "The Kharijites were mostly drawn from the Bedouin soldiery who settled in Basra and Kufa after the Persian wars. Civil life wrought little change in their unruly temper. Far from acknowledging the peculiar sanctity of a Qurayshite, they desired a chief of their own blood whom they might obey, in Bedouin fashion, as long as he did not abuse or exceed the powers conferred upon him."[10] It can thus be seen that the Islamic state had not found willing acceptability among the desert people. In the initial period (until the conditions vastly changed after the wars of conquest brought the large provinces of Roman

[8] Baladhuri, *Futuh al-Buldan,* Urdu tr. by Syed Abulkhair Maududi, Vol. I, Darut Taba' Jami'ah Usmaniyah, Hyderabad, 1932, pp. 150-51.

[9] Sir William Muir, *Annals of the Early Caliphate*, quoted by Sayed Athar Husain in *The Glorious Caliphate, op. Cit.*, p. 22.

[10] R.A. Nicholson, *A Literary History of the Arabs*, Cambridge University Press, 1969, p. 209.

and Sassanid empires under the Islamic rule) the tribal factor kept the Islamic state democratic in spirit (if not strictly in form in its modern connotation) as the caliphs were subjected to the frank criticism in the Arab tribal tradition.

Suyuti narrates an interesting episode in this connection. He says, "'Umar one day said (Umar was the second caliph) by God I do not know whether I am a king or a caliph, if I am king it is better. Someone from the audience said, O Commander of the Faithfuls, there is a great difference between a king and a caliph. Thereupon 'Umar inquired of the difference. The man said the caliph is one who does not extract (money) unjustly nor does he spend it unjustly and you are like that. A king, on the other hand, oppresses (his subjects) to pay and spends whimsically. Hearing this Umar became silent"11 (tr. mine).

This incident shows that the Arabs were not temperamentally prepared to accept the institution of kingship easily and, like the head of their tribe, wanted their caliph to be accountable to his people. The tribal roots of the Islamic state, until the foreign influence with empirical traditions became all pervasive, remained very strong. Ordinary people from the desert could call upon the caliph publicly to explain his conduct. The history of the first four caliphs is replete with such incidents. These caliphs undoubtedly showed high character and were inspired by their faith to act as they did but, nevertheless, the significance of the situational context also cannot be ignored in understanding a socio-political phenomenon.

At the time of Abu Bakr's death, the questioon of succession again became important. Abu Bakr nominated 'Umar, his close associate and trusted lieutenant, as his successor, a practice which even the Prophet had not followed. But, it must be said to the credit of Abu Bakr that in that difficult situation he made a very appropriate choice. Many senior companions of the Prophet expressed their displeasure at the choice. They told Abu Bakr on his death-bed that he had appointed a harsh and rude person (*fazzun ghaliz*) over their heads. 'Umar was strong headed and man of determination who did not believe in mincing words. Abu Bakr's choice was later on ratified by the people of Medina by swearing allegiance to him. It was not a king nominating his successor. The person chosen had to seek people's approval before he could assume the responsibilities of a head of state. Moreover, Abu Bakr had nominated his colleague, not his son or even a relative.

[11] Suyuti, *op. cit.,* p. 145.

'Umar's period as a head of Islamic state is extremely important in its history. Abu Bakr had to devote his energies in crushing the rebellion of the Bedouin tribes and setting things right after the death of the Prophet. Abu Bakr died within less than three years after being installed as caliph. He hardly had time to resolve other problems. It was during 'Umar's time that the Muslim armies conquered vast territories and brought back home, along with them, fortunes the Arabs had not seen before. The wars of conquest were good diversion for the turbulent Bedouin tribes who lived in harsh desert conditions. These conquests, in turn, created complex problems which could not have been tackled without a ruthless and determined leadership like that of 'Umar. There were no well built institutions when 'Umar took over from Abu Bakr. The state had recent origin and everything had to be learnt from experience in the fast changing situation. Some times the know-how of the experienced administrators from the conquered provinces had to be utilized to cope with the situation.

The riches the conquests yielded baffled 'Umar. He summoned his colleagues for advice. 'Ali, in keeping with the old tribal tradition, advised him to distribute the booty to the last penny among the deserving people.This advice was not in keeping with the changed situation. 'Uthman opined that if proper system was not established, the multiplying wealth might aggravate the situation. At last it was decided to establish registers, fix daily allowances for the people, and the surplus was reserved for the welfare schemes for the Muslims.[12] 'Umar had to cope up with many such difficult situations. The Arabs who became masters of a vast empire had to learn to rule. No trained adminstrators were available at hand. 'Umar was in favour of keeping a strict check over the governors, lest they should become corrupt and arrogant. Once while distributing money from the treasury to the people he was surrounded by a dense crowd. Sa'ad bin Abi Waqqas, a prominent companion of Prophet Muhammad who had played an important role in conquering Persia, came and forced his way up to 'Umar through the crowd. Sa'ad's behaviour implied that he had, by virtue of his position, precedence over others. This enraged 'Umar who flogged him right there and said, "If you are not afraid of the power of Allah, His power is also not afraid of you." It was 'Umar's desire to treat all the Muslims equally including the members of his own family.[13]

We are also told that whenever he appointed any governor he strictly

[12]Dr Taha Husain, *Ibid.*, pp. 21-22.
[13]*Ibid.*, p. 19.

warned him not to ride (expensive) Turkish horse, not to eat delicious food, not to wear fine clothes and not to close his doors over the complainants and if he did not conform to these instructions, he had to face severe punishments.[14] No one could escape the wrath of 'Umar. It is not that he exempted himself from such rigorous conduct. Taha Husain says :

> It is a fact that Umar was very strict with the people in the matters of God but he was far more strict as far as his own self was concerned. In the whole of human history, excepting the great Prophets (Ulul 'Azm), I have not found any other human being who sees danger for himself from things normally not feared, who considers as his fault something which would be hardly taken as such, who inflicts such rigorous discipline upon himself hardly any other person would do. It is well known that when there was great famine in 'Amar Ramad he gave up all comforts and took to hard life and ate very little coarse food, if at all he ate. When he came to know that Ghee (clarified butter) is not available he gave up its use and took to oil and dry crumbs of bread. But even the use of oil went against his conscience and so he told his slave to cook without oil [15] (tr. mine).

All this is undoubtedly true. But 'Umar did not succeed in building up a just and equitable social order. The march of events overtook him. Once, seeing the gap between the rich and the poor widening, he said, "Had I done first what I did later, I would have taken away the wealth from the rich and distributed it among the poor."[16] The important companions of the Prophet themselves had gradually amassed huge fortune and still it was thought to be within the bounds of law.

Ibn Khaldun gives the account of the wealth accumulated by some of the Prophet's companions. He says, "In the days of 'Uthaman, the men around Muhammad acquired estates and money. On the day 'Uthaman was killed, 1,50,000 dinars and 1,00,000 dirhams were in the hands of his treasurer. The value of his estates in Wadi al-Qura and Hunayn and other places was 200,000 dinars. He also left 1,000 horses and 1,000 female servants. Talha's income from Iraq was 1,000 dinars a day, and his income from the region of ash- Shrah was more than that. The stable of 'Abd-ar-Rahman b. 'Awf contained 1,000 horses. He also had 1,000 camels and 10,000 sheep.

3rd Caliph

[14]Suyuti, *op. cit.*, p. 131.
[15]Dr Taha Husain, *op. cit.*, p. 17.
[16]*Ibid.*, p. 21.

One-fourth of his estate after his death amounted to 84,000. Zayd b. Thabit left silver and gold that was broken into pieces with pickaxes, in addition to the (other) property and estates that he left, in the value of 100,000 dinars. Az- Zubayr built himself a residence in al-Basrah and other residences in Egypt and al-Kufah and Alexandria. Talhah built one in al-Kufah and had his residence in Medina improved. He used plaster, bricks and teakwood. Sa'd b. Abi Waqqas built himself a residence in Medina and had it plastered inside and out. Ya'la b. Munyah left 50,000 dinars and estates and other things the value of which amounted to 300,000 dirhams."

After quoting this from al-Mas'udi, Ibn Khaldun, makes an interesting comment: "Such were the gains people made. Their religion did not blame them for (amassing so much), because, as booty, it was lawful property. They did not employ their property wastefully but in planned way in all their conditions, as we have stated. Amassing worldly property is reprehensible, but it did not reflect upon them, because blame attaches only to waste and lack of planning, as we have indicated. Since their expenditure followed a plan and served the truth and its ways, amassing (so much property) helped them along on the path of true and served the purpose of attaining the other world."[17]

The distribution of wealth is a matter of state policy and, in case of Islam, also related to religious doctrine. 'Umar was in a dilemma. The tribal practice required almost instantaneous and equitable distribution of the war booty whereas the interest of state policy was otherwise. Nevertheless, tribal traditions were too strong to be ignored and a large part of the war booty (which was pouring in from all direction in ever larger quantities) had to be distributed. Those who had embraced Islam earlier (*al-Sābiqūn al-Awwalūn*), those who had acquired great prominence as the companions of Muhammad, had to be given larger shares than others. Moreover, Islam had permitted—even encouraged—trade. Many of these prominent Muslims invested their monies in commercial transactions for which the conquests had thrown open new opportunities. So again the rich started growing richer—a process which was strongly condemned in the early verses of the Quran in Mecca. The torrential flow of wealth had perhaps aggravated these income differentials.

But, as Ibn Khaldun rightly maintains, it was perfectly legitimate as their religion approved of it. *Zakat,* which was fixed at two-and-a-half per cent,

[17]Ibn Khaldun, *Muqaddimah*, Eng. tr. by Franz Rosenthal, abr. by N.J. Dawood, Princeton University Press, 1970, p. 163.

even if paid honestly, could not wipe out the aggravating disparities of income. *Zakāt*, no doubt, was a sort of income and wealth tax, but income was not taxed separately and so the differences multiplied very fast. To top it all the collection of *zakāt* by the state was stopped during the period of the third caliph 'Uthman as there was enough money in the state treasury and it was not possible to maintain accounts of all the citizens' wealth. The individuals were expected to pay *zakat* to the poor and needy directly.

The new disparities in income created fresh tensions in the society and ultimately plunged it into civil war as we shall see later. A few companions of the Prophet like Abu Dharr al-Ghifari exhorted the newly sprung up class of rich not to hoard and to spend in the way of God. Rodinson says about him: "The extremist tendency found its backing, during the Muslim Middle Ages, in one of the Companions of the Prophet, Abu Dharr al-Ghifari. Statements were attributed to him according to which, for instance, everyone ought to spend on the service of God, or in charity, the whole of his wealth or income beyond the minimum needed for subsistance. He was said to have shocked people; about ten years after the Prophet's death, by maintaining that the threatening verses in the Quran about rich men unwilling to give alms were applicable to leading members of the Muslim community no less than to the Jewish and Christian clerics aimed at in the preceding verse. He is said to have been banished to a remote locality, as a danger to society."[18]

Abu Dharr is often taken resort to by the socialist and communist Left in the Muslim world today. Though Rodinson considers him semi-mythical, there cannot be any doubt about his existence and radical pronouncements from the point of view of that period. The theologians and the rightists are equally conscious of the role of Abu Dharr and try to project him as the true champion of religion and that Islam transcends the modern systems called capitalism, socialism and communism. The Shaikh al-Azhar Shaikh 'Abd al-Halim wrote a book *Abu Dharr al-Ghifari and Commmunism* trying to paint communism in the blackest colour and presenting Ghifari as the great champion of Islam. What lies behind such an attempt is the popularity of the socialist ideas among the people.

It can thus be seen that 'Umar, the strong man of Islam, with all his strict enforcement of Islamic teachings and ruthless measures for prevention of corruption, could not check the growth of concentration of wealth and concomitant imbalances in the socio-economic structure of the early

[18] Maxime Rodinson, *Islam and Capitalism*, Allen Lane, 1974, p. 25.

Islamic society. Under the impact of the new forces generated as a result of the conquests, the peninsular Arabian community with its primitive tribal structure, was shaken and began to assimilate the new mores. The forward thrust of these powerful historical forces could not be held in check by a single individual, however strong his will. Moreover, Islam with its universal teachings and no less emphasis on this worldly aspect of life (renunciation and asceticism, in fact, has been disapproved by the Prophet) paved the way for these developments.

The conquests had great impact on the evolution of the Islamic state, which, as we have already seen, was not a pre-determined concept revealed from God or conceived by the Prophet. It was ever growing and developing under the impact of events. Conquests of the foreign lands, therefore, had the most telling impact on its evolution. 'Umar, the second caliph, never felt shy of adopting the new procedures and institutions of administration from the conquered lands, although it is also true that he got the books on theoretical sciences from the conquered lands destroyed. Ibn Khaldun thus say, "Where are the sciences of the Persians that Umar ordered to be destroyed?"[19] It is because he thought that God, through revelations, had taught human beings all that was there to be taught as far as moral code and the related theoretical matters were concerned.

In the Islamic system, right from the beginning, there was total absence of the feudal institutions as in a desert there was no question of landed estates to grow. In the oases the land was owned collectively by the tribes. But in the conquered provinces of the Roman and Sassanid empires, the nobles possessed the landed estates and the cultivators were mere serfs. 'Umar, in the conquered provinces, ordered such a system to be abolished and the cultivators were left in possession of the lands they cultivated. 'Umar issued instructions to confiscate all the lands left behind by the Roman rulers and to be given to the native cultivators.[20] This was a revolutionary step which widened the base for the Muslim invaders among the natives. 'Umar prohibited all the Muslim officers from acquiring landed property in the conquered lands even by purchases from the natives. This rule remained in operation for quite some time. He also prohibited them from cultivation. He issued instructions to all the military officers, that as the daily allowances had been fixed for all no one should be allowed to cultivate land.[21]

[19]Ibn Khaldun, *op. cit.*, p. 39.

[20]Maulana Shibli Nu'mani, *Al-Farouq*, Kutubkhana Hamidiyah, Delhi,1968, P. 301.

[21]*Ibid.*

As a result of this policy, one who cultivated the land and paid *kharaj* on it was recognized as its owner. Dr I. H. Qureshi says, "Islam regards the cultivator as the owner of land. There is a well-known hadith in Musnad Imam Ahmad and also narrated by Bukhari which lays it down unambiguously that the person who brings dead land to life is its owner, provided it has no previous owner....The Muslim jurists have based their rulings mainly upon this vary hadith. The most famous of these is Imam Abu Yusuf whose *Kitab-ul-Kharaj* considers the person who pays the kharaj as the owner of the land for which he pays it....Indeed the principle of ownership of land resting in the cultivator has been so universally accepted by the jurists of Islam that it seems redundant to discuss the problem at all."[22]

A French scholar quoted by the Shibli is also of the opinion that the Islamic conquests had much to do with kharaj (land tax). Muslim conquerors gave relief to the cultivators who had to pay heavy taxes to their Roman masters and hence they willingly supported the Muslim invaders. The resistance to the Muslim attacks came from the rulers and not from their subjects. The Copt peasants of Egypt in fact actively helped the Muslim invaders as against their Roman masters. In Damascus and Hams the Christian residents closed the gates of the city wall on the armies of Heraclitus and told Muslims that, We rather prefer your rule to that of the tyrant Romans."[23]

'Umar's was great contribution in establishing the just land revenue system and restoring ownership of land to the cultivators. But, perhaps, the historical forces were yet not ripe to let this progressive land-tenure policy to last as outside the tribal Arabia there were advanced feudal institutions (this term I have rather used loosely for want of any better term as the other term "Asiatic mode of production" is eqully unsatisfactory) very well-entrenched and these institutions, as we shall see, soon became the integral part of Islamic state. The Islamic rule, after all, could not have altered the productive forces. 'Umar's strict injunction to the Muslim conquerors not to acquire land even for cultivation was extensively violated after his death and ultimately abandoned.

'Umar, as pointed out above, always made it a point to consult non-

[22]Dr I. H. Qureshi "Land Tenure in Islam," *International Colloquium Papers, op. cit.*, pp. 149-50. For this Qureshi quotes Imam Abu Yusuf, *Kitab al-Kharaj*, Cairo, 1302 A.H. pp. 35-38.

[23]Shibli Nu'mani, *op. cit.*, p. 302.

policy of Kharaj different in Persia

Muslim poples in matters where he and his associates lacked experience and such occasions arose very frequently as the complex problems had to be faced in administrating the conquered lands. Maqrizi tells us that while deciding about the administrative measures for Iraq, 'Umar summoned two prominent persons from Iraq along with interpreters.[24] Similarly he called a Copt from Egypt to consult him for divising Egypt's administration.'Umar's pragmatism as a statesman has an interesting dimension. Egypt, Damascus, etc., were governed by the Romans before being conquered by the Muslims and hence the native population hated the foreign rulers. Their landed estates were confiscated and distributed to the native cultivators. However, the same policy was not strictly followed in case of Persia where the ruling class was native. Shibli says that those who were landlords and manorial lords called *dihqān or marzbān* in Persian language were left intact by Hadrat 'Umar. Their rights and privileges were also protected.[25]

Thus it can be seen that 'Umar who consolidated the Islamic revolution and state was guided in his state policies, apart from the Islamic teachings, by practical considerations also. In fact no ideological state (theocratic in this case although Dr. Taha Husain of Egypt maintains it was not theocratic) can be assiduously built on strictly ideological considerations whatever its theoreticians may say. Prophet Muhammad and his close companions were also, more often than not, guided by practical considerations. Here we can see that if 'Umar had followed the same policy of land tenure as he did in the case of Roman provinces, he would have alienated the ruling classes which in this case were native and so not thought to be enemical by the local people whereas the Arabs were alien and conquerors. Thus it would be wrong to maintain that the Islamic state was based only on the revealed injunctions and the Prophet's sunnah. Practical considerations in the changed situation were equally important in shaping its policies and structure.

State Revenues

With the expansion of Islamic state, the sources of its revenue were changing. It is important to note this change in the sources of revenue as ultimately the character of the state can be ascertained only by the methods it follows to extract surplus from the people. When the Prophet founded a confederate community in Medina on the basis of a mutual agreement there

[24]Maqrizi, vol. i., pp. 74-75, quoted by Shibli Nu'mani, *op. cit.*, p. 303.
[25]Shibli Nu'mani, *op. cit.*, p. 293.

was no definite source of revenue. Even the concept of zakāt in the beginning was that of charity and purification and not that of a state tax. Then gradually, for Muslims, zakāt became a compulsory levy which they had to pay annually, to the Prophet and became part of state treasury. People in Medina were engaged in commerce and cultivation of date-palms in various oases or rearing of camels, sheep, goats etc. Zakāt was levied on cash, gold, silver as well as animals. Cultivation was peripheral for the economy of Medina and was mainly carried out by the Jews. Therefore, the question of a proper system of land revenue did not arise. When Khaiber, a fertile oases, was conquered by the Prophet, the Jews pleaded with him to let them cultivate the land and in return they agreed to pay half the produce.[26] Some Muslims who cultivated land were required to pay *ushr* i.e. one-tenth of the crop or its equivalent value. The income of the state treasury was also supplemented by booty one-fifth of which was given to the Prophet.

During Abu Bakr's time large scale conquests had not begun and hence the sources of revenue remained more or less stagnant except that the war booty increased. However, during 'Umar's reign, as we have seen, large scale military expeditions were undertaken and important provinces with mainly agricultural base brought under Muslim control. In these provinces, as against the Arabian peninsula, the main source of state revenue was agricultural produce. From Iraq province alone the land revenue collected was ten crores twenty thousand dirhams. According to Baladhuri, the revenue from Jordan was 1,80,000 dinar,[27] from Palestine 3,50,000 dinar, from Damascus 4,00,000 dinars and from Ḥams, Qinissirin and al-'Awasim it was 8,00,000 dinars and according to some sources 7,00,000 dinars.[28]

Since these provinces yielded rich revenue, as can be seen from the revenue estimates given above, it was necessary to organize them administratively in a proper way. 'Umar devoted himself to this task. After the Muslim armies conquered Iraq, the first question that arose was what to to with the conquered lands. Many associates of 'Umar argued that the land be divided among the military men who had conquered it and this was how the war booty used to be divided according to the tribal customs. But that would have meant depriving the state of permanent source of revenue. Naturally Umar hesitated to accept this point of view and put the matter

[26] Baladhuri, *op. cit.*, p. 37.

[27] One dinar is approx. about 15 dirhams.

[28] Baladhuri, *op. cit.*, p. 324.

before a wider assembly of important people in Medina. After prolonged discussion 'Umar's point of view was accepted and the state was allowed to take charge of conquered land.[29] This also clearly shows that such important decisions were arrived at by discussion keeping the concrete situation in view and it was never argued that people cannot take decisions of a legislative nature.

After this vital matter was decided, 'Umar turned towards devising administrative measures to rationalize the revenue system. It was his wont to first thorougly acquaint himself with the local system prevailing from pre-conquered period and, as far as possible, retained it with necessary reforms, if any. 'Umar, in order to organize the revenue system better, issued orders to undertake measurement of land. The Arabs were not naturally acquainted with land survey system. According to Qadi Abu Yusuf (his book *Kitab al-Kharaj* gives details of this) two Arabs from Iraq who were acquainted with land revenue system were chosen for the task and great care was taken in completing the survey. The admeasured area of Iraq was worked out to 30,000 square miles.[30]

After the measurement was completed revenue was fixed according to the type of crop. According to Baladhuri, 'Uthman bin Hanif fixed ten dirham for one jarib (0.75 acres) of date-palm cultivated, four dirhams on one jarib of grapes, two dirhams for one jarib of barley as kharaj and Umar approved these rates.[31] Baladhuri also tells us that 'Umar declared all the land belonging to Kisra (the defeated ruler of Persia), those killed from his army and those who fled as state land. Income from these jagirs was around seven lakh dirhams[32] which was used for public works and welfare schemes. All these decisions were naturally dictated by practical considerations. 'Umar, we are told by the early historians (Abu Yusuf in his *Kitab al-Kharaj*, for example), exhorted his provincial governors not to be harsh in extracting the land revenue. When he received revenue from Iraq, he would call ten reliable persons from Kufah and ten from Basrah to testify that no injustice was done in collecting the revenue either from Muslims or dhimmis (i.e. protected non-Muslims). It is said that because of just methods employed, the land revenue from Iraq touched an all time high during 'Umar's reign. It went on declining thereafter.

[29] Shibli, *op. cit.*, pp. 289-90.
[30] *Ibid.*, p. 291. See also Baladhuri, *Ibid.*, p. 465.
[31] Baladhuri, *op. cit.* p. 465.
[32] *Ibid.*, p. 471.

From what has been discussed above it can be seen that the source of revenue of the early Islamic state underwent a basic change after the conquests. Earlier the source of revenue was mainly from urban area and was very scanty. Now it came mainly from rural areas and was abundant. The base of revenue thus shifted to agriculture. But still everything was in flux. Large scale conversions to Islam had not taken place and cultivation was done by non-Muslim peasantry. Non-Muslims were treated as dhimmis and had no effective say in administration (for that matter even converted non-Arab Muslims, despite their equal status in theory, were treated as *mawalis* i.e. clients of Arab tribes), it being Muslims' duty to protect them. Morevoer, the old land-holding class was in total disarray and most of them had fled. The new land-holding class of Muslims had not shaped as 'Umar had restrained the invading Arabs from acquiring land in the conquered provinces. Thus though the surplus now mainly came from peasantry, the land-holding class as such, had no domination over the state.

The political power was wielded by the Arabs in the large empire carved out by them. The natives from the Byzantine as well as Sassanid provinces were entitled for protection in exchange for the jizya (protection money or poll-tax) paid. Thus it would be wrong to characterize, as many Muslim writers often do, the early caliphal rule as democratic in spirit taking the entire area governed by it into consideration. Like the British empire, the metropolitan area was undoubtedly democratic in spirit as the important representatives and senior persons were consulted by the caliph which resulted in free and frank discussion before the final decision was taken and in many instances the caliph had to decide against his personal opinion. One should not, therefore, confuse between democratic-like functioning (not democractic functioning involving elective principle based on adult franchise) in Medina, the metropolitan city and the seat of Arab power with the state of political subjugation in the conquered provinces.

The conflict between the Arabs and non-Arabs developed much later (when the great majority from the former Byzantine and Sassanid provinces embraced Islam more out of sheer inducement or religious conviction than brute force as often alleged) assuming various forms--ranging from mere intellectual protest like that of the *Shu'ubiya's* to the armed struggle as that of Abu Muslim Khurasani or that of Ibn Muqanna'a or that of Qaramita or of Zanj. There was no question of such conflict emerging on surface during the reign of 'Umar as in the conquered provinces then the exploiting classes were in total disarray and the exploited classes were welcoming the Muslim rule as already pointed out. In that period even in the metropolitan centre no definite classes had yet emerged to influence the state policies in a decisive way. Many of them had commercial interests but in the new circumstances they found the military career more rewarding as it brought much coveted war booty with which commercial profits could hardly compare. Moreover, in these military expeditions a large number of Bedouin tribes also joined who had hardly any other interest than getting the war booty.

The social structure in the metropolitan area was more of a primitive tribal type than a cohesive and pronounced class structure. In this context it would be interesting to note that the caliph 'Umar, in view of this social reality, followed different policy in the Arabian peninsula from that in the former Byzantine province as regards the style of living of the state functionaries. Whereas in Arabia he demanded strict observance of simplicity in the style of living and punished those violating this rule severely, he did not strongly reprimand Mu'awiyah, the Umayyad governor of Syria, who lived in pomp and ostentation. He only mildly reproached Mu'awiyah for his style of living and accepted the latter's explanation that here in the former Roman province one cnnot govern if one lived as in a desert. It is quite obvious that the new rulers wanted to conform to the advanced culture of the old ruling class. A section of the rich traders of Mecca had long been cherishing the desire to take to the ways of sophisticated and stylish living of the Byzantine and Sassanid ruling classes with whom they often had to deal. Some of the early verses of the Quran describing the paradise and its pleasures are also a pointer in this direction:

> He will reward them for their steadfastness with robes of silk and the delights of Paradise. Reclining there upon soft couches, they shall feel neither the scorching heat nor the biting cold. Trees will spread their shade around them, and fruits will hang in clusters over them. They shall be served with silver dishes, and beakers as large as goblets; silver goblets which they themselves shall measure; and cups rim-full with ginger flavoured water from the Fount of Selsabil. They shall be attended by boys graced with eternal youth, who to the beholder's eyes will seem like sprinkled pearls. When you gaze upon that scene you will behold a kingdom blissful and glorious.[33]

This is a highly imaginative description of the luxuries of life. In fact, the

[33] The *Quran*, 76 : 12 to 21, Penguin Books, *op. cit.*, p. 17.

ruling classes of the Byzantine and Sassanid empires and their client states of Ghassanids and Lakhmidites lived in these luxuries and the Meccan Arabs had been observing this for long in their transactions with the rich and the nobles of these empires and client states. Now, thanks to Islam, they had defeated the Byzantine and Sassanid rulers and themselves had become the masters of a vast empire. Thus the Umayyads and some other Qurayshites soon adopted the ways of the former ruling classes and justified them on the basis of the cultural milieu prevailing there. Even 'Umar, the iron man of Islam, had to reconcile himself with the soft and easy ways of the new Muslim ruling elite in Syria and Egypt. He could enforce his directives on an egalitarian and a simple way of living with some degree of success only in the Arabian peninsula. The primitive tribal ethos of the people in the peninsula was more in keeping with the spirit of these directives. But even Mecca and Medina could not insulate themselves for long from the rising tide of wealth pouring in from all directions.

Until Abu Bakr's time, neither was there a paid army nor paid bureaucracy or the regular police force. But after the large scale conquests and the vast armed forces these expeditions required, these services could no longer be efficiently maintained purely on voluntary basis. Even the state-treasury was not established during Abu Bakr's time as whatever amount was received by way of war booty or zakāt was immediately distributed. No police force was created either. But during the 'Umar's reign the situation became much more complex and it became necessary to organize regular army, police and state treasury. A pucca structure was constructed to house the state treasury which was kept adjacent to a mosque to avoid theft.[34] As per Walid bin Hasham's advice, the Syrian model was adopted for establishing the state treasury.[35]

Similarly, until that time, there were no regular judicial and police services. Most of the cases were brought to the Caliph who decided them on the basis of the Quran, *hadith*, *sunna* or, if there were no precedents, by *qiyās* (analogy) and *ijtihād* (interpretation). If the Caliph found it difficult, he would consult the other senior companions of the Prophet like 'Ali or 'Abd-allah bin 'Abbas. Of course, the Caliph's decision was final. There was no separation of judiciary and executive and, God alone being the legislator, there was no question of Caliph or anyone else having the legislative powers. The Caliph was also installed in office by *bay'ah* (oath

[34]Shibli, *Ibid.*, p. 325.
[35]*Ibid.*, p. 324.

of allegiance) not for any fixed term, but for life. There was no regular police force either to keep watch against crimes. The cases were voluntarily reported. Until the rise of Islam and the state based on it, the tribal assemblies used to perform these functions according to the age- old traditions. The Arabs, therefore, lacked experience in running an elaborate state apparatus.

In view of the fast changing situation after the conquests of the former Byzantine and Sassanid provinces which had known well established administrative structure, the pressure was felt for a thorough organization of similar administrative apparatus for the new state. 'Umar, the second Caliph, made a beginning in this direction. He established a separate police service under Sahib al-Ahdāth (the chief of police). The functions of Ahdāth included maintaining watch over weights and measures, preventing people from constructing houses on the public roads or erecting other obstructions, stopping over-loading of animals, enforcing prohibition, etc.[36] There were no prisons. The punishments prescribed by the Quran (called *hudud*) were in keeping with the social ethos of the tribal Arabbia i.e. life for life, tooth for tooth, eye for eye, etc., as prescribed by God in *Torah* also. For theft the Quran prescribed amputation of hand and for illegitimate sexual intercourse hundred lashes. Umar, however, established prison-houses. According to Maqrizi he bought the house of Safwan bin Umayyah for 4,000 dirhams and converted it into a prison house.[37] According to Shibli 'Umar made certain changes in prescribing punishments. Abu Muhjin Thaqafi, for example, was put into jail for drunkenness, rather than being publicly lashed (The Quran, of course has not prescribed lashing for drinking). It clearly shows that lashing can be replaced by imprisonment and what is important is the spirit behind the punishment rather than its mode, but the orthodox *ulama* would not budge.

'Umar also organized the judicial service. He appointed a chief Qādi and number of qadis under him. It would be interesting to quote here from the letter 'Umar wrote to the governor of Kufa, Abu Musa Ash'ari on the principles of justice. He wrote:

> ...administration of justice is a necessary duty. Treat people equally be it in private audience or public sitting in matters of justice so that the weak should not despair of your justice and the strong should not hope for

[36]*Ibid.*, p. 322.

[37]Maqrizi, vol. ii., p. 287, cited by Shibli, *Ibid.*, p. 322.

favour. It is for the plaintiff to produce proof and it is for the defendant to deny on oath. Compromise is permissible provided it does not violate what has been permitted or prohibited (by *shari'ah*). If you have passed any judgement yesterday there would be nothing wrong in reversing it today on second thought in the interest of justice. If it is not there in the Quran or hadith contemplate over it deeply taking into account examples, similar cases and drawing analogies. Fix a time limit for the plaintiff to produce proof. Justice be done to him if he produces proof or else, his case be dismissed...[38] (tr. mine).

While the above letter of 'Umar shows his deep concern for justice without discriminating between the weak and strong, it also throws light on the primitive state at which the administration of justice was in the Islamic state at that time. 'Umar took pains for organizing the department of justice and fixed high salaries for the judges to insulate them from temptation of corruption. He was also careful in the choice of qādis, his main criteria being Islamic learning and personal integrity.

'Umar also fixed regular salaries for the soldiers and their officers. Soldiers got around 300 dirhams per year whereas their officers around ten thousand per annum—a difference of over thirty times. The salaries were paid in cash and were distributed through the reliable persons of the tribes to which the soliders belonged. Revenue registers were maintained in Persian, Syrian and Copt as Arabic language until then lacked the necessary vocabulary for the purpose. It can thus be seen that although the Prophet founded the first ever state in Arabia, its structure was extremely primitive in view of the limited functions it had to perform in a predominantly tribal society. His was, however, essentially a religious vision and he left behind him laws, inspired by this vision, many of which had universal validity while some were a product of local milieu. His successors, however, had to confront very complex problems after the conquered provinces of Byzantine and Sassanid empires were integrated into the Islamic state. It was then that a complex structure of the Islamic state began to be built up by assimilating, integrating or devising institutions unknown before in the simple and unsophisticated milieu of tribal Arabia. Also the state had to assume more and more repressive functions not needed before but now felt necessary as the class composition of the society changed. In pre-Islamic Mecca, a new mercantile class was emerging but was still too weak compared to the tribal structure to assume any

[38]'Allama Abul Ishaq Shirazi in his *Tabqat al-Fuqaha'*, cited by Shibli, *Ibid.*, pp. 310-11.

repressive functions by forming political organs like state. But of course they dominated the tribal senate. But now the whole social composition changed and new classes began to come into existence which were far more viable and stronger as compared to the tribal structure and hence the state had to assume more and more repressive functions in practice to maintain order in the newly emergent socio-economic structure although in theory it continued to be motivated by the divinely revealed laws. Also, what is important to note is that these laws were by no means barriers to the development of new property relations or growth of productive forces although certain checks and balances (based on the new morality of which Islam was harbinger) did operate as prescribed by Allah.

The class composition of the society was changing so fast that it was becoming increasingly difficult to reconcile different interests and during the reign of the third Caliph 'Uthman, the conflict began to surface. 'Umar was a strong man and ruled with an iron hand. It was no easy task to keep the Bedouins in check who were basically passionate lovers of personal freedom and had known no dominating state authority and also to promote the interests of those townsmen who were fast becoming rich due to the new opportunities opened up by the conquests of new provinces. 'Umar tried to rigorously impose the Islamic morality which was egalitarian in spirit due to its tribal roots. He meted out severe punishments to the offenders to check the corrupt practices and he seemed to succeed. But, as the later events proved, his success was more apparent than real.

It seems 'Umar himself was aware of this. He could not, unlike his predecessor, nominate his successor unhesitatingly. Maulana Maududi says:

> Haḍrat 'Umar became apprehensive during his last days that these tribal loyalties (which had not been totally obliterated despite the revolutionary influence of Islam) may be re-awakened and Islam may be faced with a new maelstrom. He, therefore, once told Ḥaḍrat 'Abd-allah bin 'Abbas while talking about his possible successors. 'If I suggest 'Uthman as my successor, he would inflict Bani Abi Mu'ayt (Bani Umayyah) on the people and they will violate the injunctions of Allah. By God if he did that (i.e. appoint 'Uthman) he would certainly do that and if 'Uthman did that people would rise in revolt and kill him.'[39]

[39]Sayyid Abul 'Ala Maududi, *Islami Riyasat*, compiled by Khurshid Ahmed, Islamic Publications Ltd., Lahore, 5th ed. 1974, p.431. Maududi has quoted Ibn 'Abd al-Barr *Al-Isti*'ab, vol.ii., published by Diratul Ma'arif, Hyderabad 2nd ed., p. 467.

Thus the new forces in the womb of the society were working in a different direction. 'Uthman, as 'Umar predicted, could not control these new forces and soon a dangerous situation developed plunging the society into a civil war. According to Dr Taha Husain there developed four groups namely (1) the Quraysh of Mecca, (2) the Helpers (Ansar), (3) the nomadic Arabs and (4) the subjects of the conquered countries. These groups contended against each other for more power and control over material resources. The most dominant group was that of the Qurayshites. The Qurayshites had been rich businessmen and skilled diplomats. Other Arabs were dependent on them for a number of reasons, most important being their livelihood. The Qurayshites now considered it as their monopoly to rule over others and control all the resources. This naturally created resentment among the non-Qurayshites. 'Uthman further aggravated this by giving all the key positions to Umayyads, a section of the Qurayshites.

The second group was of the Ansars. They fought along with the Prophet against the Qurayshites of Mecca and made sacrifices in the cause of Islam. Although some important leaders of this group were consulted in all important state matters, the new generation of Ansars which came of age when 'Uthman took over as caliph strongly resented their secondary role and nursed grievance against the Qurayshites. The third group was that of the nomadic Arabs to whom the new state was like a fetter to their freedom inflicted on them by the townspeople. They had rebelled soon after the death of the Prophet but their rebellion was crushed. They provided soldiers for the invading Muslim armies but the power was wielded by the Qurayshites. In the civil war the Bedouin soldiery became the mainstay of the Kharijite movement of which we have spoken earlier.

The fourth group was that of non-Arab peoples from the conquered provinces which was worst of all as it had no say in the state affairs monopolized only by the Arabs. Kufa, a huge military camp in Iraq, became centre of non-Arab mawalis captured in various wars. They were highly discontented. Moreover, new pressures developed when the children born of the female slaves in various expeditions came of age. Kufa thus became a great centre of turmoil. Uthman took another decision of far reaching economic consequence. In order to induce the Hejazis settled in Kufa to go back to the Hejaz to ease pressure of population on Kufa, he permitted them to exchange their lands held in Iraq with those holding in Hejaz. 'Umar had wisely disallowed this. Many shrewd people took advantage of this opportunity and exchanged their barren lands in Hejaz for the most fertile lands in the provinces and in no time became big

Uthman & the emergence of a feudalist élite.

land-holders. Some of them made most of it in Hejaz also by acquiring huge chunks of lands and importing slaves from outside to work. The slaves captured in the wars were easily available to work on the fields. The slave labour converted even the barren land of Hejaz into a fertile land. Thus came into existence in the Islamic society a class of big land-owners. This was the beginning of feudalism in Islam. In Mecca, Taif and Medina a class of wealthy land- owners came into existence which did not work and lived off the labour of slaves and workers. They had plenty of leisure and now passed their time in all sorts of worldly pleasures. The old base of Islamic morality based on simple and unostentatious living gave away, under the pressure of easily gotten wealth, to pomp and luxury. Dance, music and poetry which were disapproved by Islam were now in vogue right in the birth place of Islam.[40]

Here it would not be out of place to further quote Dr. Taha Husain who is a perceptive Muslim historian of this centurty:

> 'Uthman's economic revolution [referred to above] gave opportunity to the rich to invest their capital in some ventures and so they soon became owners of great enterprises and acquired a great deal of wealth. And, in no time, big landed properties came into existence and this way the affluence (and the resultant decadence) plagued Islam right in the beginning what had plagued the Roman empire at its end. What was responsible for the fall of the Roman empire was also responsible for the decline of the Islamic republic....In short the consequences of the system brought into existence by 'Uthman did not remain confined to politics alone; it not only created a super-rich class which exploited people and divided them into groups and sects in order to rule over them but also affected the whole society. Thus this revolution created a class society in which the ruling class had extraordinary wealth and means of production. This class controlled political power too. On the other hand there was the exploited class which toiled for the interests of the upper class and between them was the middleclass living in towns which took part in the military expeditions and guarded the borders. It was this middle-class which was sought to be manouvered by the rich class and divided into separate groups and sects....But at last the decisive struggle took place between the rich and middle classes[41] (tr. mine).

[40]Dr Taha Husain, *Ibid.*, pp. 113-25.

[41]*Ibid.*, pp. 154-55.

p 38 The process of class formation once set in motion by the historical forces never looked back and despite repeated struggles on the part of the Kharjites and others to recreate the early Islamic republic, the wheel of history could not be turned back. The civil war at last resulted in the victory of dynastic rule established by Mu'awiyah and the Islamic republic vanished into oblivion of the tribal past.

3. Islamic State Through Medieval Ages

The Islamic "republic" lasted for about thirty years after the death of the Prophet. As we have seen in the last chapter with the new conquests and the land-exchange policy followed by the third caliph 'Uthman, there emerged a wealthy and powerful class of landlords in Medina as well as in the provinces which could now influence state policies although it would be wrong to think that it was the most influential class. We do not propose to analyze various factors which led to 'Uthman's murder by the rebels as it is not our subject matter; suffice it may be to say that the policies followed by 'Uthman under pressure from the vested interests most of whom belonged to his own clan, led to this disaster.

'Ali was elected to be the fourth caliph after the death of 'Uthman. However, the forces unleashed by the formation of new classes and groups, could not be brought under control by him although his honesty, integrity and devotion to the cause of Islam cannot be disputed. 'Ali wanted to shape his policies in keeping with the teachings of Islam, especially its egalitarian spirit. But an individual, whatever the strength of his will and character, cannot change the course of history when the tide of historical forces is against him. The flow of wealth and formation of the powerful groups of big landlords had, forever, brought an end of the classless tribal structure of the Arabian society. The conquest of the provinces outside Arabia was the beginning of this process. 'Umar, for certain period of time, could keep the situation under control as the powerful groups had yet not emerged partly due to the wise policies he followed and partly due to the fact that it was the beginning of the process of emergence of the new historical forces. However, as we have seen in the last chapter, he also had to bow to the pressure mounted by the forces led by Mu'awiyah and allow them to consume more and lead ostentatious life.

By the time 'Ali became caliph, these forces were very well entrenched and the egalitarian structure of the Arabian society had been nearly shattered. He found it extremely difficult to execute his policies and he too,

Dynasic Rule

fell prey to the sword of an assassin. The assassin belonged to an extremist group called Khawārij (i.e. seceders) most of whom were Bedouin soldiery. To these desert nomads the institution of state dominated by the townspeople hardly made any sense. Over and above it the various groups and parties were now locked in battle to capture the state machine. The Bedouins who had no such interests found it utterly senseless, raised the slogan *la hukma illa lillah* (sovereignty is only for God) and revolted.

In Syria, the former Byzantine province, Mu'awiyah had consolidated his position and begun adopting the imperial ways for which, as indicated above, the new property relations were paving the way. Mu'awiyah was a shrewd politician and an astute diplomat. Though a companion of the Prophet, he was least concerned with the ideology of Islam and devoted his energies to gain the position of a supreme ruler in the new empire. This he sought to do with the help of the propertied classes and the emerging bureaucracy which held key administrative positions and governorships in various important provinces. 'Ali, on the other hand, tried to sincerely follow the egalitarian path emphasized by Islam which had found easy acceptance among the people who had not been divided into classes—at least it had not become the predominant reality. Thus the emerging property relations were not in keeping with the early Islamic course 'Ali wanted to follow. And so in this decisive historical struggle 'Ali lost and Mu'awiyah won.

Mu'awiyah, with the support of the new forces in the society and through his astute diplomacy—in this sense he was one of the best representatives of the Qurayshite tradition—succeeded not only in consolidating his position but also in getting his son Yazid nominated to the august office of *amir Al-Mu'minīn* (i.e. the commander of the faithfuls, the title used for the caliph since the time of 'Umar). This was in the gross violation of the Arab tradition which had not known dynastic rule. This act was shocking, to say the least, for many pious and senior companions of the Prophet who were then alive but the conditions which sustained the Islamic theo-democracy --to use Maududi's term,[1] were no longer operative and the emergence of the new property relations on the model of Byzantine and Sassanid empires were paving way for the triumph of dynastic rule. Thus we see that with the change in the historical conditions the earlier theo-democratic form of the government changed into a kind of secular-dynastic rule.

[1]Sayyid Abul Ala Maududi *Islami Riyasat*, compiled by Khurshid Ahmed, Islamic Publications, Lahore, 1974, p. 130.

Now the Umayyad dynasty, after crushing the rebellions of Husayn (the son of 'Ali and the grandson of the Prophet), Mukhtar and 'Abdullah bin Zubayr which, in one way of the other, were attempts to defeat the alien dynastic system and restore the early elective system of Islam firmly established itself. In the changed circumstances any attempt or rebellion to restore earlier form of government was difficult. The new system was more congenial to the new provinces of Syria and Iraq. The political centre, therefore, shifted from Medina to Syria during the Umayyad rule and later on to Baghdad during the Abbasid period. The concept and form of the Islamic state was now completely transformed with the growth of new classes, productive forces and property relations. Although the ruler was still called *Amir al-Mu'minin* (commander of the faithfuls), he was no more than a monarch. In the metamorphosed state set-up there was nothing more Islamic than the fact that the ruler professed Islam and enforced certain provisions of the *Shari'ah* in personal and criminal matters. It was the result of such circumstances that a number of traditions were coined justifying any regime which did as little as enforcing the Islamic way of prayer.

Thus *Muslim* has recorded such traditions. One such tradition says: "The Prophet said you will be governed by the rulers who would enforce justice only partly and partly would indulge in evil. Those who expressed their displeasure at them, shall acquit themselves and those who disapproved of them shall also save themselves but those who approved of them and followed them would be accountable (before God). When some people asked (the Prophet) should we not fight against them? The Prophet said no as long as they pray."[2] (tr. mine.) There are similar other traditions recorded by *Muslim* which clearly prohibit fighting against the unjust rulers as long as they continue to pray i.e. nominally profess Islam.

The state was otherwise getting increasingly feudalized in as much as more and more landed properties came into existence. The rulers were no longer inspired by the Islamic vision nor did they show much concern about it. They adopted all the feudal customs prevalent in imperial courts. Prof. Hitti says, "One hundred years after the death of the founder of Islam his followers were the masters of an empire greater than that of Rome at its zenith, an empire extending from the Bay of Biscay to the Indus and the confines of China and from the Aral Sea to the lower cataract of the Nile....Damascus, which young Muhammad according to tradition hesitated to enter because he wished to enter paradise only once, had

[2]*Ibid.*, pp. 187-88. Maududi has cited these traditions from Muslim.

become the capital of this huge empire. In the heart of the city, set like a pearl in the emerald of its gardens, stood the glittering palace of the Umayyads, commanding a view of flourishing plain which extended south-westward to Mount Hermon with its turban of perpetual snow. Al-Khadra' (the green one) was its name. Its builder was none other than Mu'awiyah, founder of the dynasty, and it stood beside th Umayyad Mosque....In the audience chamber a square seat covered with richly embroidered cushions formed the caliphal throne, on which during formal audiences the caliph, in gorgeous flowing robes, sat cross-legged. On the right stood his paternal relatives in a row according to seniority, on the left his maternal relatives. Courtiers, poets and petitioners stood behind."[3]

The early Islamic caliphate, as we have seen, had not known such kingly courts and differences in ranks. The Arab traditions strongly influenced by the nomadic environment around were totally against all this. So the first four caliphs heading the Islamic state strictly observed these traditions. It was not only the rulers or the members of their dynasty who took to luxury and courtly ways but also the ruling classes. Prof. Hitti says: "With this increased flow of wealth the two Holy Cities became less holy. They developed into a centre of worldly pleasure and gaiety and a home of secular Arab music and song. In Makkah was established a kind of clubhouse patronized by guests who, we are told, had facilities for hanging their outer garments on pegs—apparently an innovation for al-Hijaz—before indulging in chess, backgammon, dice or reading. To al-Madinah Persian and Byzantine slave songstresses (qiyan) flocked in incresing numbers. Amorous poetry kept pace with other new developments. Houses of ill repute (buyut al-qiyan) flourished in al-Madinah and were patronized by no less a poet than al-Farazdaq of national fame. As these female slaves sang and played soft melodies for the entertainment of their wealthy masters and guests, the latter, attired in colourful robes, reclined on square mattresses or cushions while they inhaled the perfume of burning spices and sipped from silver goblets the ruddy wines of Syria.[4]

Despite many attempts by the Kharijites and other puritanic 'Ulama to restore early conditions and strengthen the moral foundations of the state, nothing much could be achieved. The Abbasid period outdid the Umayyad period in wealth and splendour. "Especially on ceremonial occasions, such as the installation of the caliph, weddings, pilgrimages and receptions for

[3] Philip K. Hitti, *History of the Arabs*, Macmillan and Co., London, 1958, p. 215, cf. Aghani, vol. iv. p. 80.

[4] *Ibid.*, p. 237.

foreign envoys," says Hitti, "did the courtly wealth and magnificence make its fullest display. The marriage ceremony of the Caliph al-Mamun to the eighteen-year-old Buran, daughter of his vizier, was celebrated in 825 with such fabulous expenditure of money that it has lived in Arabic literature as one of the unforgettable extravaganzas of the age. At the nuptials a thousand pearls of unique size, we are told, were showered from a gold tray upon the couple who stood on a golden mat studded with pearls and sapphires. A two-hundred-roll candle of ambergris turned the night into day."[5]

In short, we can say that the Umayyad or Abbasid rule, in substance as well as in form, was no different from the Byzantine or Sassanid rule which it had overthrown with revolutionary zeal. The earlier simplicity and puritanism could not be restored as the material conditions had totally changed and new classes had emerged with powerful interests in maintaining the system. *Kharaj* (land tax) was the main form of revenue although trading activities also supplemented it. It means the system was based on exploitation of the peasantry. The area where Islam originated was not agricultural; in fact there was no production of any sort except date-palms in a few scattered oases. The Meccan economy mainly depended on profits made by exchange of goods and not their production and hence trade was highly encouraged by Islam. According to one tradition recorded by Tirmidhi an honest trader will be in the company of the prophets and martyrs.[6]

Now the whole basis of economy had changed, and so did the composition of the ruling class. As it was not possible to change the new productive forces and hence the structure of the state, the political theory of Islam was made to conform to suit the new conditions. These theories also underwent changes from the rise of the Umayyads to the decline of the Abbasids as during this period spread over several centuries many political changes occurred. These theories reflected these political changes.

When the Umayyads usurped power and confined it to their dynasty against the Islamic tradition, the *'ulama* at first strongly resented this move and kept themselves aloof from the rulers. Some 'ulama who had high character continued to boycott the rulers and could not be swayed either by temptation or fear for their lives. Imam Ghazali (d. A.D. 1111) wrote

[5]Philip K. Hitti, *The Arabs*, Gateway Edition, Chicago, 1962, p. 111.

[6]'Allama Yusuf al-Qardawi, *Al-Halal wa al-Haram fi al-Islam*, Urdu tr. Shams Peerzada, Al-Darus Salfiyah, Bombay, 1977, p. 184.

in his *Ihya al-'Ulūm,* "In our time all or nearly all the possessions of rulers are unlawful. And why not? Only *zakāt, khums* and war booty are lawful and of these there is no trace in our times. Now remains only jazya (only lawful source of income) and that too is extracted by use of force and hence becomes unlawful" (tr. mine). Then about paying visits to the monarchs he says, "One should keep away from them (rulers) so that they cannot see them nor they should see him (i.e. ruler) and this is obligatory as this is the only way to guard one's religion. Their tyranny should be hated and their survival condemned and they should not be praised. One should not inquire about them nor one should keep relations with those who meet them"[7] (tr. mine). In the same work Imam Ghazali has quoted several instances of those *'ulama* who kept away from the Umayyad rulers and if summoned to the court admonished them.

But most of the *'ulama* veered round the view that in order to preserve law and order or social stability it is necessary to support government whatever its form or character. We have noted above Ghazali's views about keeping away from salātins (rulers) as they are tyrants and do not conform to the Islamic laws. But even according to his political theory caliphate, even though dominated by sultan, is necessary for keeping law and order in the society. It is also necessary for ensuring collective security and historical continuation of the Muslim community.[8] We will discuss Ghazali's theory of Islamic government little later. Before this some light should be thrown on the political situation when the modified theories of the Islamic government were propounded.

After the decline of the Umayyad power, Abbasids organized an armed rebellion and succeeded in seizing power with the help of discontented Persian forces mainly from the province of Khorasan. The Abbasids soon consolidated their position and made attempts to legitimize their rule with the help of *'ulama*. Like the Umayyads they had not been "elected" to the office of the caliph but had siezed power by organizing an armed uprising. Though the learned theologians, as pointed out above, had not approved of the Umayyad rule, they had veered round the view that rebellion against the established authority should not be permitted in the interest of stability. Number of traditions (many of them forged) were cited in support of this

[7]Quoted from *Ihya al-'ulum* by Shibli Nomani in *Al-Ghazali,* Nami Press, Kanpur, nd., pp. 232-33.

[8]Leonard Binder *"Al-Ghazali's Theory of Islamic Government,"* Urdu tr. by Sayyid Abid Ali Abid, *Qurun-e-Wusta ke Musalmanon ke Siyasi Nazarye,* Iqbal Academy, Lahore, 1958, p. 18.

stand. Even some of the verses of the Quran were subjected to different interpretation to suit the political exigency.

The famous Quranic verse, *"Believers, obey Allah and the Apostle and those in authority* (emphasis mine) among you. Should you disagree about anything refer it to Allah and the Apostle, if you truly believe in Allah and the Last Day,"[9] was extensively used to argue that whosoever is in authority must be obeyed, in some cases adding the rider, that as long as the ruler prayed (as laid down by Islam). However, the Abbasids had rebelled and captured power. But when they became the effective authority the same verse of the Quran was used to demand obedience from the Muslims. The *'ulama* took the same view once again and prohibited rebellion against the Abbasid rulers. But the situation became much more complicated when the Abbasid caliph became a nominal head. The Islamic theoreticians once again had to use their ingenuity to legitimize the new complex situation. Al- Mawardi was the most systematic political theorist of Islam of that period. Before discussing Al-Mawardi's theory it would be interesting to quote some of the traditions which were current in those days. These traditions, ascribed to the Prophet, were circulated to bolster the authority of any ruler who cared to install himself in office with the help of sword.

Ibn al-Muqaffa', another great political thinker of early Islam, has quoted some of these traditions in support of his theory. While emphasizing complete and unconditional obedience to the caliph, he quotes the following tradition: "One who obeys me, indeed he obeys God; and one who obeys the Imam, indeed he obeys me." (Here Imam means the caliph of the time.) Again, according to another tradition, "Even if a nose-cleft negro slave is made your sovereign, hearken to him and obey him." Ibn Muqaffa' maintains that loyalty to Imam is essential even if he happens to be a tyrant, because it is in keeping with the will and desire of God. He further narrates a tradition from Ibn 'Abbas that the Prophet said: "When God intends good to a people, He appoints over them governors who are forbearing and puts their properties in the hands of tolerant men; and when He wants to put them to ordeal, He appoints over them stupid governors and entrusts their goods into the hands of avaricious men."[10]

The traditions quoted above clearly imply that whatever the character of a ruler and even if he is a tyrant, it is obligatory to obey him as this is what

[9] *Quran* 4:59 tr. by N.J. Dawood, Penguin Books, 1966, p. 363.

[10] For this and previous two traditions quoted see Qamaruddin Khan's *Al-Mawardi's Theory of the State*, Bazm-e-Iqbal, Lahore, nd.

God desires. Although such a position was clearly in flagrant contradiction to the practice of the close companions of the Prophet who were associated with the first four caliphs. These caliphs were publicly criticized, reprimanded and opposed by the Muslims; they tolerated and in some cases even welcomed such criticism but never demanded uncritical obedience. If the Prophet had favoured blind obedience as these traditions purported to do, his companions would have known better and so could have easily silenced the critics and opponents. However, during the medieval ages, the whole historical situation had changed and the state had acquired, under the hegemony of propertied classes and bureaucracy, a thoroughly repressive character. The political theories of Islam, evolved during this period, must, therefore, be seen in this light. Another tradition ascribed to the Prophet expresses the real intentions of the rulers of the time very explicitly: "Do not abuse your governors, for if they do good, for them is the reward and for you is to be *grateful* (emphasis supplied); and if they do evil, on them lies the responsibility and for you is to endure; and indeed they are the vengeance of God, with them. He strikes anyone He likes; therefore do not invite the vengeance of God with your defiance and anger, but welcome it with submission and humility."[11] This tradition hardly needs any comments and clearly rules out any rebellion. If the ruler rules justly it is God's boon and if he is a tyrant it is God's wrath and in either cases defiance is not permitted as his defiance would amount to God's defiance and this no Muslim can ever contemplate.

Al-Mawardi's Political Theory[12]

Al-Mawardi was acclaimed as one of the ablest men of his age. He was not only a distinguished judge but also an author of great repute. He wrote mostly on law and politics. His views on the political theory are propounded in *Al-Ahkām as-Sultaniyah* which is his *magnum opus*. Only a small portion of the work is devoted to political theory, the rest being devoted to details of administration and rules of government. But this small portion is extremely important as it was first ever attempt at propounding the theory of Islamic state and left enduring influence on the Muslim political thought until our own time.

According to Mawardi the institution of Imamate is necessary as a

[11] See *Kitab al-Kharaj* by Abu Yusuf, p. 11 quoted by Qamar-ud-Din Khan, *Ibid.*, pp. 13-14.

[12] See Al-Mawardi's *al-Ahkam as-Sultaniyah* and Qamar-ud-Din Khan's *Al-Mawardi's Theory of the State, op. cit.*, for the account of Mawardi's theory.

requirement of the *Shari'ah* and not as a requirement of reason. The appointment of an Imam by the consensus of the Muslim community is obligatory.[13] The Imamate is instituted by means of election and the electoral college shall consist of persons with special qualifications (these qualifications are justice, knowledge of religion and wisdom).[14] Al-Mawardi, to suit his political exigency, omits the case when a licentious person is elected as Imam. This omission is deliberate as the Buwayhids, who actually wielded political power, were appointing caliphs to suit their selfish ends. In fact it was in the interests of the Buwayhids that caliphs should not take any interest in the affairs of the state and should indulge in pleasure-seeking so as to leave them alone to exercise political authority.

Again, as against the *Kharijites* who believed in "complete democracy and universal franchise," al-Mawardi advocates the view that those living in the capital have priority in electing the caliph as the death of the previous caliph is first known there, and political considerations require immediate appointment of a new caliph, and also as most of the people possessing the necessary qualifications for the imamate generally reside there.[15] Further, the principle of election of a caliph is not consistently followed as Mawardi says that the Imam is appointed in one of the two ways: (a) he may be elected by the electoral college (b) he may be nominated by the ruling Imam.[16] In the first case some scholars maintain that the Imam must be elected by the members of electoral college from all cities whereas others opposing this view feel that Abu Bakr was elected only by the people of Medina. Some even say that only five people are sufficient to elect the Imam as it happened in the case of Abu Bakr and 'Uthman. But in Mawardi's opinion even one person is enough to elect a caliph.[17] Mawardi's opinion gets support from al-Ash'ari. But it is essentially a concession to the changed situation when the Islamic state stood feudalized.

Al-Mawardi also maintains that the election of a less qualified person in the presence of a more qualified person is perfectly legal, provided the former fulfils all the conditions of the Imamate.[18] This has been done

[13]Al-Mawardi, *Al-Aḥkām as-Sultaniyah*, p. 3, see Qamar-ud-Din Khan, *op. cit.*, p. 25.
[14]Al-Mawardi, *op. cit.*, p. 4.
[15]Al-Mawardi, *op. cit.*, p. 5.
[16]*Ibid.*
[17]*Ibid.*, p. 7.
[18]*Ibid.*, p. 10.

obviously with a view to give free license to the Buwayhids to choose most worthless and rotten caliphs to tow their line. It was also directed against the Shi'ahs who believe that an inferior person cannot have precedence over a superior one. In fact this doctrine of inferior person taking precedence over superior became the agreed opinion of all the Sunnite jurists and theologians. Also, according to Mawardi existence of two Imams contemporaneously is illegal[19] although al-Ash'ari maintains that two Imams at a time are possible if their territories are far-flung and widely spread and separated by an ocean, which hinders easy communication between the two. Al-Mawardi was anxious not to let the Fatimids of Egypt and the Umayyads of Spain to claim legitimacy., But today al-Mawardi's theory in this respect cannot be accepted.

Further, al-Mawardi maintains that the Imam can nominate any suitable person as his successor, provided he does not happen to be his father or son. The concurrence of the *Ahl al-hall wa al-'aqd* (persons of responsibility and wisdom) must be obtained in case he nominates his son. Also, he can nominate any other relation without requiring the concurrence.[20] Commenting on this Qamaruddin Khan says, "It was the theory of nomination that cut at the very root of democratic ideals in Islamic polity. It has been persistently resorted to by every Muslim ruler after the days of the Pious Caliphate, to perpetuate dynastic and despotic rule among the Muslim peoples. Thus apparently the structure of the Caliphate was maintained by the Umayyads, the Abbasids, the Fatimids, and the Turks but the spirit of Islamic democracy was buried in the coffin of Ali, the last of Pious Caliphs."[21] The historical conditions which gave rise to that spirit could not be revived and so the pious caliphate vanished from reality into the oblivion of history.

Writing on the privileges of the caliph, al-Mawardi says that when a person is duly elected as Imam the people should entrust all their affairs to him and must give him their unquestioning obedience. The Imam may not consult them in the affairs of state, yet they must obey him.[22] This was also in violation of the practice of the first four caliphs and also against the clearly laid down injunction of the Quran (Take counsel with them in the conduct of affairs, 3:159 and see also 42:38). The monarchy strictly controlled by the Bywayhids with their military might could not have

[19] *Ibid*, p. 11.
[20] *Ibid.*, pp. 14-15.
[21] *Ibid.*, pp. 29-30.
[22] *Ibid.*, p. 27.

savoured consultation with the people in what they considered as their personal privilege. Al-Mawardi accordingly had to twist his theory to suit the era of despotism.

Al-Mawardi also lists the duties of an Imam foremost among which is to enforce Islamic Shari'ah as understood and propounded by the consensus of ancient authorities, innovation being disallowed. All the Muslim rulers throughout the Islamic history have followed, or at least pretended to follow, this path of enforcing the Shari'ah as propounded by the consensus of earlier *'ulama* and, in almost all the cases, this has been considered *raison d'etre* of the Islamic state. Whatever the form or content of the policies of the government, if it proclaims its intention to enforce, or practices, Islamic Shari'ah, it is considered *ipso facto* an Islamic state. We will discuss more of it in the subsequent chapters.

Among other duties of an Imam are: (1) dispensation of justice and disposal of all litigations in accordance with Shari'ah and thus putting the strong and weak on the same pedestal, (2) maintenance of law and order to make it possible for the people to lead peaceful life, and proceed in their economic activities freely, and travel in the land without fear, (3) enforcement of the criminal code of the Quran so that people do not violate the prohibitions of God; this in fact is subsumed in the first duty itself to enforce Shari'ah, (4) defence of the frontiers against foreign invasions to guarantee the security of life and property to Muslims and non-Muslims both in the Islamic state, (5) organization and prosecution of religious war against those who oppose the call of Islam or refuse to enter the protection of the Islamic state as non-Muslim subjects as the Imam is bound by the covenant of God to establish the supremacy of Islam over all other religions and faiths. Such a duty enjoined on the caliph by Mawardi was alright as a theory in the medieval period but even then the practice had to deviate from this line and, of course, many would not agree with Mawardi that the head of an Islamic state is bound by the covenant of God to establish the supremacy of Islam over other religions. And, as for the modern times, even the most orthodox Islamic state like Saudi Arabia cannot proclaim any such intention, let alone practicing it.

Collection of kharaj and *zakat* in accordance with the laws of Shari'ah without extortion or pressure, fixing of allowances and stipends from the state treasury (Bait al-Mal) to those who deserve, appointment of honest and sincere men to the principal offices of state to secure sound and effective administration and lastly to personally look into and apprising himself of the affairs of his dominions so that he may himself direct the national policy without engrossing himself in luxury or religious devotion are also the important duties of an Imam, according to Mawardi.[23]

In the circumstances in which he lived, al-Mawardi legitimizes the Buwayhid control of state by saying that if the Imam is overpowered by one of his counsellors and assistants, who appropriates all authority to himself, but does not openly defy the Imam, the Imam will continue in his office, provided the usurper rules in accordance with the injunctions of the Shari'ah, and in deference to the accepted norms of justice. This is to ensure that the functions of the Imamate should continue to be performed, and that the people do not fall prey to the ways of evil on account of the non-enforcement of the laws of the Shari'ah. Mawardi further says that if the governor or the usurper declares his allegiance to the caliph and promises to maintain the unit of the caliphate, enforces the laws of Shari'ah, and cooperates with the Imam against the foes of Islam, the caliph shall recognize his absolution by conferring on him the deed of investiture formally and publicly. This arrangement had no precedence in the practice of Islamic history but, then, the actual operative conditions have logic of their own. Mawardi was just trying to adjust his theory to the objective conditions.

Botched political thinking

But there is one relieving feature in al-Mawardi's theory of Islamic state which distinguishes him from the other medieval Muslim thinkers. He does not make it obligatory to obey an unjust ruler. In his opinion obedience is due only when the order of the ruler is in keeping with truth. He clearly advocates disobedience when the Imam either falls an open prey to sensual passions or becomes sceptic of the basic creed of Islam.[24] But Qamar-ud-Din Khan points out, "No machinery has been proposed by means of which the will of the people may be ascertained or the Imam may be voted out of power. There is no precedent in Islamic history when an Imam may have been removed from office by legal or peaceful means. And since Imam is the supreme authority, not responsible to any tribunal, it is obvious that he cannot sit to impeach himself or allow others to interdict him. On the contrary, there are numerous examples in history when tyrant Imams persecuted pious and innocent people and even sent them to the gallows."[25]

But, unfortunately, Mawardi does not spell out a clear case of rebellion against an unjust or a tyrant Imam. His provision, therefore, that an unjust

[23] *Ibid.*, pp. 27-31.
[24] *Ibid.*, pp. 31-32.
[25] *Ibid.*, p. 47.

Al - Ghazali

Imam need not be obeyed is, at best, of an academic interest. In fact he was a civil servant and, even if he wanted, he could not have advocated an open rebellion against the ruler. His failure, therefore, to elaborate a theory of rebellion may not have been wilful as Qamar-ud-Din maintains. Moreover, at his heart, he was for the impotent Abbasid caliphs vis-a-vis the Shi'ite Buwayhids who exercised actual power. His advocacy of rebellion would have further weakened the position of the Abbasids.

Al-Ghazali is another major thinker who has expounded his views on the necessity and functions of Islamic state. As against the Mu'tazalites who maintained that the basis of caliphate is reason rather than Shari'ah, al-Ghazali, like other Sunnite theologians, emphasizes that Shari'ah is the real basis of caliphate.[26] Being well versed in philosophy he presents his views more logically and systematically than others. He is of the opinion that the caliphate should be necessarily utilitarian and that appointment of Imam must be first, on the basis of ijma'a (concensus) and then on the basis of the intention of the Prophet. Ghazali thinks that the Prophet's intention is the basis of the community's concensus. The Prophet wanted to establish an Islamic society and for this it is necessary to protect both life as well as source of livelihood and hence the necessity of state.[27] This clearly implies that the establishment of state is a social necessity and is not necessarily theocratic in origin.

According to al-Ghazali the main purpose of caliphate is to enforce the provisions of Shari'ah through which alone one can achieve liberation and in order to enforce Shari'ah social stability is a must and hence the necessity for a centralized and repressive power which can enforce law and order in the society. According to Ghazali without an Imam the provisions of Shari'ah with respect to religious rites, economic and political matters etc. cannot be implemented as in the absence of a caliph no decision or agreement of a qadi (a Muslim judge) can be implemented. In other words the qadi derives his authority, not from any worldly potentate but from the Imam appointed as per the concensus of the community.[28] Thus, according to him, in the absence of Imamate, all human relations will result in "sin" and anarchy and such a state of affairs will affect the chances of indiviual human liberation too. Although Ghazali is an orthodox Sunnite and a bitter

[26]Al-Ghazali, *Al-Iqtisad fil I'tiqad*, Cairo, nd., pp. 104-9.
[27]Leonard Binder, "Al-Ghazali's Theory of Islamic Government," *op. cit.*, p. 11-12.
[28]Al-Ghazali, *Al-Iqtisad fil I'tiqad,* op. cit., p. 107.

critic of Isma'ilis, in this respect he comes closer to their position. The Isma'ilis too hold that the existence of Imam is highly necessary in order to enforce Shari'ah. Of course, the Isma'ilis do not, unlike Ghazali, believe in the appointment of Imam by ijma'.

Al-Ghazali also lays stress on the fact--looking to the realities of his time this was inevitable--that a jurist is forced to acknowledge the existing power (which was wielded, not by caliph but by the Turks) since the alternative is anarchy and stoppage of social life for lack of a properly constituted authority.[29] Thus the caliphate in Ghazali's theory stood for the whole of Islamic government, and contained three elements, the caliph, the sultan (i.e. one who actually wields the power), and the *'ulama*, who by their approval of the sultan's choice of caliph in the bay'a and by their fatwas (religious opinion) expressed the functional authority of the Shari'a.[30]

Al-Ghazali's *Nasihat al-Muluk* (*Counsel for Kings*) written in or shortly after 1109-10 for Sanjar, who was then governor of Khurrasan on behalf of the Seljuq Sultan Muhammad, contains his view on the Sultanate as distinct from the Caliphate. Ghazali changes the interpretation of the Quranic verse "Obey God, obey the Prophet and those in authority among you" to mean obedience to God, the prophets, and emirs, i.e. the temporal rulers. Now the caliph is no longer there and the Sultan is endowed with divine effulgence, and obedience to him as the chosen of God is incumbent upon the people, but only he who practices justice is the true Sultan. Further he maintains in the above book that religion is made strong by kingship, and kingship by the army, and the army by wealth; wealth is assured by making the country populous and flourishing, and this result is achieved by justice. Ghazali, moreover, wants the Sultan to be strong to maintain law and order. He divides the duties of the ruler into his duty towards God and his duty towards the people. The former includes the performance of canonical religious duties, the avoidance of innovation, and the suppression of heresy.[31] Thus we see that even the most eminent 'alim like al-Ghazali legitimized a purely feudal institution like kingship for which there was no place in the theory and practice of early Islamic political thought.

[29] G.E. Von Grunebaum, *Medieval Islam*, Chicago, 1964, pp. 168 cf. *The Legacy of Islam*, ed. by Joseph Sacht with C.E. Bosworth, Oxford University Press, 1974, p. 414.

[30] A.K.S. Lambton, "Islamic Political Thought," in The *Legacy of Islam, op. cit.*, p. 414.

[31] See A.K.S. Lambton, *Ibid.*, p. 418.

Ibn Taymiyya (d. 1328) is another eminent Muslim thinker who tries to come to terms with the political realities of his time. He is comparatively more progressive in his views. Although he says that if religion and power are separated it would result in disorder but, unlike other conservative Muslim thinkers, he rejects the view for a single and universal Imam and for the possession by him of ideal qualities. He comes very close to the modern day political realities by holding the view that the real unity of the community does not consist in a *fictitious political unity* but in the confessional solidarity which each autonomous state experiences by belonging to an organic whole. He makes it obligatory on Imam to take recourse to consultation (shura') as required by the Quran and subjects, while participating in the life of the community and administration of state, must ensure obedience to the Imam.[32]

However, Ibn Taymiyya is no less enthusiastic in accepting the institution of kingship. He calls sultan the Shadow of God upon earth, a title which was widely used by the Muslim kings during the Middle-ages and he is of the opinion that even an unjust or ignorant ruler is to be obeyed. Disobedience, according to him, is only permissible in the event of the ruler's decision being manifestly contrary to the Quran, the *sunna*, and the consensus of the earlier *'ulama*. For him disobedience resulting in *fitna* (general disorder) is an unforgivable sin. Thus we see that even on Ibn Taymiyya's thinking the deep impress of the medieval period is evident.

With the rise of the Abbasids the Sassanid elements entered into the thought system of the caliphate. Abu Yusuf, who was appointed qadi of Baghdad in 782, wrote the *Kitab al-Kharaj* addressed to Harun al-Rashid. This book is an implicit protest against the adaptation of the principles of Islamic ideology to Sasanian influences. He discusses the problems of constitutional theory in the introduction to this book. However, his protest remained ineffective as the historical forces were moving in a different direction altogether. The dilemma for Abu Yusuf was as to how to legitimize a government which was siezed by force of arms by the Abbasids as in the theory of Islamic state a caliph had to be elected or appointed by consultation or consensus.

Abu Yusuf sees no other way and thinks that perhaps it is the will of God.[33] He is very particular about the observance of religious injunctions

[32]*Ibid*., p. 415 and H. Laoust, Essai Sur les doctrines Socials et politiques de Ibn Taimiyah, Cairo, 1939 and Le Traite de droit public d'Ibn Taimiyah, Beirut, 1948 for a full discussion of the theory of Ibn Taimiyah.

[33]Abu Yusuf, *Kitab al-Kharaj*, second ed., Cairo, 1352 A.H., p. 5

and clearly says that if the Caliph follows the path of true religion he and his dynasty will remain in full control of government.[34] He roundly condemns a licentious caliph and indirectly says that it is not necessary to obey him. He is also particular in emphasizing that it is obligatory for a caliph to look after the spiritual welfare of the Muslim community. According to Qamar-ud-Din Khan, "He (Abu Yusuf), however, does not lay down any direct and material check which may restrain the caliph from absolute despotism. The caliph is responsible only to God. After asserting this view, Abu Yusuf vainly attempts to warn the caliph against the judgement of God on the day of Resurrection."[35]

Nizam al-Mulk (d. 1092) was a secretary of state of vizier to Alp Arslan and then to Malikshah. His political thought was deeply influenced by the Sassanid practices. This is obvious from his book *Siyāsat-Nāma*. He was more a bureaucrat than a political theorist and hence was more interested in administrative affairs. Greater part of Siyāsat-Nāma has been devoted to administrative matters. But he also deals with political theory. Nizam al-Mulk is not concerned with who rules but how he rules. He also does not show much concern about the way a ruler occupies the seat of power. For him what matters is the maintenance of the present social order which has been devised by God.[36] Thus we see that Nizam al-Mulk is essentially status quoist. This is also to be borne in mind that the type of social system he has in mind is not the one advocated by Islam--in theory at least there is no place for feudal relations of production in Islam--but the one representing the Sassanid heritage.

There are some striking features of the political theory of Nizam al- Mulk which must be noted. As pointed out earlier, powerful propertied classes both, feudal as well as mercantile, feudal of course predominating, had emerged during the period of pious caliphs. But the orthodox *'ulama* had not formally integrated the class concept into their religio-political thinking and had maitntained the concept of equality of all the faithfuls. But Nizam al-Mulk, a bureaucrat carrying the deep impress of the Sassanid social system, made the class system integral part of his political theory. He feels that if the class differences are maintained the ends of justice would be met and the best of social system would come into existence. He

[34] *Ibid.*

[35] Qamar-ud-Din Khan, *Ibid.*, p. 14.

[36] Leonard Binder, "Nizam al-Mulk's Political Theory," Urdu tr. by Sajjad Rizvi in *Qurun-e-Wusta ke Musalmanon ke Siyasi Nazariyat*, Bazme-Iqbal, Lahore, 1958, p. 51.

does not clearly state the nature of classes he has in mind but he includes the Abbasids and Alids in the list of nobles. He talks about *'ulama* as if among them there is priestly hierarchy like that of Zoroastrian priests. From different indications we come to know that apart from the Saljuqis, he included those who wield pen or sword and those who serve the ruling dynasty, in the class of nobility and emphatically advises the Sultan to employ people from this class only. He puts the subjects at the lowest rung of the society and, not surprisingly, does not distinguish, at this level, between Muslims and non-muslims.[37] Thus with Nizam al-Mulk the concept of nobility and other social classes systematically entered into the political thought of Islam.

In the neo-Iranian system of Nizam al-Mulk, the king is absolute and source of all power. He is answerable to none save God. All other functionaries of state possess limited powers delegated by the king which they cannot exceed. The king rules by godly privilege and maintains the social system on earth devised by God. If the sultan fulfils his duties properly he wins respect and kingdom of God. Thus we see that in Nizam al- Mulk's system king's supremacy is accepted not only as a *de facto* authority but as *de jure*. Now the king or sultan, instead of the cliph, becomes the direct representative of God on earth. The feudalization of Islamic state was, thus, complete in theory too.

So far we have discussed the theories propounded by the 'ulama, jurists or administrators. Let us now consider the theories of Islamic state formulated by the idealist Muslim philosophers. Nearly all the Muslim philosophers of that period fall under the influence of Greek philosophy. Al-Farabi (d. 950), an eminent Muslim philosopher, is called the second teacher in contradistinction to Aristotle, the first teacher. He sought to harmonize classical political philosophy with Islam and to make it intelligible within the context of revealed religion.[38] Farabi's political philosophy is idealistic and far from real life. "In his oriental way of looking at things," says De Boer, "the ideal Republic of Plato merges into the Philosopher as Ruler'. Men having been brought together by a natural want, submit themselves to the will of a single person, in whom the State, be it good or bad, is, so to speak, embodied. A State therefore is bad, if the head of it is, as regards the principles of the Good, either ignorant or in

[37]See *Siyasat-Nama*, tr. by Scheffer, chapter 22, quoted by Leonard Binder, *Ibid.*, p. 52-53.

[38]M. Mahdi, 'Al-Farabi', in *History of Political Philosophy*, ed. L. Strauss and J. Cropsey, New York, 1963, pp. 160-61.

error, or quite depraved. On the other hand the good or excellent State has only one type, that namely in which the philosopher is ruler."[39]

His most famous work is *al-Madīna al-Fāḍila* (The Good City). In this book he is concerned with attainment of happiness through political life. He is also concerned with the relation between the best regime as Plato understood it and the divine law of Islam.[40] In this perfect city perfect happiness is achieved by a perfectly led and administered ideal state ruled by the philosopher who is identical with the Law giver and Imam. Al-Farabi divides the citizens of the virtuous regime into three classes, (*i*) the wise and the philosophers, who knew the nature of things by means of demonstrable proofs and their own insights, (*ii*) the followers of the first class, who trusted their insight and accepted their judgement, and (*iii*) the rest of the citizens, who knew things only by means of similitudes. The ruler assigns to each their specilized duties, gives them laws, and commands them in war, and seeks by persuation and compulsion to develop in everyone the virtues of which he is capable, and orders them hierarchically so that each class attains that perfection of which it is capable.[41]

According to al-Farabi, morality reaches perfection only in a State which at the same time forms a religious community. Not only does the condition of the State determine the temporal lot of its citizens, but also their future destiny. The souls of citizens in an "ignorant" State are devoid of reason, and return to the elements as sensible Forms, in order to be united anew with other beings—men or lower animals.[42] Thus we see that al-Farabi is mainly concerned with moral perfection and spiritual happiness in an ideal city. In one of the passages of this book he explains that the final aim of the State on earth is to make soul happy in the next world. The souls of the citizens belonging to th ideal city would assemble generation after generation in the next world and their happiness would increase according to increase in their number.[43] Farabi's political theory is nothing but the Islamic version of Plato's utopian Republic and is, therefore, far removed from the facts of life. It did not thus affect the practical policies of Islamic states. However, al-Farabi profoundly influened the later philosophers and

[39]Dr T.J. De Boer, *The History of Philosophy in Islam*, tr. by Edward R. Jones, Dover Publications, New York, 1967, pp. 122-23.

[40]M. Mahdi, 'Al-Farabi', *op. cit.*, pp. 160-61.

[41]*Ibid.*, pp. 164-65.

[42]Dr T.J. Boer, *op. cit.*, p. 123.

[43]M. Saeed Shaikh *Studies in Muslim Philosophy*, Pakistan Philosophical Congress, Lahore, 1962, p. 85.

thinkers like Ibn Sina (Avicenna, d. 1037), Ibn Rushd (Averroes, d. 1198), Fakhr al-Din al-Razi (d. 1209) etc. all of whom, in one way or the other, projected the philosopher king as the ruler of an ideal Islamic State and Shari'ah being the revealed law of that State perfectly harmonizing with reason. But, as far as the actual practice of Islamic rulers is concerned, these idealistic and perfectionist theories had very little influence.

Ibn Khaldun, the famous 14th century Muslim historian, commenting on the idealistic politics says: The meaning of this idealistic politics in the opinion of philosophers is that each citizen of this society should be so perfect in his behaviour that he will no longer need any ruler at his head and the philosophers call such a society "al-Madīna al-Faḏila" (i.e. the Good City). The philosophers do not mean by this what is generally expected of a society motivated by the common interests as it is different from it. Such a "Good City" is very difficult to be established and they talk of it merely as what ought to be.[44]

Now we will throw some light on the view of Ibn Khaldun regarding the concept of an Islamic State. According to him society is a must for a man and the society cannot dispense with the control of a ruler. On the one hand this rule derives its legitimacy from the revealed law of God whose obedience is compulsory and, on the other hand, from the politics based on reason to which people have to submit as they expect the ruler to establish an order in general interest. By submitting to the former (i.e. the revealed law) a person benefits in this as well as in the world hereafter whereas by submitting to the later, he derives benefit only in this world.[45] Ibn Khaldun further subdivides the politics based on reason in two categories. In one case the politics is based on the interest (of people) in general, and, on that of the ruler, in particular. In another case the interest of the ruler is supreme and his rule is based on oppression and exploitation and the interests of people are secondary. Generally this is the pattern of rule imposed in all the societies in the world, Muslim or otherwise. The Muslim rulers of course try, to the extent possible for them, to implement the laws of *Shari'ah.*[46]

Ibn Khaldun also deals with the question of the necessity of an Imam. He does not agree with those who maintain that observance of religious laws is enough by itself and there is no necessity for Imam. He, like other

[44]*Al-Mujallad al-Awwal min Tarikh al-Allama Ibn Khaldun,* Dar al-kitab Allubnani, Beirut, 1960, p. 540.

[45]*Ibid.*

[46]*Ibid.*, p. 541.

medieval thinkers, finds nothing wrong in power being wielded by a royal authority as long as there is no violation of justice and fair play. He says:

> It should be known that the religious law does not censure royal authority as such and does not forbid its exercise. It merely censures the evils resulting from it, such as tyranny, injustice, and pleasure seeking....Now, all these things are concomitants of royal authority, too. Thus, censure attaches to royal authority only on account of some of its qualities and conditions, not others. (The religious law) does not censure royal authority as such, nor does it seek to suppress it entirely. It also censures concupiscence and wrathfulness in responsible persons, but it does not want to see either of these qualities relinquished altogether, because necessity calls for their existence. It merely wants to see that proper use is made of them.[47]

Thus, to Ibn Khaldun, exercise of governmental control is very necessary. He does not agree with those who say that "the restraining influence comes into being only through a religious law from God, to which the mass submits as a matter of belief and religious creed."[48] According to him, "The restraining influence comes into being as the result of the impetus of royal authority and the forcefulness of the mighty, even if there is no religious law."[49] Ibn Khaldun was a penetrating observer. He knew that a society divided vertically into rich and poor classes and horizontally into various racial and linguistic groups could not stand united merely by observance of the provisions of Shari'ah. A repressive state machinery, to protect the interests of the dominant classes and racial or linguistic groups, cannot be dispensed with in such a society. So Ibn Khaldun, a pragmatic analyst, sees nothing wrong in the repressive character of the State machinery as, without it, proper control cannot be exercised over the people.

After establishing the necessity of Imamate, Ibn Khaldun lays down four conditions governing this institution namely: (*1*) knowledge, (*2*) probity, (*3*) competence and (*4*) freedom of the senses and limbs from any defect that might effect judgement and action. About the fifth condition i.e. Qurayshite descent, there is no unanimity among the Muslims but Ibn Khaldun accepts the contention of those who maintain that such a descent

[47]Ibn Khaldun, *The Muqaddimah*, tr. by Franz Rosenthal, vol. 1, Routledge and Kegan Paul, London, 1958, p. 389.

[48]*Ibid.*, p. 390.

[49]*Ibid.*

is not necessary. In his opinion what is most necessary for the stability of any government is the group feeling (*'asabiyah*) and cohesion. In the early period of Islam this group feeling was strongest among the Quraysh and hence the Prophet thought it necessary to confine the Imamate to it. But now the conditions have changed and other groups and people have emerged and so Qurayshite descent is no longer necessary. Ibn Khaldun says:

> If it is established that Qurayshite (descent) as a condition (of the Imamate) was intended to remove dissension with the help of (Qurayshite) group feeling and superiority, and if we know that the Lawgiver (Muhammad) does not make special laws for any one generation, period, or nation, we also know that (Qurayshite descent) falls under (the heading of) competence. Thus, we have linked it up with (the condition of competence) and have established the over-all purpose of (the condition of) Qurayshite (descent), which is the existence of group feeling. Therefore, we consider it a (necessary) condition for the person in charge of the affairs of the Muslims that he belongs to people who possess a strong group feeling, superior to that of their contemporaries, so that they can force the others to follow them and the whole thing can be united for effective protection.[50]

It is clear from the passage quoted above that Ibn Khaldun is far from dogmatic in his approach. Whatever is laid down by the lawgiver is not meant for merely one generation or one period and if it has to apply in the changed conditions for the coming generations suitable changes or adjustments must be made in whatever has been provided for by the lawgiver. Ibn Khaldun approaches all the problems related with the state and the business of governance in the same pragmatic spirit within the frame-work of the Islamic laws. He clearly takes the stand that "The religious law would hardly ever make a requirement in contradiction to the requirements of existence."[51] If Ibn Khaldun appears to favour strong (and even repressive) government making it obligatory for the people to submit to its authority, it is because he was a hard pragmatist, above everything else. He himself was deeply involved in the politics of his day (he was associated with many rulers who assigned diplomatic missions to him) and hence he was no mere visionary to indulge in idealistic talk. He accepted the necessity of the

[50] *Ibid.*, p. 401.
[51] *Ibid.*, p. 402.

institution of State approving the form it had acquired in his day while making it clear that the historical changes might necessitate changes in its form. As a thinker and a historian he never confined himself to the phenomenon but penetrated behind it to trace out its social and historical roots. In mundane matters like those of state, he, unlike the 'ulama, never allowed himself to be blinded in his thinking by the dogmas but, through his analytical thinking, got at the essence of the matter. At one place in his history Ibn Khaldun says that what we are discussing here is not the provisions of Shari'ah about the functions of kings or sultans but what is in keeping with the nature of society and human existence in general. He also feels that a Muslim jurist has to take all the political and situational factors into account, and not only the provisions of Shari'ah, while judging the functions of Islamic state.[52]

Shi'ah Theory of Imamat

The thinkers and theoreticians we have dealt with so far are all of Sunnite religion. The Shi'ah thinkers and jurists fundamentally differ from the Sunnites on the question of caliphate and Imamate. According to the Shi'ah doctrine, the Imam cannot be elected. Ibn Khaldun says, "The tenet on which they all agree (i.e. the Shi'ahs) is that the Imamate is not a general (public) interest to be delegated to the Muslim nation for consideration and appointment of a person to fill it. (To the Shi'ah), it is a pillar and fundamental article of Islam. No Prophet is permitted to neglect it or to delegate (the appointment of an Imam) to the Muslim nation. It is incumbent upon him to appoint an Imam for the (Muslims). The Imam cannot commit sins either great or small."[53]

Thus the cardinal principle of Shi'ah religion is Imamate by nass (appointment) and not by election and that the Imam is m'asum i.e. above the possibility of committing sins. Prophet Muhammad appointed Ali, his son-in-law, as his successor and thereafter the Imamate continued in his progeny the preceding Imam appointing his successor by divine inspiration. All others who claimed to be caliphs were usurpers and hence deserve to be condemned. Again, according to the Shi'i doctrine, like the Prophet, an Imam enjoys absolute powers and, being m'asum, his actions or motives cannot be questioned by the people. He is like a king, his word being a law, although he is bound by the provisions of Shari'ah. The Imam, however,

[52] *Al-Mujallad al-Awwal min Tarikh al-'Allama Ibn Khaldun, op. cit.* p. 418.
[53] Ibn Khaldun, *The Muqaddimah, op. cit.*, p. 403.

enjoys the right to interpret Shari'ah and, in this regard too, his word will be final. Thus Imam being the final authority in religious as well as political matters, there isn't much of controversy about the political theories among the Shi'ahs generally. The structure of the state would also be monolithic with Imam as its head. Unlike Sunnites, it is not obligatory for him to consult others in matters of state policies although he may do so if he so desires.

There are many sects among the Shi'ahs too the principal being the twelvers (Ithna asharis) and the Isma'ilis. As far the concept of Imama is concerned, there is hardly much difference between the two. Both are in agreement as far as the doctrines of nass (i.e. appointment through divine inspiration) 'ismah (being above error or infallible) etc. are concerned. However, the twelver Imams never came to power and the theory was never practiced. But the Isma 'ili Imams established their rule first in the North-West Africa and then in Egypt. Their rule, like that of the Abbasids, was dynastic, it being known as the Fatimid dynasty. Again, like the Abbasids, the Fatimid caliphs, to begin with, were in full command of the affairs of the state; but gradually the military-machine came to acquire more and more importance and ultimately the Turkish and the Berber generals reduced the Fatimid caliphs to the status of mere puppets. However, unlike their Sunnite counterparts, there was much more cohesion and near unanimity among the Isma'ili theoreticians on the questions of political theory and the structure of state on the lines indicated above. Despite the harsh political realities, for the faithfuls, the Imam continued to be absolute master, the sole interpreter of Quran and Shari'ah. In the Isma'ili theory of state, it is interesting to note, there os also an utopian element. As the Marxists believe that the state will wither away once the classes are eliminated from the society, the Isma'ilis hold that once people become murtad (i.e. self-controlled, perfect) there will be no need for any external coercion either in the form of Shari'ah (which in the Isma'ili terminology is called *siyasat al-nafs* i.e. discipline of soul) or in the form of political authority i.e. *siyasat al- 'ammah*. This millenial period is called *dawr al-kashf* (literally a period of discovery, revelation) i.e. when nothing will be hidden and people will have overcome their ignorance.[54]

Thus we see that the Islamic state which originated as democratic, un-

[54] There are numerous Isma'ili books of *Ta'wil* and *Haqiqat* giving exposition to these theories. Of particular importance is books like *Ithbat al-Imama* by Sayyidna Ahmad Nisaburi, *Rahat al-'Aql* by Hamid ad-Din Kirmani, etc. P.J. Vatikiotis, in his *The Fatimid Theory of State* has also discussed many of these aspects.

repressive and open state with its head accountable to the community of Muslims, in the historical conditions as they prevailed in Arabia then was transformed into a highly repressive, bureaucratic and despotic rule during the Middle Ages as the historical conditions and the relations and forces of production changed. The earlier form of the Islamic state could not be restored and the 'ulama and political theoreticians had to suitably adjust their theories to suit the new historical conditions.

4. Islamic State in the Modern Era

We have seen in the last chapter that the concept of Islamic state changed with the change in historical conditions.What began as a non-repressive collective organization in the semi-nomadic and tribal conditions of Arabia in the early period of Islam was transformed into a highly repressive feudal state when the conquests shifted the centre of power from the holy cities of Arabia to the heartland of feudalism first in the Roman province of Syria during the Umayyad period and later to Baghdad during the Abbasid period. In the changed historical conditions and with the emergence of new productive forces, the old social composition also underwent profound changes and so did the nature of the state. The elective principle of early caliphate was replaced by hereditary monarchial one and still later sultāns, who captured power by sheer might of arms, came to wield actual political power. *'Ulama,* the theoreticians of Islam, accordingly modified their theories of the Islamic state in order to suit their realities. Now they made it obligatory for all the faithfuls, as we have seen in the earlier chapter, to make anyone who wilded power provided he professed the religion of Islam and enforced Islamic prayer.

By the beginning of sixteenth century, almost the entire Arab world came under the domination of the Ottoman empire. Egypt, Syria, Tripoli, Tunis and Algiers in the North and the Yemen on the southern end of Arabian peninsula were incorporated into the empire lorded over by the Ottomans. The Turkish rulers were called sultāns and the myth of caliphat which survived through the Mamluke period in Egypt finally vanished. The 'ulama once again accepted the new reality and found justification for the Ottaman rule. The Turkish suzerainty over the Arab provinces ended only during the First World War in 1918 with the help of the British power. It was only during this period that the Muslim people, along with others in the colonial countries, started developing a new sense of nationalism. It would be interesting to briefly narrate the important developments which occurred during the nineteenth century in the Islamic world dominated by the Turks in order to enhance our understanding of the forces which were developing in the womb of the old society. It will also help us in fixing the direction of change.

The Ottoman empire was "not so much a single community as a group of communities each of which claimed the immidiate loyalty of its members. These communities were regional, religious or functional;or, to some extent, a mixture of all these."[1] The religion followed by majority of the subjects of the Turkish empire was, of course, Islam. The Sultān—the Ottoman monarch—projected himself as the protector of the faith vis-a-vis the Christians of Europe who threatened the supremacy of the empire. A large number of the Turkish subjects were the Arabs. The Turkish Sultan used religion to ensure the loyalty of the Arabs who, in one way or the other, resented non-Arab political domination. Earlier, the Arabs were the masters of the Islamic empire and non-Arabs, especially the Persians, had resisted their political supremacy. Though the Islamic empire further expanded under the Turks, the Arabs hardly took notice of the glory of Islamic empire under them. For the Arabs, whatever may be the theoretical position, Islam is their national religion; in fact Islam and Arabism are closely interwined (we will refer to this phenomenon again in a later chapter). Prof. W.C.Smith says:

> The synthesis is close: an identification, at times unconscious, of Islam and Arabism. On the one hand, an Arab need not be pious or spiritually concerned in rder to be proud of Islam's historic achievements. Indeed, he need not even be a Muslim; Christian Arabs have taken a share in that pride. On the other hand, Muslim Arabs have never quite acknowledged, have never fully incorporated into their thinking and especially their feeling, either that a non-Muslim is really a complete Arab, or that a non-Arab is really a complete Muslim. Arab Islam has never given much serious thought to either group. It is uninterested in and virtually unaware of Islamic greatness after the Arab downfall. For it, in 1258 (the fall of

[1] A. Hourani, *Arabic Thought in the Liberal Age 1798-1939*, London, 1962, p. 29.

Baghdad), or for Egypt in 1517 (the Turkish conquest), Islamic history virtually came to an end.[2]

The Arabs similarly never took any interest in other Muslim empires like that in Persia or India. For them 1258 was the terminal point of the Islamic history and although the Turks were the defenders of the faith but never the integral part of Islamic history. Most of the Egyptian writers think and feel about the period after 1517, as the period of Egyptian history, not that of Islamic history. Thus those who advocate Islamic brotherhood whether they belong to Ikhwan al-Muslimin of Egypt or the Jamat-e-Islami of Pakistan should note the fact that a religious ideal simply does not wipe-out the racial and national differences. At times national considerations override those of religion. Here it would be interesting to quote the instance of the Ḫijāz railway. In 1906 Abdul Hamid (the Turkish sulṯan-caliph) proposed to build the Ḥijāz railway and landed a force at the head of the gulf of Aqaba to lay claim to the whole of the Sinai peninsula. However, most of the patriotic Egyptians saw no point in abandoning Sinai, which had widely come to be regarded as Egyptian territory, for the rather nebulous cause of Islamic solidarity.

The Arabs remained Ottoman subjects for four centuries but there was no open hostility between the two races as it began to happen during the last phase of the declining Turkish empire. Their mutual relations were non-antagonistic. The absence of hostility was due, partly, to religious fellowship; but only partly it could be explained on that basis. A comprehensive explanation will have to take several other factors into account. In order to attempt a critique of the present day Muslim fundamentalists who maintain that the Islamic solidarity in the spiritual sense over-rides all other considerations it would be necessary to understand this phenomenon in greater depth. We will also have to bear it in mind while discussing the views of fundamentalist theoreticians like Maududi of Pakistan. Here we will throw some light on it.

The Ottoman rule did not mean slavery for the Arabs in any sense of the word. A section of the Arabs was part of the ruling class. As there was close affinity between Arabism and Islam and the Arabs had presided over the grand Islamic empire until yesterday, they could not be treated as culturally inferior by the ruling Turks. Although Turkish was the language

[2]W.C.Smith, *Islam in Modern History*, The New American Library (Mentor Book) New York, 1957, p. 99.

of administration throughout the Ottoman empire, Arabic had its own importance as a sacred language of Islam. God had chosen that language to reveal His message to the Prophet. In fact the Arabic-speaking provinces were regarded by the Ottoman ruling class, at least in the beginning, with a certain deference which they did not accord to the rest of the sultān's dominions—for the very reason that its inhabitants did speak the sācred language, while most of them at the same time professed the dominant religion.[3]

This was as far as the religio-linguistic factors were concerned. Another important factor was the nature of the Ottoman state. Needless to say, it was feudal. Many Arabs belonging to the pre-Turkish ruling class were given fiefs and thus assimilated by the Turkish ruling class. Peter Mansfield says, "Under these circumstances there was no question at this stage of the Turkification of these Arab societies. Turkish may have become the language of government but Arabic retained its honoured status and in practice a large share of political power passed into the hands of the local elite of shaikhs, 'ulama and landowners."[4] The peasantry, Arab or non-Arab, or, Muslim or non-Muslim, for that matter, continued to be exploited by the Turko-Arab ruling class. The peasantry, exploited through the ages, developed a resigned attitude despairing of any improvement in its lot. Thus, in a sense collusion between the Turkish and Arab ruling classes--although a latter was playing a secondary role--kept the conflict within the manageable proportions. However, with the dawn of modern era and new forces therewith, the nature of relationship between the Turks and the Arabs started changing and conflict began to emerge to the surface. We need not go into those details here as it is not the subject matter of our book.

The new challenges emerged on the scene after the western colonialists began to establish their domination over various Muslim countries which were part of the Ottoman empire. The Ottoman rulers, in view of the changed balance of forces in the world, began to adjust. They had not only to come to terms with the western powers but also with the aspirations of the people at home and in other parts of their empire. The western colonial powers, on the other hand, kept on consolidating their position in the areas heavily populated by Muslims. Peter Mansfield observes, "In the last quarter of the nineteenth century the crisis of Islam became much more acute. It was no longer possible for Arab intellectuals to take a detached

[3]H.A.R. Gibb and H. Bowen, Islamic Society and the West, London, 1950, vol. 1, p. 160.

[4]Peter Mansfield, *The Arabs*, Penguin Books, 1978, p. 75.

attitude towards the West as it became apparent that France's occupation of Algiers was not an isolated incident in a relatively remote regency of the Ottoman Empire but a prelude to the imposition of a Western hegemony along the whole southern coast of Mediterranean."[5]

When faced with the serious modern challenges, there emerged some Muslim thinkers who made a serious bid to come to grips with these challenges. The most influential of these thinkers was Jamal al-Din al-Afghani (1838-97) a man of electrifying personality and the capacity of a true revolutionary. According to W.C. Smith in him "are typified and fused two tendencies—internal reform and external defence."[6] While the new historical forces were generating pressure for reform and change, the imperialist onslaught had made it necessary to defend against the external threats. Afghani set out to meet the external threat with his pan-Islamism. This, however, does not mean that he undervalued nationalism. In fact he advocated both local nationalism as well as pan-Islamism. Afghani had known the sentiments of the Egyptian and other Arabs and hence could not ignore their nationalist aspirations. In his writings and speeches, Afghani lays due emphasis on *watan* i.e. national home land. He says, "a people without unity and a people without literature is a people without language. A people without history is a people without glory, and a people will lack history if authorities do not rise among them, to protect and revivify the memory of their historical heroes so that they may follow and emulate. All this depends on a national (*watani*) education which begins with "the homeland" (*watan*), the environment of which is "the homeland," and the end of which is "the homeland."[7]

It is also to be noted that al-Afghani's concept of pan-Islam was incompatible with despotic rule. He wanted Muslim masses to take their destiny into their own hands by uniting and forcing their rulers to govern them in their own interests and defend them against acquisitive and exploitative foreigners. He, therefore, attacked most bitterly those rulers who were mainly concerned with their own powers and privileges neglecting the welfare of people. Mansfield maintains that "He was a revolutionary in that he introduced a wholly new concept into the world of Islam—that of

[5] *Ibid.*, pp. 160-61.

[6] W.C.Smith, *op. cit.*, p. 54.

[7] Muhammad al-Makhzumi, *The Opinions of Jamal al-Din al-Afghani* (Arabic), Beirut, 1941, p. 257. Peter Mansfield, *op. cit.* has quoted this from Sylvia Haim, Arab Nationalism : An Anthology, London, 1962, p. 13.

secular politics. He himself was a sceptic—even an agnostic."[8] According to Hourani Afghani's centre of attention is no longer Islam as a religion, it is rather Islam as a civilization. The norm of human action is not the service of God; it is the creation of human civilization flourishing in all its parts. The idea of civilization is indeed one of the seminal idea of nineteenth-century Europe, and it is through al-Afghani above all that it reaches the Islamic world.[9]

Afghani's pan-Islamism was a reaction to the West's invasion of the World of Islam. This concept, which, in a way, was more secular than religious, stirred the feelings of the Muslims throughout the Islamic world and Afghani acquired great deal of influence. Abdul Hamid, the Turkish sultan-caliph, sought to exploit Afghani's influence over the Islamic world for his own ends. He invited him to Istanbul with the intention of harnessing his potent influence of his claim to pan-Islamic leadership. However, Abdul Hamid, a despot, did not like Afghani's diatribes against despotism. The result of this was that al-Afghani, while treated with honour, ended his days virtually as the Sultan's prisoner. But, not surprisingly, Afghani, who considered assassination as a legitimate political weapon, got the Shah of Persia physically eliminated. It must be remembered that the Shah had deported him from Iran for his revolutionary activities.

W.C. Smith perceptively remarks about Afghani: "Yet his contribution was not as a thinker, either creative or systematizing; nor even on the practical side, as an organizer and planner. It was not what he introduced into the development of the Islamic world that gives him significance, so much as what he brought into focus--focus so sharp that it was able to ignite. He is important because he summed up in himself so wide a sweep of the contemporary Muslim world in difficulties, and then reacted against those difficulties with a prodigious energy."[10] Afghani's restless personality could create such an impact because: He was embracingly catholic; in his concern for the community's probelms, impinging impartially on its various elements, he transcended its traditional divisions and would turn attention from them. He was the firebrand agitator; taking deeply to heart the then condition of Islam, he sensed with a passionate

[8]Peter Mansfield, *op. cit.*, p. 164. It is difficult to agree with Mansfield that al-Afghani was an agnostic. He, in fact, wrote a book *al-Radd' al-Dahriyin* (Refutation of the Materialists) vide Mahmudul Haq's *Muhammad 'Abduh--a Study of Modern Thinker of Egypt*, Institute of Islamic Studies, Aligarh, 1970, p. 8.

[9]Hourani, *op. cit.*, p. 114.

[10]W.C. Smith, *op. cit.*, pp. 54-55.

poignancy the plight of his fellow Muslims, and in his rebounding zest stimulated them to a keen consciousness of their situation and to a determination to redress it.[11]

The Islamic world had fallen into a state of 'non-responsible quietude' as Smith aptly puts it.[12] Afghani urged the Muslims on to self-directing determination. He inspired them to act for creating the kind of Islamic world that ought to be. He enthusiastically employed the by now unemphasized, if not altogether forgotten, Quranic verse "Verily, God does not change the condition of a people until they change their own condition" (13:11). Afghani also sought to induce Muslims to action by conjuring up with great passion the grandeur of the Islamic past. It was his passionate mission to awaken the Muslims out of their deep slumber. However, it would be wrong to think that Afghani drew inspiration only from the past and wanted to turn the wheel back. His vivid evocation of the greatness of past was meant to enthuse people into action and his spirited appeals did have an electrifying effect in one Muslim country after the other. Prof. Smith remarks, "Indeed, in addition to internal reform and external defence, this recalling of erstwhile Muslim grandeur has become a third dominant trait of modern Islam."[13]

Undoubtedly, the three traits mentioned by Prof. W.C. Smith have played important role but, what must be noted in the present context is the fact that 'internal reform' has not received the attention it deserves from the Muslim intellectuals. External defence also has assumed the beaten track of apologetics rather than serious thinking and creative assimilation. This would be possible only when there is a sincere and honest attempt at internal reform. Prof. Smith has elsewhere in the same book has very aptly remarked that there are attempts to re-think defences of Islam rather than re-thinking Islam. Thus we see that internal reform took the back seat and eulogizing past became the prominent trend with the Muslim thinkers. Rashid Rida, an Egyptian thinker of whom we shall talk later, noting the absence of any serious attempt at internal reform, had to remark that the absence of ijtihad (i.e. creative interpretation) is responsible for the relapse into Bedouinism or near-Bedouinism (i.e. nomadism) no less than for Europeanisation, heresy and atheism.[14] As for glorifying the past Dr Iqbal

[11] *Ibid.*, p. 55.
[12] *Ibid.*, p. 57.
[13] *Ibid.*, p. 56.
[14] See *Some Reflections on the Separation of Religion and Politics in Modern Islam* by Erwin I. J. Rosenthal, *Islamic Studies*, Journal of the Central Institute of Islamic Research, Karachi, vol. III, September 1964, p. 259.

has pithily observed, "...a false reverence for past history and its artificial resurrection constitute no remedy for a people's decay." Then Dr Iqbal goes on to quote a modern writer, "The verdict of history is that won- out ideas have never risen to power among a people who have worn them out." [15]

However, it would be wrong to think that al-Afghani only emphasized the past glory of Islam. He was equally sincerely concerned with the problem of jettisoning Islam of feudal accretions and, instead, assimilating the modern scientific values. Afghani's pan-Islamism, as we have already seen, never under-valued the importance of local nationalisms—Irani, Arab, Indian, etc. Prof. Smith observes: "Further, Afghani exhibited a partial appreciation of intellectualism and of Western values and particularly Western science and techniques. He saw the West as something primarily to be resisted, because it threatened Islam and the community, but secondly, in part to be imitated. He was vigorous in inciting his Muslim hearers to develop reason and technology as the West was doing, in order to be strong."[16] Thus Afghani was no obscurantist, merely revivifying past. But, in the feudal environment of the most of the Muslim countries, this is what survived of Afghani's teachings. While his glorification of the Islamic past survived, his emphasis on Western reason and technology were quitely forgotten. Similarly, Afghani's pan-Islamism, for its wider emotional appeal, continued to be appreciated long after he was dead. It must, however, be said that Afghani was no systematic thinker and he had no clear programme or ordered philosophy. But he did have abounding energy and inspiring personality--the latter largely due to his sincere and devoted missionary zeal.

Before we proceed further, it will be interesting to throw some light on the nature of Islamic society so as to better understand the relative strength of nationalism and pan-Islamism. Even today, despite emergence of new forces, mainly bourgeois, pan-Islamic sentiments continue to be popular. The Arab world, as we have seen in the first chapter, was basically a commercial grouping, with Egypt as the only great "peasant" exception. The ruling class was, of course, mainly urban, made up of court officials, merchants, religious leaders, and around them that little world of craftsmen and petty clerks which is typical of Eastern cities. Everywhere (we are talking of the Arab countries here) it shares the same language and the same

[15] Dr Sir Muhammad Iqbal, *The Reconstruction of Religious Thought in Islam*, Lahore, 1960, p. *157*.

[16] *W.C.Smith*, *op. cit.*, p. 56.

profoundly Islamic culture, which, moreover, is orthodox Sunni. This class is highly mobile, being able to move from Tangier to Damuscus without ceasing in the slightest to feel at home. It is this class that has created "Arab Civilization."[17]

Naturally, its prosperity is bound up with that of long distance trade. The latter is the basis of its alliance with the nomadic tribes, its caravan escorts. This explains the isolation of the agricultural areas, which retain personalities of their own, either linguistic (Berber) or religious (Shi'a) (Iran, for example), but play no important part in the civilization of the Arab world. Except in Egypt the peasantry enters little into the system, and is subjected only episodically and slightly to the levying of tribute. "This Arab world," says Ahmad El Kodsy, "is thus both divers and profoundly unified—by its ruling class. It is not to be compared to feudal Europe of the Middle Ages, which was thoroughly "peasant" in character. This is doubtless why Europe was to evolve toward the formation of separate nations, for the ruling classes of Europe, living as they did on the surplus taken from peasant communities, were bound to emphasize the diversity of the peoples of Europe. In contrast to this, in the Arab world, because the peasants did not play this role, unity was preserved."[18]

This unity was preserved upto the nineteenth century under the umbrella of the Ottoman empire. The colonial powers of the West then established their hold on its different parts and ultimately created different countries in the Arab world. It was after the First World War that the British and the French created separate countries of Iraq, Syria, Lebonan and Transjordan. Strong bourgeois class had not emerged in these countries (although the traditional mercantile elements did exist and exerted some pressure) to champion the cause of nationalism as we understand today. However, when the Arab world was divided as a result of Western imperialist conspiracy, the sentiments of Arab unity became strong and, it ought to be noted, the concept of Arab unity included the religious minorities like Christians. This was an important development and that the Arabs formed a nation in the twentieth century meaning of the word was a novel idea and it was necessary to show that all the ancestors of the Arabs from pre-Islamic times had contributed to the Arab heritage. Feisal, the son of Sharif Hussein of Mecca, did develop a rudimentary theory of Arab nationalism as he struggled to preserve a united and independent Arab Syria. "We are Arabs

[17] Ahmad El Kodsy, "Nationalism and Class Struggle in the Arab World," *Monthly Review*, July August 1970, New York, pp. 16-17.

[18] *Ibid.*, p. 17.

before being Muslims, and Muhammad is an Arab before being a Prophet," he would say. In a speech in Aleppo in June 1919, he declared: "There is neither minority nor majority among us, nothing to divide us. We are one body. We were Arabs even before the time of Moses, Jesus and Abraham."[19]

We will return to this subject later. We have seen above the popularity of al-Afghani's slogan of pan-Islam. For him, it was an important weapon to forge unity among Muslims and present a consolidated front to the formidable imperialist powers of the West. In this struggle his most trusted disciple was Muhammad 'Abduh (1849-1905). 'Abduh was deeply influenced by the political thought of al-Afghani and for quite some time was actively associated with him. When Afghani was expelled from Egypt by Khedive Tewfik, with British encouragement, he went to Paris via India. Muhammad 'Abduh joined him there and both together published an influential Arabic periodical *al-'Urwa al-wuthqa* (The Indissoluble Link). However, later on their relations cooled and 'Abduh devoted his energies to social reforms.

Mahmudul Haq says in the preface to his book on Muhammad 'Abduh that he 'was a pioneer amongst the Muslim modernist at the turn of the present century. At this period of the penetration of Western culture the reformer, through his liberal and humanitarian interpretation of Islam, prepared the minds of the Muslims and particularly of his countrymen to accept modern science and rationalism and give up the moribund tradition of the past. In fact, Muhammad 'Abduh's contribution as an Islamic modernist is so significant that a close study of his system of thought seems viable for an understanding of the development of modern Islamic reform movement not only in Egypt but also in the Muslim world in general.'[20]

In a way 'Abduh can be described as a forerunner of the modern nationalist movement. His liberal interpretation of Islam, his emphasis on spreading education and use of journalism to educate the public opinion created a new consciousness among Muslims and prepared their minds for accepting the modern political institutions. Moreover, brought up in the tradition of al-Afghani, he was very much in the forefront of the political movement in Egypt which was directed both against the British domination as well as the Turkish overlordship exercised through the Khedive.

[19]Quoted in Sylvia G. Haim, ed. *Arab Nationalism: An Anthology*, London, 1962, p. 35, cf. Peter Mansfield, *The Arabs, op. cit.*, pp. 261-62.

[20]Mahmudul Haq *Muhammad 'Abduh*, Institute of Islamic Studies, Aligarh Muslim University, 1970, p. IX.

Muhammad 'Abduh agreed with those colleagues who held the view that the country was on the verge of ruin, the *fellahs* (peasants) were miserable, that the growing interference of European powers in the internal affairs of the country was ruining it, that the cancer of corruption was very widespread resulting in misgovernment and that the government was following a policy of discrimination against the Egyptians in the army thus resulting in the domination by the Turkish and Circassian elements.[21]

Muhammad 'Abduh participated in the revolt led by 'Urabi Pasha in 1882. The revolt failed and he was tried along with Colonel 'Urabi and others and was exiled for three years to Syria where he settled down in Beirut. It is from here that he went to Paris in 1884 to join his teacher al-Afghani. 'Abduh does not specify his views on the form of government but one can, from his writings infer that he was in favour of a democratic set-up. 'Abduh, in certain respects, was great admirer of the West. He even welcomed the advance of westernization since the time of Khedive Isma'il resulting in the introduction of new codes of law and Western political institutions. But, at the same time, he was no blind imitator of the West. He did not endorse the idea of dividing society into two different water tight compartments i.e. of the profane and the holy. He felt deeply concerned about the fact that while the domain of the former was widening, that of the latter was shrinking. The problem which agitated his mind was to bridge this gap.

'Abduh was, no doubt, a great admirer of the West, especially its material aspect but he was against the *ipso facto* acceptance of European laws and institutions which, as he claimed, bore no relevance to the customs and habits of the people or to the Islamic norm.[22] However, he stood for the reinterpretation of the laws of shari'ah in keeping with the changed conditions lack of which, he felt, had widened the scope of westernization. He was highly critical of the stagnation of shari'ah in the hands of the Muslim jurists. He also advocated the view that in Islam there is nothing like the absolute religious authority. He says: "I say that in Islam there is no such thing as religious authority. The caliphs or the Qadis or the muftis or the shaykh al-Islam are civil officials only. Whatever authority is held by any one of these is civil authority, though it is the Islamic-Law that defines their powers and duties."[23]

Muhammad 'Abduh felt suffocated in the medieval practices of his own

[21] *Zu'ama'*, p. 298, quoted by Mahmudul Haq, *op. cit.*, p, 17.
[22] Mahmudul Haq, *op. cit.*, p. 56.
[23] *Al-Islam*, pp. 64-65, 67, quoted by Mahmudul Haq, *op. cit.*, p. 57.

country and to that extent he looked towards Europe for inspiration. According to Rashid Rida, his exile was a blessing in disguise for him as it led to his widening of mental horizon. So inspiring did 'Abduh find his travels in Europe that in later years he returned to Europe again and again whenever he felt the need of refreshing his mind. He never went to Europe, 'Abduh said, when there did not revive in him the hope for the change of the present state of his co-religionists for something better. These hopes admittedly weakened in him when he returned to his own country. Yet, as he tells us, when he again went to Europe and remained there a month or two, these hopes came back to him and the attainment of that which had been counted as impossible seemed possible to him.[24] 'Abduh also vigorously devoted himself for the feminist cause. He opposed polygamy and believed in equality of man and woman. Again, as opposed to the orthodox 'ulama, 'Abduh held the view that it was not necessary to follow the Prophet's opinion in worldly matters. He quotes the tradition "I am only a human being, when I give you a command in religious matters, you should obey it, but when I give you a command in daily affairs, then remember that I am only a human being" in his support. Thus if Abduh's interpretations are accepted, the scope of reconstructing the socio-political ideas of Islam is greatly widened. But unfortunately there have not been many liberal 'ulama like him championing the cause of creatively integrating modern scientific and social values with the past heritage thus helping inner growth of the Islamic institutions in harmony with the urges and inspirations of the new era.

'Abd al-Rahman Kawakibi (1854-1902) was a contemporary of 'Abduh. A Syrian Arab, he was opposed to any form of despotism and hence a staunch opponent of the Turkish domination over the Arabs. He has elaborated his political ideas in his *Taba'i' al-Istib-dad and Umm al-Qura'*. In his writings he appears to be a supporter of the cause of Arab nationalism. He was, like Tahtavi, great admirer of the French Revolution and the western parliamentary institution. Tahtavi was sent to France by Muhammad 'Ali of Egypt and thus had observed the functioning of the French political institutions himself personally. Both Kawakibi and Tahtavi were great admirers of the western type of democracy.

More than Tahtavi, Kawakibi was totally opposed to despotism and he remained uncompromising towards the Turkish despotism over the Arabs. He was convinced that without ending the Turkish despotism it was not

[24]Al-Manar, VIII, pp. 416, 465, 466, cf. Mahmudul Haq, *op. cit.*, p. 41.

possible to establish truly democratic institution in the Arab countries. Kawakibi, in fact, devoted his whole life to fighting against the Turkish despotism over the Arabs. Kawakibi was of the firm opinion that the parliamentary form of democracy was in keeping with the concept of Islamic government whereas despotism was totally against it. He held that the medieval period's concept of Islamic government that "sultan was the shadow of God on earth" or that the ruler was inspired by God was wrong. He also vehemently opposed the 'ulama's opinion formed during the Middle Ages that "tyranny is better than anarchy!". Thus he completely disagreed with the political thought of the 'ulama of the medieval period. In other words he wanted to re-interpret Islam in order to bring it more in harmony with the modern period.[25]

Kawakibi was an enthusiastic supporter of modern ideas and political institutions. However, to make them acceptable to the Muslims of his period, he sought to establish their legitimacy on the basis of Quran. He found certain verses in the Quran which supported his point of view. H.Z.Nuseibeh says, "This seems a cumbersome, indirect way of assimilating new ideas. Considering all the factors involved, it was probably the most feasible course."[26] Kawakibi even maintains that since oppression and despotism is totally alien to Islam, a just non-Muslim ruler is preferable to a tyrant Muslim ruler. It is for this reason that the Prophet took pride for having been born in the period of Nushirwan, the just.[27]

Kawakibi, in support of his above claim that a just non-Muslim ruler is better than a tyrant Muslim despot quotes an event from Ibn Taqtaqi's book *Al-Fakhri fi al-Adab as-Sultaniya wa al-Dawal al-Islamiya:*

> When in A.H.656 (A.D.1258) the Mongol conqueror Hulagu who was not a Muslim, conquered Baghdad, he inquired from the 'ulama of the school of Mustansariya who is better of the two rulers: a kafir but just or a Muslim but tyrant? None could reply it satisfactorily. Then Radi ad-Din b. Tawus, when his turn came, lifted up that piece of paper (on which the question was written) and wrote down that a ruler who is kafir but just is preferable to a ruler who is Muslim but tyrant. Thereafter all other muftis

[25]Mahmudul Haq, *'Abl al-Rahman al-Kawakibi-Zindagi aur Afkar*, Institute of Islamic Studies, Aligarh Muslim University, 1972, pp. 176.

[26]H.Z. Nuseibeh, *The Ideas of Arab Nationalism*, London, 1956, p. 110, cf. Mahmudl Haq, *Al-Kawakibi*, p. 177.

[27]Al-Kawakibi, *Umm al-Qura*, Aleppo, 1959, p. 33, cf. Mahmudul Haq, al-*Kawakibi*, p. 177.

put their signature over it thus giving their consent to it.[28]

This opinion, it would be recalled, is in sharp contrast to the Prophetic traditions in circulation during the medieval period that even a Negro slave must be obeyed although he may be a tyrant as long as he enforced salat (i.e. a Muslim way of prayer). There has rarely been unanimity among the Muslim theologians even on such crucial matters.

Kawakibi was, as pointed out earlier, a great opponent of despotism. He wrote a book against it (*Taba'i' al-Istibdad*) and gave elaborate arguments from political, social, ethical and religious point of view. According to him despotism is destroyer of everything that is positive in human life. Kawakibi says that a despot rules according to his own whims in complete disregard of people's will or welfare. Since a despot is a tyrant, he mercilessly supresses the people's voice and their just grievances. A despotic ruler is a deadly enemy of truth and freedom. He always desires that the ruled should humiliatingly surrender and behave like humble dogs and sycophants. He also desires that his subjects people should never see the light of truth because he knows that they will submit to him only as they are drowned in ignorance and darkness.[29]

It is pertinent to note here that Kawakibi does not spare those who justify despotism in the name of religion. He says that the religious group also belongs to this clique of despot's supporters. They go to the people in the disguise of religion and tell them that the tyranny and hardships they are facing (which in fact is the product of despotic rule) is the will of God and we should patiently bear it. They in fact collude with the despotic ruler and are richly rewarded for their services in the form of fat salaries and thus they also become part of the exploiting machinery which sucks the blood of the people.[30] Kawakibi propounds the view that the despotic rule is supported by the class of nobles which is especially favoured and that the theologians also get similar favourable treatment as a price for their support for the despotic regime. The masses, on the other hand, feel totally helpless in the face of oppression and exploitation and quietly go on suffering. Only the 'uqala' (i.e. intellectuals) keep the banner of freedom aloft and fight against despotism. Thus we see that among the nineteenth cantury Muslim thinkers, Kawakibi declares war against the Eastern despotism and shows

[28]*Umm al-Qura, op. cit.,* p. 33.

[29]Kawakibi, *Taba'i' al-Istibdad,* pp. 9-10, quoted by Mahmudul Haq *al-Kawakibi,* p. 179.

[30]*Ibid.*, p. 56, cf. Mahmudul Haq, p. 180.

great passion for freedom and democracy. He gives great importance to individual freedom and even approvingly quotes J.J. Rousseau that "Man is born free and everywhere he is in chains."[31] Thus we see that Kawakibi not only exposes the hypocricy of the mullahs and 'ulama but also takes an uncompromising attitude towards all despotic forns of government.

Generally the Muslim thinkers as well as theologians, despite their antagonism towards the ruling Turks, had considered the Ottoman empire as a great Muslim empire which needed to be protected vis-a-vis other major non- Muslim powers, especially of the West. But Kawakibi totally condemned it as a despotic regime which deserves no sympathy as it has imposed over other Muslims a despotic rule and is not interested in the welfare of the non- Turkish Muslims. The Turks hate Arabs and consider them inferior subjects. Kawakibi was, as opposed to the despotism of the Ottomans, all praise for the western parliamentary form of government based on the cardinal principles of secularism and democracy. Thus we see that, unlike many other Muslim thinkers, Kawakibi is not opposed to the idea of separating religion from government and adopting secularism. In fact he considers the western parliamentary democracy as the fulfilment of man's old dream of freedom and equality.

Kawakibi, it must also be noted, was basically an Arab nationalist. For him Islam is the national religion of the Arabs and they are its best defenders. Turks are mere pretenders who use Islam to serve their vile political ends. Arabs are more genuinely concerned with revival of Islam. Kawakibi was of the firm opinion that the Turks had no right to the Islamic caliphate. He wanted Mecca to be its centre and an Arab to be caliph. But Kawakibi did not want to vest the caliph with temporal powers over the peoples of different areas. He wanted him to be a figure-head concerned with religious and spiritual matters. The actual political power, in this setup, would be wielded by the Sultān or leader of that area. In other words the national states enjoying full autonomy would exist under the caliph's spiritual headship.[32] Kawakibi's concept of confederation of the Islamic states under the spiritual headship of an Arab at Mecca was rather new for his period. He wanted to establish the united states of Muslim countries like the United States of America with the states enjoying complete autonomy and the head of the united states having powers limited to the religious sphere only. Also his main emphasis was on democracy and justice and

[31] *Ibid.*, p. 77, cf. p. 183.
[32] Mahmudul Haq, *al-Kawakibi, op. cit.*, pp. 210-11.

prefered a non-Islamic government with these virtues to an Islamic government lacking them.

Before we discuss the views of some other twentieth century thinkers on the subject of Islamic State, a few general observations will be in order. Most of these thinkers were of the opinion that Islam must be jettisoned of the medieval accretions and its pristine purity restored. None of these thinkers, in must be noted, talk of *reformation*; he is interested in *restoration* of the Islam of the salaf, the first Companions and Successors of the Prophet. These thinkers also show their concern for integrating four different orthodox Sunni schools of law into one universal one through the process of ijtihad. To this Rosenthal remarks: "But, as every student of Muslim law and jurisprudence knows, this is much more complicated and difficult in practice than would appear in the way its protagonists use it—almost as a magic wand. The practice of *taqlid* (imitating) over a long period has not only made the 'ulama' subservient to their rulers, Muslim as well as European, but—even worse—incapable of facing the modern world and meeting its challenge by the only legitimate means, namely, ijtihad. This, at least, is the considered opinion of Rashid Rida.[33] Another trait of these thinkers worth noting is that they do not accept separation of politics from religion in theory but do not mind it in practice. Let us now turn to some of these thinkers.

We have already discussed above the views of Muhammad 'Abduh. Rashid Rida was his most eminent disciple. His treatise is called al-Khilafah aw al-Imamah al-'uzma.[34] This work, according to Rosenthal, "can be considered not only as the programme of the reformist party but also as the authoritative pronouncement on the attitude of modernism to politics. As the latter, it is a significant document which has lost nothing of its topical character."

In keeping with the classical theory of the khilafah, Rashid Rida makes the distinction between Khulafa Rashidun (i.e. the first four guided caliphs) and the Umayyad and 'Abbasid caliphs, including the condemnation of Mu'awiyah (he was the first caliph to introduce dynastic rule by nominating his son Yazid). However, he acknowledges the signal services to the spread and growth of civilization which these "temporal" caliphs rendered.

[33]E.I.J. Rosenthal, "Some Reflections on the Separation of Religion and Politics in Modern Islam," *Islamic Studies*, Journal of The Central Institute of Islamic Research, Karachi, vol. III, September 1964, no. 3, pp. 251-52.

[34]Here we have referred to Cairo 1923 edition. E.I.J. Rosenthal has referred to this as well as its French tr. by Henri Laoust, published from Beyrouth, 1938. The first figure refers to Arabic text, the second to Rosenthal's article *op. cit.* in *Islamic Studies.*

Riḍa, a Syrian Arab, considers the Qurayshite descent as an essential qualification for becoming a caliph. This must be seen in the background of the Turkish domination and Rida's strong attachment to the Arabs and Arabism.[35]

Rashid Rida's main emphasis is on *ijtihad*-i.e. (creative) reinterpretation. This *ijtihād*, according to him, has two dimentions: (*1*) ridding Islam of later accretions to restore its pristine purity and (*2*) to make it more acceptable to the reqirements of the modern age. Again, for Rashid, *ijtihād* means an entirely fresh and new interpretation of the primary sources of Islamic law without which no effective answer can be found for the very different outlook and needs of our time. He, therefore, advocates opening of institute where the future mujtahids (i,e, correct interpreters)could be trained. According to him these mujtahids should be so mentally equipped as to enable them to interpret and apply the Shri'ah in the spirit of pure, early Islam and in keeping with the requirements of our age. Rashid Rida divides his generation into three groups: (*1*) the servile imitators of the four different law schools; (2) admirers of European laws and organizations and (*3*) the reformist party (al-Afghani, Muhammad 'Abduh, Abu'l Kalam Azad, Zaghlul Pasha and others).[36]
Thus we see that Rashid Rida lays equal emphasis on return to early Islam as well as assimilation of the spirit of the modern age (as we shall see later, an eminebt Urdu poet-philosopher Iqbal advocated similar point of view almost at the same time in India). Rida, it is intersting to note, appealed to the Indian Muslims to supply money and men to carry through the reform and renewal of Islam. While advocating assimilation of the modern spirit, he was strongly anti-Western. He detested Europeanization and accused its advocates of trying to efface "the last vestiges of Muslim law," and makes European education responsible for the opinion that religion was incompatible for contemporary politics, science and civilization and that a majority of them wanted a lay state, suppress the caliphate and weaken the religion in the nation.[37] Rashid Rida, of course, speaks here as a theoretician and thus makes idealistic statements ignoring practical aspects. Religion, as the experience in the modern world of Islam shows, has never been a viable force of nation-building though it does provide a sentimental bond which can occasionally rise to great emotional pitch.

[35] Cf., pp. 66/254.
[36] Cf. pp. 59/255.
[37] Cf. pp. 62f/256.

For Rida the Islamic state is the best and this not only for the Muslims but for the whole of mankind, since it stands for justice, equality and legitimate aspirations and interests of everybody. Rashid Rida of course makes idealistic statement without taking into account complex interplay of forces in the real world. Similarly he does not take into account the intractable financial and economic problems of the modern capitalist economy when he posits Zakat (which is levied at 2 1/2% on wealth as well as income of an individual) as the Islamic solution of the social scourges which are inherent in materialist and atheistic governments. The Shari'ah issues pertaining to finance, banking and investment will have to be fundamentally rethought if social justice is to be insured. Zakat can be a part of the solution, not whole. Modern capitalist economy cannot ensure social justice without certain far reaching measures.

His attitude to the new Turkish government is also ambivalent. On the other hand he denies Kamal Ataturk the rights to decide Muslim law, since this is and must remain the prerogative of the 'ulama who, according to him, surprisingly, constitute the jama'at al-Islam (The Party of Islam). One of the examples he quotes deserves notice since it concerns the important question of women's right to do the work of men. The head of the Turkish government obtained the fatwa in favour of women. But the head of the government, Kamal Pasha, according to Rashid Rida is neither expert in the theory nor in the practice of Islamic law with all his courage, prowess and superb military and political leadership.[38] On the other hand Rashid Rida feels that the Turkish government having proved itself capable of preserving the integrity and freedom of its territory is well qualified to effect the needed reform of Islam.In other words it means that Rashid Rida considers the members of the Grand National Assembly at Ankara as properly qualified to carry out *ijtihād* to effect reforms. Thus one will find in Rashid Rida's work complementary and contradictory strands inter-oven.

What is more congenial to the modern age in Rashid Rida's thinking is his conviction, unlike many of his predecessors or contemporaries, that Islam grants legislative powers in political, military and financial matters i.e. in all matters outside the cult in its widest connotation. This lagislative power is entrusted to the community and is to be exercised through consultation by all those who possess knowledge and judgement.[39] Rashid

[38] E.I.J. Rosenthal, cf. p. 257.
[39] Cf. pp. 90ff/257.

Rida too, like al-Kawakibi, is partisan of the Arabs. For him too, the Arab nation is the vital principle of Islam; without it there can be no unity of purpose and action among the Muslims.[40] There is obvious contradiction in his attitude towards the caliph also. On one page of this book one finds that the caliph is purely temporal ruler called upon to defend Islam under the Shari'ah, and on the other page that the caliph is the fountainhead of power, with the right and ability to legislate by *ijtihad*.[41]

Here, it would be relevant to quote Rosenthal's realistic assessment of Rashid Rida and his work: "His own work in this direction is significant, but less for its actual results than for the spirit that animated it. As stated earlier, we owe to him a number of fatwas. But we may justifiably ask whether their scope and content really touch the fundamentals of modern life or whether his reforms—these they certainly constitute—are, in fact, rather confined to more peripheral matters? With the exception of the concession on credit and of his interpretation of *riba* as compensation for service, following Muhammad 'Abduh and Ibn Qayyim al-Jawziyah, it is largely the latter, for his decision that art (music and painting) is canonically permisable hardly shows a sense of urgency in the face of pressing economic and social problems affecting the peace and stability of a modern state and nation, no matter how progressive such a fatwa is; and its importance should not be belited."[42]

Rashid Rida, it can be said, despite his fervent advocacy of *ijtihad* keeping in view the *maslahah* (common weal) does not go much beyond Imam Ibn Taymiyyah and Ibn Qayyim al-Jawziyah. He, like many other Muslim apologists and thinkers, maintains that since Islam teaches social justice, there is no need for modern socialism. He has no doubt that if our modern socialists had known Islamic law properly they would have converted to Islam and become ardent defenders of their new faith.[43] Rashid Rida, as pointed out above, has contradictory attitude towards western modernism. On one hand he considers Islam as the upholder of social justice and humanism which are essentially modern concepts as Islam, during the middle ages, was devoid of them (at least as far as its political philosophy was concerned) and, on the other, he denounces the Westernisers as heretics. In his opinion they would reduce Islam to a cultural and national bond, bereft of all religious meaning and obligation. He, therefore,

[40] Cf. pp. 70/258.
[41] Cf. pp. 77/259.
[42] E.I.J. Rosenthal, cf. pp. 259-60.
[43] Cf. pp. 99/261.

proclaims the necessity of an Islamic government, entirely free from European influence, its laws and traditions, except those which in matters of administrative organization agree with the religious law and there are no different among the nations. The caliphate should have the right of organizing Muslim propaganda, apply legal sanctions, yet assure complete religious liberty.[44]

About the powers and duties of a caliph heading the Islamic state, Rashid Rida's ideas lack consistency. At one place he says that the caliph in fact should have authority over education and personal status, that is, not over any of the members usually under the authority of political governments. But in another place he is said to be a purely temporal ruler[45] and in the third place his spiritual guidance is compared to that if the Pope.[46] Thus at times he approves of separation of religion and politics and at other times he does not with the result that it is difficult to expect any clear guidance from him on this question. This contradiction becomes sharper when he further on asserts that the caliph is the vicegerent of the Prophet, must be a *mujtahid*, defend Islam as religion an law and has coercive power to enforce the law of Islam. He also pleads that the state should entrust all religious matters to independant religious societies and properly trained persons and, to this end, an institute of propaganda and direction of conscience is to be set up which is divorced from politics.[47]

While Rashid Rida avers that the laws vary with time and place and with the religious and temporal situation of the nations, there is no doubt that the Shari'ah is the binding force for the Muslim at all times. New legislation is safe-guarded through the principle of *ijtihād*, and he vigorously attacks *taqlid* and its practitioners throughout the history of Islam. His insistence on *ijtihād* clealy points to his orthodox concept of Islam as "at the same time a spiritual principle and a social and political ideal."[48] Thus we see that Rashid Rida, grounded as he is in the classical Islamic concept, has to become apologetic when confronted with the new realities of modern age. The political realities of the modern world, after Rida wrote his treatise, has become more complex. It would certainly amount to over-simplifying the issue to maintain that only if the pristine purity of Islam is restored through *ijtihad* and certain modern requirements kept in view, it would be

[44]Cf. pp. 119/261.
[45]Cf. pp. 126/261.
[46]Cf. pp. 103/261.
[47]Cf. pp. 119/262.
[48]Cf. pp. 66/262.

possible to establish an on-going and viable Islamic state fully equipped to meet the new challenges.

Another important political thinker is 'Ali 'Abd al-Rāziq. In his writings we find an unequivocal assertion of purely religious character of Islam. He maintains that as against religious doctrines, the religious community is the creation of Muhammad; the imamah or *khilafah* is neither a dogma in Islam nor demanded in the Qur'an and the Sunnah. He says that the theory of the imamah or *khilafah* is the work of theology and jurists and is strictly separated from the history of the khilafah. He clearly maintains that the application of Muhammad's religious massage has nothing whatever to do with politics which is exclusively man's rational task. Abu Bakr, according to him was a *malik* i.e. merely a temporal ruler and there was nothing specifically Islamic in the "calihpate" and Islam has nothing to do with politics. Thus he finally rejects the religious and political unity of Islam which has been claimed by jurists and even by Ibd Khaldun by whom he is otherwise strongly influenced. He, therefore, makes an uncompromising demand for separation of religion from politics as a basis for a modern state and for the premanence of Islam as a religion.[49]

As al-Rāziq does not consider *khilafah* a religious institution, he applies historical criticism to the period of first four rightly guided caliphs as well and does not, like other jurists, begin the criticism from Mu'awiyah onwards. For, he confines pure Islam to the Prophet whom he does not count among the usual political categories. Muhammad, according to him was an exclusively religious leader and his political activity was accidental to his religious mission i.e. *d'awah*, in fact it shares with political activity nothing but the name. He also maintains that creative and normative religious "mission" has ceased with the Prophet's death. The unity of Arab nation is, therefore religious, not political.[50]

Rosenthal comments on al-Raziq's views: "Whether one agrees with 'Abd al-Rāziq's reading of Qur'an and *the Sunnah* and of the history of the Islamic empire or not, it is undeniable that he adopts a definite position which leads him to assign Islam a momentous role in the life of the Muslim believer, but apart from politics. The strength of this attitude is that it starts from first principles and, by taking Islam as a religious *d'awah* out of national and nationalist politics, safeguards the purity of Islam as a universal faith which Rashid Rida strove to recover. But, whereas for Rashid Rida

[49]E.I.J. Rosenthal, *Ibid.*, p.266.
[50]*Ibid.*, p.267.

this purity was represented by the imamah of the Khulafa' Rashidun which he wanted to restore in the twenteeth century, 'Ali 'Abd al-Raziq rejected the canonical necessity of the imamah, together with the actual caliphate, as contrary to the nature and intention of the original Islam of the Prophet Muhammad.[51]

In view of his unorthodox views, 'Abd al-Raziq aroused great hostility. Although the history of Islamic state as we have traced out in earlier chapter, tends to support him, all through the medieval period the concept of theocratic state was sustained and it had become an integral part of the Islamic tradition. All through the Shari'ah was considered as the basis of an Islamic state and now what 'Ali 'Abd al-Raziq said denied this very basic role to the Shari'ah. The 'ulama's condemnation of his views was, therefore, quite natural. However, whatever the traditional view-point, it would be wrong to condemn al-Raziq's views as untenable, if the Quran is made the basis of this theory. The Quran, as we have seen earlier, does not advocate any particular form of state. Besides, the Quran does not aim to create a state but to create a society. It aims at a just society. What is important is to realise this Quranic goal, not necessarily through a kind of theocratic state traditionally upheld by the Muslim jurists.

'Ali 'Abd al-Raziq has propounded his views on the Islamic state in his treatise *al-Islam wa-usul al-hukm*. All the Muslim jurists down to his time have maintained the necessity of an Imam as a doctrinal requirement. But al-Raziq denies that the doctors of Islam proved the necessity of having an Imam from the Quran. Against Rashid Rida he maintains that there is no basis for the institution of the caliphate in the Sunnah and *ijma'a*, on which the institution of *imamah* or *khilafah* could be based. It has no authority in tradition either. Again he says that though undoubtedly authentic, these *ahadith* (traditions) do not constitute a valid argument for the *imamah* as a religious obligation, but simply speak of *imamah, bay'ah jama'at al-Muslimin* (the society of Muslims) as existing in fact.[52]

Under the influence of Ibn Khaldun, the author appreciates the paramount role military force and personal power, based on the active support of family, clan or tribe, play in politics. He also frankly admits that 'brute force has always been the support of the institution of the caliphate.[53] According to him the Muslim historians clearly demonstrate

[51] *Ibid.*
[52] *Ibid.*, p. 269.
[53] Ali 'Abd al-Raziq *al-Islam wa-Us. al-Hukum*, Cairo 1925, p.25 *ul* Cf. E.I.J. Rosenthal, *Ibid.*, pp.269. In subsequent references the first number will indicate al-Raziq's above work and later number Rosenthal's article quoted above.

that there was always opposition to the caliph for the Muslims only submit to Allah voluntarily, but accept the rule of the caliph-supported as it is by force-under duress. So, like a modern political theorist, he comes to the conclusion that the caliphate rests on force rather than on any religious authority. And no doubt, the entire history of Muslim caliphs and sultans bears him out. Even the first caliph Abu Bakr's rule did not go unchallenged. 'Abd al-Raziq himself quotes many examples from the history of the Umayyads, 'Abbasids, Mamluks and other dynasties. He approvingly quotes Ibn Khaldun who says that the Khilafah disappears with the 'asabiyyah.[54] (Partisan spirit)

He then comes to the conclusion that Allah does not want His religion to be subjected to a specific form of government nor to a particular group of rulers.[55] Religious observance, he feels, is independent of caliphate.[56] Thus 'Abd al-Raziq accepts, without any hesitation, and based on the realities of history, separation between religion and politics. Power and authority, according to him, are not necessary for the practice of religion. And yet, he admits that Islam has not only theoretically formulated laws, but has obliged its adherents to practice them. These laws are founded on brotherhood and equality.[57]

'Ali 'Abd al-Raziq, whatever the position of the Muslim jurists, comes much nearer to the truth as seen historically. His is not merely theocratic approach as accepted for centuries by the 'ulama and the jurists; his is, on the contrary, most realistic and historical approach to this otherwise much controversial problem. However, it does not mean that al-Rāziq, in any way undervalues the significance of religious problem. He is of the opinion that the Prophet's authority was spiritual and moral and hence, unlike the caliphs and worldly rulers, his authority was unique which was not based on brute force. He distinguishes between a religious authority deriving from revelation, and political power based on force. He also stresses the fact that that Islam is a *d'awah* to Allah aspiring to a religious unity (*wahdah diniyah*) of all mankind, but not to a political unity, one world government. It was in order to further religion and to support his preaching (*d'awah*) the Prophet made use of means which we would call political actions in other men. He claims that the rules of Islam have absolutely nothing in common with the method and measures of political government

[54]Cf. pp. 36/270.
[55]Cf. pp. 38/270.
[56]Cf. pp. 35F/270.
[57]Cf. pp. 27/270.

and civil administration. The Prophet did not designate a successor; he died after he had accomplished his mission as the apostle of Allah.[58]

He clearly rejects Ibn Khaldun's view that in Islam alone religious and political authority are united. He maintains that if it were so we would have known a good deal more about the political organization and administration of the state founded by the Prophet who acted from Divine revelation. He sums up his argument from the Quran, the *Sunnah* and history in an eloquent exposition of the universality of Islam which is, a religious unity, a unity of faith and a religious way and direction, and not a political unity and temporal-royal institutions and directions. Muhammad, he asserts, never mixed in their affairs, never deposed a governor, nominated a judge (*qadi*) or regulated economic affairs. What Islam teaches in principles, social relations, ethics, legal punishments and so forth is only religious law (*shar'a dini*) directed towards Allah and man's religious welfare (*maṣlaḥah*). Neither the religious law nor the Prophet are concerned with the political welfare of man (*maṣlaḥah madaniyah*) which is not relevant to it. Moreover, the *Shari'ah* only created religious unity but politically, socially and economically they were different peoples.[59]

In Muhammad al-Ghazali we again encounter views similar to those of Rashid Rida. Like him, he is also convinced of the religious and political unity of Islam and exhorts Muslims to apply the teachings of Islam to their political and social life. He comes very close to the Muslim Brotherhood and condemns West for its separation of religion and politics. Also, modern nationalism is condemned by him as the dangerous foe of Islam. He wrote a treatise *Min huna n'alam* (Our beginning in wisdom) in reply to Khalid Muhammad Khalid's *Min huna nabda'* (From Here We Start) to condemn separation of religion from politics. According to him this separation is the result of western imperialist influence out to destroy Islam by isolating it from legislation.[60]

Al-Ghazali is of the opinion that in order to be successful Islam must gain political power, like the French and Russian Revolutions. He says that the Prophet began as a preacher and ended up as a ruler: "...this happened to the great Prophet, the master of this *Shari'ah*, for he began as a preacher, an announcer and warner, but ended as a judge and ruler (*hakim*) ...his messengership turned from d'awah to dawlah...(State).[61] About the first

[58] Cf. pp. 59f/271.
[59] Cf. pp. 83ff/274.
[60] From preface to the second edition of *Our Beginning in Wisdom*. Washington, 1953 (American Council of Learned Societies), Eng. tr. by Isma'il R. al-Faruqi pp. 11/Cf. Rosenthal p. 276.
[61] Cf. pp. 23/276.

four caliphs also he maintains that God and His Book, not power, guided them in establishing a government safeguarding Islam and applying its principles. It was, in his opinion, traditional enmity of Europe towards Islam that they separated it from state and projected it as a religion. For him the separation of religion from the state is bid'ah, heresy. He is convinced that Islamic government alone answers the need of the world for it guards revelation. For him religion without power would be powerless. Thus he feels that any nationalist government which separates state from religion would be irreligious and it is the duty of the Muslims to fight such a government and replace it by a religious one. He thus clearly speaks the language of Ikhwan al-Muslimin and Jama'at-e-Islami of Pakistan. He is totally opposed to the concept of nationalism and holds it responsible for the loss of Islamic unity." "the nationalist attitude is the most important thing we copied from the West, and formed the cornerstone in establishing the modern state."[62]

Here it will also be interesting to examine the blue-print of an Islamic government prepared by Said Halim Pasha in 1927. According to him: "In Muslim society, where there are no class rivalries, where the ideals and social aspirations are the same for all, national representation must of necessity assume a form quite different from that which it has assumed in western society, different in spirit and objective, in its composition, its rights and its prerogatives." He, therefore, feels that "national representation in Muslim society should be secured by an assembly of which the composition must be such as to ensure that political peace and concord, founded on that fraternity between classes which is one of the distinctive features of Muslim society, shall reign within that assembly. It must establish and maintain in the political sphere the solidarity which is found in the social sphere."[63]

The author, needless to say, completely ignores the present day social realities and tries to wish away the social conflicts and tensions by employing the high sounding ideals. We will subject these ideas to critical examination in a later chapter. According to Pasha in the Muslim parliament there will be no communists, no socialists, no republicans and no monarchists. There will be only men of good-will all cherishing the same ideal and aim: to apply to the best of their ability the wise commandments of the *Shari'a*. They will be men differing among themselves only as to

[62]Cf. pp. 68/278.
[63]Said Halim 'Pasha, "The Reform of Muslim Society," Islamic Culture, the Hyderabad Quarterly Review, 1927, p. 129.

the choice of means wherewith to serve the common ideal (this idealistic dream looks like Farabi's *al-Madinah al-Fadilah* i.e. The Good City).

As for the rights and prerogatives of that Parliament, they will be extensive enough to allow its exercising the widest, most complete and most effective control over the government. *But the faculty of legislation will not be among them* (emphasis mine). The recognition of such a right in national representation would be contrary to the spirit of the *Shari'ah* whose perfect wisdom and justice never could admit that a group of political men, however high their character, should be charged with the making of the laws. Besides, the special reasons, for which that right is ascribed to Parliament in the Western society, do not exist in Muslim society (Pasha does not care to explain those special reasons). In fact, the Muslim Parliament would not have to spend its time in facilitating transformations, which the fluctuating state of the western community demands, by passing laws appropriate to such changes. National representation in Muslim society would thus be a *controlling, not a legislative power* (emphasis supplied); for its aim would be to secure a wise and honest administration for the society, to promote the reign of the greatest justice between individuals, and thus to aid the nation in its task of constant progress.[64]

Moreover, Said Halim Pasha is of the view that since in Muslim society, the function of legislation is essentially a social function of the first importance, a function in which the political character is not predominant as it is in Western society, the right to legislate must belong to him who knows how to make laws-i.e., to the legist; for it is not a question of majority, but simply one of competence (Pasha obviously does not give any importance to the aspirations of the masses of people.) What matters most for Said Halim Pasha and men of his ilk is the deep knowledge of *Shari'ah* as handed down from generation to generation and only those possessed of the knowledge of static body of the juristic corpus will be eligible to frame, accept or reject, any legislation. In addition to this, Said Pasha lays down that they should also possess high moral qualities, moderation, prudence, impartiality, in short, should have wisdom. They must also have the intimate knowledge of the soul, the mind and temperament of the people. Only then the laws will be live, loved, respected and feared.[65]

He also feels it necessary that in Muslim states, more than anywhere, authority should be strong. And, one of the conditions of the strength,

[64] *Ibid.*, pp. 128-29.
[65] *.Ibid.*, p.129.

according to him, is that it must reside in one person. And it is just as necessary that it must reside in one person. And it is just as necessary that the person holding authority should be chosen by the nation. That is one of the nation's most. Halim Pasha says, incontestable rights, arising from the nation's duty to take care that the administration functions properly, which can only happen if the supreme power is entrusted to the man most worthy to wield it.[66] He holds that the chief of the state should be personally responsible both to the representatives and guardians of the *Shari'ah*-whatever be the body charged with those functions-and to the nation (this is distinctive feature of the Muslim organization, according to Pasha); while his delegates are responsible to the representatives of the nation and those of *Shari'ah.* Thus in the Muslim political regime, the responsibility of the Executive Power to Parliament and to the Legislative Assembly is established.[67]

There is no reference to *ijtihad* in Said Halim Pasha's above political system. It, therefore, appears that he accepts the provisions of *Shari'ah* without any reinterpretation unlike 'Abduh and Rashid Rida. Like other idealistic thinkers, Pasha also thinks that laws and ethical norms are borne in human mind or divinely revealed without any reference to the objective social situation and once these laws are given the objective situation-whatever it may be-can be made to confirm to them. Thus Islamic *Shari'ah* once formulated by the early Muslim 'ulama does not stand in need of any reinterpretation or change and if it is not being observed the fault lies with those who do not enforce it rigorously. Once the top political executive is made responsible to the council of 'ulama, everything would fall in place and *Shari'ah* would be properly observed. The Parliament elected by the people would have no legislative powers; neither will 'ulama enjoy that power. Parliament will only exercise supervisory functions and 'ulama would ensure that the decisions taken by the highest executive strictly conform to the provisions of *Shari'ah.*

Said Pasha's views on Islamic state, needless to say, are over- simplified and imply the presumption that social conflict, if any, can be resolved by application of *Shari'ah* and not by removing those causes whose roots are in the social structure and maldistribution of material resources. Neither does he understand the nature and force of private property which is considerably different in the modern industrial society from the period to

[66] *Ibid.*, p. 130.
[67] *Ibid.*, p. 131.

which Islam belonged and the compulsions of the social and historical situation in which the Prophet upheld the right to property (we shall have more detailed discussion on this in a subsequent chapter). Pasha, on account of his lack of knowledge of these modern complexities of socio-economic forces, suggests that in an Islamic Parliament there would be neither communists nor socialists or any other political parties and the absence of these parties and groups would ensure smooth functioning and all that is needed is a sincere enforcement of the *Shari'ah.* More of it later. The only progressive aspect in Pasha's theory is his acceptance of nation-state which many other Islamic theorists deny.

So far we have considered the views of those Muslim theoreticians on Islam and state who belonged to either wholly Muslim or Muslim majority countries. Naturally, therefore, their views on Islamic state were deeply influenced by their own situation. Now we shall throw some light on the views of Maulana Abu'l Kalam Azad, an eminent Muslim scholar from India. Azad, although a traditional scholar of Islam, held views, like Muhammad 'Abduh of Egypt, which were, in many ways, closer to our own time. Azad did not see any conflict between Islam and modern secular nationalism. In fact Gandhiji said that Azad's faith in nationalism was "as robust as his faith in Islam."[68] Azad did not stress a separate Islamic character of state. According to him the essence of the Prophet's message lay in monotheism and belief in *Din* (i.e. essential religion). Maulana Azad refers to a Prophet's tradition: "O God I bear witness that all people are brothers to one another. Differences they might have created among themselves, but you have united them together with a single bond of humanity."[69]

Most of the Muslim thinkers, as we have seen, base the Islamic state on *Shari'ah.* Moreover, seen in general, these thinkers consider *Shari'ah* as the axis around which the religion of Islam revolves. Maulana Azad, on the other hand, distinguishes between Din and *Shari'ah* treating the former as the essence of Islam. *Shari'ah,* according to him, varies from nation to nation and people to people. He says: "*Din* in reality was devotion to God through righteous living, and was no exclusive heritage of any single group of people. On the other hand, it was the common heritage of all mankind, and knew no change. Actions and customs are but secondary to it. They have changed and are liable to change from time to time and vary from

[68]Moin Shakir "Political Ideas of Maulana Azad," *Azad Islam and Nationalism,* Kalamkar Prakashan, Delhi, n.d. p. 18.

[69]Moin Shakir, *Idid.*

country to country under the exigencies of time and circumstances. Whatever differences one may notice between one religion and another, they relate particularly to this sphere of life."

Then quoting a verse from the Quran "Why do you give so great an importance to ceremonials? God had prescribed different ceremonials at different times and for different countries. Whatever was appropriate to a particular situation was prescribed," Azad corroborates his argument that *Din* and *Shari'ah* are different and that whereas the former is unchangeable and universal the latter is variable depending on time and place.[70]

Maulana Azad, as is well-known, had enthusiastically participated in the *Khilafat* movement in the early twentieth century. He had, along with other fellow 'ulama, advocated that the Ottoman ruler be made the caliph of the Muslim community throughout the world. However, later on the Maulana realized the futility of such an international caliphate and abandoned the idea. How did this transformation occur in his outlook? I am inclined to agree with Dr Alam Khundmiri that "...a great and profound religious and spiritual transformation took place in the mind of Azad during the days of his forced withdrawal from active life when he was interned in Ranchi and the result was a new Azad who had discovered a clue to the understanding of Islam. He was able to hold fast to the true orthodox basis of Islam and to find a new solution to the political situation of the country...Even conceding the influence of political events on the development of his thought it must be recognized that he never let the political events determine the course of the development of his thought...His insight into the real and timeless Islam stops him from joining that chorus of anti-Westernism which denounces new science and new modes of political thinking. On the contrary, his orthodox religious outlook leads to that fundamental discovery that Islam cannot be tied up to a particular culture or a particular phase of history."[71]

Maulana Azad, while adhering to the essential teachings of Islam, did not tie it down to any particular form of government, nor did he consider it necessary to advocate theocracy. He believed in the theory of composite nationalism and found justification for it in the Prophet's agreement which he entered into with Medinese Jews, Christians and pagans thus laying the foundation of a new community in Medina (vide chapter 1 for the clauses

[70]Maulana Abdul Kalam Azad, *The Tarjuman al-Qur'an*, Eng. tr. by Syed Abdul Latif, Asia Publishing House, 1965, pp. 160-61.

[71]Alam Khundmiri "Religious Philsophy of Azad," *Azad, Islam and Nationalism*, op. cit., p. 48.

of this agreement). Azad, unlike Maududi, never considered theocracy as the integral part of Islam nor the rigid form of *Shari'ah* (which is considered by many 'ulama as the basis of Islamic state) as the basis of laws of state. He explicitly states :

> The Qur'an points out that the teaching of a religion is two-fold. One constitutes its spirit; the other its outward manifestation. The former is primary in importance, the latter secondary. The first called Din: the second Shar'a or Minhaj and Nusk. Shar'a and Minhaj mean the path; and Nusk the manner or ceremonial of devotion. In practice however, Shar'a has come to mean the law prescribed by religion and Nusk merely the form of devotion or worship. The Qur'an states that the differences which exist between one religion and another are not differences in Din, the basic provision, but in the manner of giving effect to it, or in the Shar'a and Minhaj, not in the spirit of religion, but in its outward form. This difference was but natural. The essential purpose of religion is the progress and well-being of humanity....Intelletual and social aptitudes have varied from time to time and from country to country necessitating variations in Shar'a and Minhaj.[72]

Thus we see that Azad is concerned with the essence of religion and not with its outward form or manifestation, much less with the shape of the state it is supposed to stress. *Shar'a* for him is not necessarily the basis of state laws; on the contrary, with the change in time, clime and place, the laws of *Shar'a* can change. According to Azad's theory of religion a modern secular state like that of India does not come in conflict with the essential teachings of Islam which consists of "devotion to God and righteous living."[73] Maulana Husain Ahmad Madani and other leaders of Jami'at al-'Ulama-Hind which was an ally of the Indian National Congress, also accepted the concept of composite nationalism and secular character of state.

Maulana Husain Ahmad Madani has written a booklet *Muttahida Qaumiyyat aur Islam* (Composite Nationalism and Islam)[74] to justify the concept of composite nationalism on the basis of the Quran. In this booklet he has quoted many Quranic verses to show that the word qaum (people,

[72] Maulana Abul Kalam Azad, *op. cit.*, p. 158.
[73] *Ibid.*, p. 163
[74] Maulana Syed Husain Ahmad, *Muttahida Qaumiyat aur Islam*, Qaumi Ekta Trust, Delhi, n.d.

tribe, nation etc.) has always been used include all the people of a particular region irrespective of their religious beliefs. In fact this word, whenever used in the Quran includes kafirs (non-believers) also.[75] Quoting these verses he says: "In all these verses Muslims and non-believers (kafirs) have been called one people and what could be the relation between them except race or country?"[76] Syed Husain Ahmad has even approvingly quoted Sir Syed's speech on the concept of qaum in which Sir Syed has clearly emphasized that this word is applied to all those who live in one country irrespective of their religion. In this speech Sir Syed declares that the words "Hindu," "Muslim," "Christan" etc. have religious connotation but all these people living in one country constitute one nation. Gone is the time when the residents of one country were considered two different nations on the basis of religion.[77]

[75]*Ibid.*, pp. 16-21
[76]*Ibid.*, p. 21.
[77]*Ibid.*, pp. 72-73.

5. Jama'at-e-Islami and Islamic State

Our survey of the theories of Islamic state would not be complete without dealing with the ideology of Jama'at-e-Islami and the concept of theocracy propounded by it. The Jama'at has been by far the most influential in many Muslim countries, specially Pakistan. Among the rightist parties, it is the strongest and most consistent. The Jama'at was founded in 1941 by Abu-l-A'la Mawdudi in India. W.C. Smith describes the foundation of the Jama'at as "one of the most significant developments in contemporary Islam and one of the most significant forces in contemporary Pakistan."[1] Also about Mawdudi Smith says: "...perhaps the most significant Constituent of Mawdudi's position has been the gradual and continual elaboration of an impressive system of ideas. Mawdudi would appear even wonder whether his chief contribution, in the realm of interpretation, has not been for good or ill his transforming of Islam into a system—or, perhaps more accurately, his giving expression to a modern tendency so as to transform it."[2]

The Jama'at has produced voluminous literature on Islam in Urdu much of which is now being translated into English and Arabic. The Jama'at has also won over number of Muslim intellectuals in Pakistan and has trained its own cadre. Those who have acquired this religious expertise are much in demand these days in the oil-rich Arabian countries. Detlev H. Khalid says, "Libya and Saudi Arabia have failed to produce any Islamic thinker or spiritual leader of mark. For religious expertise they require specialists from abroad just as they rely on foreign manpower in other spheres of life. In matters Islamic this personnel is supplied mainly by Egypt and Pakistan and to a lesser degree by Morocco and Syria. In Egypt and Pakistan strong fundamentalist organizations (i.e. Ikhwan al-Muslimin in Egypt and Jama'at- e-Islami in Pakistan), based on a layer of neo-Wahaabism left

[1]W.C. Smith, *op. cit.*, p. 235, footnote.
[2]*Ibid.*, p. 236.

over from the branches created at the turn of the century."[3] Mawlana Maududi himself was invited by Qaddafi of Libya for his advice in framing the constitution. Khalid says: "It came, then, as a rude shock to all those in Pakistan who admired Qaddafi for his socialist pretentions when he invited, of all persons, Maududi and his party lieutenants to advise him in framing the new Libyan constitution and 'Islamize" the law.'[4]

Mawlana Maududi, the founder of the Jama'at, remained its chief theoretician and supreme leader until his death (Maududi died in September 1979). There was no other leader of the Jama'at of comparable stature to Maududi. It was Maududi who decided its policies and evolved its ideological stance. We shall, therefore, mainly discuss his views on the basis of his writings spread over more than three decades.

Maududi, although schematic in his approach and consistent in his thinking, is arch conservative. He borrows, to a limited extent, the modern methodology of social sciences to project his medieval views and thus creates deception of being modern in his approach. "It is one of the legacies of colonialism," remarks Detlev Khalid, "that enlightened thinkers such as Sayyid Ahmad Khan and Muhammad 'Abduh had necessarily to be succeeded by religio-political agitators such as Maududi in Pakistan and Benna in Egypt there reference is to Hasan al-Banna of Egypt who founded Ikhwan al-Muslimin). They are seasoned dialecticians who, in their lifelong struggle against Westernization, have acquired consummate skill and polish, availing themselves of modern categories of thought, knowing fully well that otherwise they cannot compete."[5] Detlev further remarks that the movements which they created found little following among the rural masses, but they are the best organized political parties in their respective countries. Their power base is the petty bourgeoisie which has given evidence of its ability to determine the country's destiny.[6]

Maududi and Islamic State.

The founder of the Jama'at has been, from the very beginning, an ardent advocate of a theocratic state. It was because of his views on Islamic state that he did not make common cause with Jinnah. Jinnah, in the Pakistan of his dream, wanted to establish a secular state and not a theocratic state. The Muslim League represented, it is important to note, the interests of the

[3]Detlev H. Khalid, "Phenomenon of Re-Islamisation," *Mainstream*, Delhi, 16, June 1979, p. 20,

[4]*Ibid.*, pp. 21-22.
[5]*Ibid.*, p. 21.
[6]*Ibid.*

feudal lords of North India on the one hand, and, those of the nascent class of mercantile bourgeoisie of Western India, on the other (there were no industrial entrepreneurs worth the name among the Indian Muslims at that time). Jinnah himself belonged to the mercantile Khojah community of Western India and was essentially secular in his outlook. Maududi, on the other hand, served with the Nizam state of Hyderabad and was highly conservative in his views. For him secularism is the product of modern atheistic political philosophy and as such has no place whatsoever in an Islamic society.

Maududi's writings on Islamic state spread over decades have been compiled by Khurshid Ahmad in a book *Islami Riyasat*[7] and published from Lahore. We shall mainly refer to this book in our discussion of Maududi's views on Islamic state. According to Maududi religion cannot become merely a private affair of man's life. It is nothing if not the complete system on which is based entire culture and civilization.[8] Unlike Maulana Azad's view on religion (vide chapter IV), Maududi is totally opposed to the idea of separating *Din* from *Shari'ah.* According to Maududi both are not only inseparable but the religion of Islam admits no other way of life except the one we find in the Quran and *Shari'ah* as formulated by the early 'ulama on the basis of the Prophet's tradition and *Sunnah. Shari'ah* is immutable as it is based on the divine laws. Islam, Maududi says, should become an integral part of a Muslim's life. It should be his entire life, its spirit and its moving force. One's understanding, consciousness, thinking and views cannot be other than what Islamic teachings are. Religion should guide a person from beginning of his life and through its journey to the other world (*akhirah*) and should enable him to pass through all these phases successfully.[9]

Thus we see that Maududi holds an all embracing view of religion and it is hard to find his parallel in the contemporary Islamic world. Of course by *Shari'ah* Maududi means mainly the Hanafite school (though he does not reject totally the other three Sunnite schools) and does not admit validity of the other heterodox schools of Islam. Also, Maududi is hardly inclined towards *ijtihad* or reinterpretation of various Islamic laws and he has, therefore, been rightly described as fundamentalist. As far as Maududi is concerned the gates of *ijtihad* are closed. The codification of *Shari'ah* in the early Islamic period was based on divine wisdom and divine wisdom

[7]Syed Abu'l A'la Maududi, *Islami Riyasat,* compiled by Khurshid Ahmad, Islamic Publications Ltd., Lahore (West Pakistan), 1974.

[8]*Ibid.*, p. 39.
[9]*Ibid.*

does not depend on the exigencies of situation. Many other 'ulama and thinkers, as we have seen in the last chapter, have accepted the necessity of reinterpretation and adjustment but for Maududi this is all unpardonable heresy and hence deserves outright condemnation. With great rhetoric he says ;

> If these people very well understand who is Muslim and to which group of people the term Islami Jama'at (the Islamic party) can be applied, then their, misunderstandings can be removed. Legally everyone who recites the formula (i.e. there is no gods but one God and that Muhammad is His messenger) is a Muslim but his Islam is only a matter of formality a passport to join the Islamic community and that he cannot be dubbed as kafir...But this is not true Islam. True Islam is one which envelops your heart and mind, which moulds your entire way of thinking to that of the Quranic way, makes all your values the Quranic values, makes your goal the Quarnic goal, makes you abandon all other paths and leads you on to the Islamic and Quranic path. Only then you can be said to have adopted what is described by the Quran as the *sabil al-mu' minin*[10] (the path of the faithfuls).

Thus in all this rhetoric one will hardly find any attempt to grapple with the concrete problems of contemporary life. Such rhetoric has, undoubtedly, a great appeal for an ordinary Muslim specially to one belonging to an urban petty bourgeoisie class and there lies the secret of the Jama'at's success. Maududi's entire thinking is abstract which he projects with consummate skill logically and rhetorically and thus succeeds in captivating a Muslim's mind. As far as the quality and depth of thinking is concerned, Maulana Maududi, compared to other great Muslim thinkers like Afghani, Muhammad 'Abduh, Kawakibi, Sir Syed and others, is no more than a mediocre. While these other thinkers, grappled with the concrete contemporary problems and suggested solutions in an assimilative spirit, Maududi wants to promote what bears deep medieval impress in the garb of Islam and wrapped in his fascinating rhetorics. Nowhere he comes near to grappling with the contemporary problems in all their complexities. With all his coherence he appears to move in the closed circle of his own creation. The best way of life is the one shown by the Quran and what is that way of life? the one codified by the *Shari'ah*. Well

[10] W.C. Smith, *op. cit.*, p. 236.

everything begins and ends within this circle. He couldn't care less if contemporary problems do not admit of the solutions suggested in a vastly different situation during the medieval period. His fundamentalism does not allow him to see anything beyond the early Islamic period and the Middle-Ages. Even a thinker like Rashid Rida, who was certainly more conservative than Muhammad 'Abduh appears to be much more radical in comparison to Maulana Maududi.

Here it will be interesting to quote W.C. Smith. He says :

> It is true that in the second and third centuries *hijri* some of the moral imperatives of Islam were systematized by the then religious leaders into the law. There are modern tendencies that would view even this system as dated, as inadequate in scope and too rigid in form to represent faithfully those imperatives for today; and would seek the truth of Islam also in this area more in the realm of values and dynamic, of principles and spirit. Over against these, Maududi for the first time would rather extend still further the drive to reduce Islam to a positive system-further both in the degree of reduction and in the areas covered. He presents Islam as a system, one that long ago provided mankind with set answers to all its problems, rather than as a faith in which God provides mankind anew each morning the riches whereby it may answer them itself.

One may go through thousands of pages of Maududi's writings but it would be futile to seek enlightenment in them. One will find that the Maulana repeats the same arguments again and again with different emphasis and in different forms, of course. The entire burden of his arguments repeated ad nauseum is that Islam, as presented by the 'ulama of the early Islamic period and the concepts formulated by them, aught to be accepted with complete involvement of one's heart and mind. He does not even bother to take their deep differences on many fundamental issues into account.

Maududi has his own concept of Islamic state in the modern era. This simplistic concept betrays total lack of understanding of the complexities of contemporary socio-political structure. He dogmatically refuses to take into account various interests and how they influence the policies of a modern state. Thus he says that if you wish to would your political and economic life in accordance with the teachings of Islam then you need not divide yourself into different parties. Only one party-i.e. *Hizbullah* (the Party of God)—is sufficient for all these tasks. (Needless to say all totalitarian systems advocate one party rule). Why? Because in an Islamic society there is no conflict between capitalists and workers, landlords and peasants, rulers and the ruled. On the contrary there are principles which promote co-operation between these classes. Then why not eliminate this conflict between these classes on the basis of these principles? Those who lack these principles may be compelled to jump into the fire of class war but why you (i.e. the Muslims)?[11]

If this is not oversimplification of the complex problems of the modern industrial society what else is? Of course we are not attempting here a critique of such theories which advocate elimination of class conflict merely by expression of noble sentiments and lofty ethical principles (themselves product of upper class ideology) but suffice it may to say here that these noble words cannot (Pakistan's own experience in the last thirty years of its existence is a sufficient proof of this, if any proof is needed) eliminate powerful vested interests sought to be perpetuated by certain classes at home in the third world countries, let alone much more formidable forces represented by powerful multinational corporations owned by the capitalist classes in the imperialist countries of the West. In such a situation different political parties representing different vested interests or class-interests are bound to arise or even if one party acquires dominant position (as it happens in many countries with limited or controlled democracies), it will be able to rule only and if it broadly represents the interests of the ruling classes (capitalist or feudal or both as often happens in the third-world countries to which almost all the Islamic countries belong). This at least has been the experience of all the third world countries. Maududi talks of one party i.e. *Hizbullah* but even in Pakistan the 'ulama are divided into several parties and have, fundamental differences with each other. What is most shocking is that these 'ulama could not even agree amongst themselves as to who is Muslim. The Munir report brought the sorry state of affairs to the public notice that the 'ulama were not only unfitted to run a modern state but were depiorably unable under cross-questioning even to give realistic guidance on elementary matters of Islam. The court of enquiry, and subsequently the world, was presented with the sorry spectacle of Muslim divines no two of whom agreed on the definition of a Muslim, and who yet were practically unanimous that all who disagreed should be put to death.[12]

[11]Syed Abu'l A'la Maududi, *op. cit.*, p. 47
[12]Munir Commission Report, Lahore, 1954 pp. 218-219. Cf. W.C. Smith, *op. cit.*, p. 234-35

Why Islamic State?

Maulana Maududi tries to explain the necessity for an Islamic state. He says that according to the Quran God is the master of the world– He has created the world and so it is His right to rule over it. Maududi maintains that over His own creation, over His own world, no one else has any right to rule; it will be fundamentally wrong. There is only one true path and that path is that the caliph should rule as His vicegerent according to Shari'ah.[13] We have already seen that even on matters of *shari'ah* there is no unanimity of opinion. Apart from the four traditional schools of Sunnites, there are several others as codified by various heterodox sects i.e.the Twelvers, the Zaidites, Isma'ilis,. the Kharijites, etc.

There are fundamental differences betwveen these schools of Islamic jurisprudence on various important issues. Moreover, many thinkers and 'ulama belonging to these schools want to reinterpret the traditional provisions of their respective schools in response to the contemporary challenges. It would therefore by very difficult to maintain that this is the meaning of the Quaranic injunction and hence the Islamic state law in its light has to be so framed. Hence ultimately there may be unanimity on the Islamic rule being based on the Quranic laws but not on what these laws precisely are. Then there are those Muslim thinkers like Maulana Azad who feel, not without justification from the Quran itself, that the *Shari'ah* is not an internal part of the religious faith i.e. *Dīn* which mainly consists in the belief in God and righteous actions. If it is so one can hardly maintain that the Islamic state has to be based on Shari'ah and that God's rule means enforcing Islamic *Shari'ah* as formulated in the early Islamic period. And this is exactly what Maulana Maududi means when he talks of God's rule being established on earth. God's rule in that case would mean Islamic *Shari'a*h as formulated by Imam Abu Hanifa and as interpreted by Maududi or his lieutenants.

In fact Maududi's approach is so rigid and his attitude so authoritarian that any state founded on his ideas would be a medieval dictatorship. Freedom and creative thinking would be its first victims. Maulana Maududi rigidly maintains that man has been deprived of the right to legislate as he is God's creature, His subject and necessarily under His rule. He has no option but to follow the Laws imposed on him by God, the real lord of this world. He has been given, at the most, a little leeway to fill in details within the strict limits laid down by *Shari'ah* as handed down to

[13]Maududi, *op. cit.*, p. 49.

him. But, if he transgresses these limits or chooses to follow any other law to regulate the worldly affairs he will be guilty of following the Satanic powers and that amounts to rebellion from God and His Prophet.[14] To prove his point Maududi chooses various Quranic verses without proper context. The more enlightened Muslim thinkers have used those very verses to draw different inferences. This clearly shows that it is not the monopoly of any single authority to consider his interpretation as final and sacred like the Quran.

It is the considered opinion of Maulana Maududi that any government and its laws based on any source other than that of God and His Messenger is illegitimate. All its acts are worthless, weightless and untrue. There is no legitimacy whatsoever for its acts[15] (even if these acts are based on the universally accepted principles of social justice; this is what his assertions clearly imply). Such a government deserves nothing but outright condemnation by all the "faithfuls." These faithfuls may accept such a government as a de facto government but certainly not as *de jure* because the faithfuls cannot seek any other source of legitimacy except the one emanating directly from God. Because those who do so, according to Maududi, are outside the circle of Islam. Maulana Maududi, who vexes so eloquent on the Islamic form of government, has no hesitation in accepting those traditions ascribed to the Prophet according to which one must not rebel against a ruler, however cruel or unjust he may be, as long as he formally enforces the Islamic way of prayer (*salat*). Quoting many of these traditions Maududi concludes that one ought not to rebel against a government as long as it continues to enforce prayer. This clearly implies that one cannot rebel against an unjust government simply because it technically continues to confess Islam.[16] Thus for Maududi and for his Jama'at what is of fundamental importance is Islamic formalism and not its spirit of social justice which is considered to be a cardinal principle of a socialist system. Even an enlightened capitalist state considers social welfare as one of its fundamental tasks. But for Maududi an uncritical acceptance of medieval Islam with all its feudal accretions is far more preferable to an "atheistic" socialist or welfare capitalist state. But if it comes to a choice Maududi will certainly prefer former to the later one.

Maududi considers communists as the enemies of Islam but, nevertheless, does not hesitate to adopt their tactics to wrest power from the

[14] *Ibid.*, pp. 50-51.
[15] *Ibid.*, p. 53.
[16] *Ibid.*, pp. 186-89.

opponents and establish an "Islamic state." To him religion without political power has no meaning. Islam is a comprehensive ideology and, like communism, is in need of state power to be enforced. Maududi says that it is in the very nature of Islamic way of life to replace other systems by its own and this cannot be accomplished without wresting state power. And, to achieve this objective, Muslims can adopt any means in this struggle. According to Maududi the Quran and the Prophetic traditions this is the real stand of Islam and not that of making compromises with other systems.[17]

In the light of this, Maududi makes it very clear that existence of any state other than Islam should be an open challenge to the Muslims. Others may or may not like it, it may or may not lead to cooperation or intercourse with non-Muslims (it may even mean confrontation with them), if we are sincere to our religion and faith, says Maududi, we must then struggle to impose *shari'ah,* the law of God. For Maududi, anyone who opposes imposition of God's rule as advocated by him, is an enemy like the class-enemy in the case of communists. For, Maududi maintains that cordial relations with the non-Muslims is not the real aim of an Islamic society; on the contrary, its real aim is to impose God's rule over the society even if it means confrontation with non-Muslims. In other words religious conflict is to Maududi what class conflict is to the communists. Real peace, according to Maududi, can be established only if all submit to the law of God, only when the non-Muslims reconcile themselves to the establishment of the Islamic rule.[18]

For Maududi, any rule other than the Islamic rule, is Satanic. For him any peace based on compromise with the Satanic systems is an illusion, an un-Islamic act. Islam does not accept peace established by others but the one established by itself, on its own terms. Man's security lies only in accepting this Islamic peace. Maududi also maintains that the Quranic verse that "There is no compulsion in religion" only means that others will not be compelled to accept the Islamic beliefs neither will they be forced to pray according to the Islamic system but that is about all. This verse, according to him, does not at all mean that the laws of civilization could be based on anything save that ordained by God nor that the traitors (i.e. Kafirs) be permitted to enforce Satanic rule and expect the Muslims to submit to it. In any case in such a struggle one party will have to interfere

[17] *Ibid.*, p. 62.
[18] *Ibid.*, p. 63.

in the party's religion and if the Muslims don't interfere in the religion of Kafirs, they will interfere in the religion of Muslims and as a result of this unbelief (kufr) will become a part of Muslims' lives.[19]

It is quite obvious that Maududi considers religious conflict as the basic conflict even in the modern polity. In fact it is also obvious that he has borrowed many of his ideas on organization and conducting of struggle for power from the communists whom he otherwise hates. Maududi tries to replace "class conflict" by "religious conflict" and thus betrays very superficial understanding not only of Marxism but also of religion as well as motive forces of a human society. Maududi seems to be highly impressed by the assertion of ideological superiority by the Marxists and hence he also tries to pesuade his co-religionists that one need not be apologetic about the superiority of their religion with all its attendant implications. As the communists advocate class conflict there is no reason, Maududi feels, why there should be any hesitation on the party of the Muslims to advocate religious conflict and strive and struggle, like the communists, for the final triumph of their "religion" (proletariat in the case of communists). Such an analogy might attract some people but the subjective illusion can be no substitute for the concrete reality. Maududi fails to understand that an ideology is no mere mental construct or a moral vision unconnected with the concrete social realities. Even Ibn Khaldun, the great Muslim historian, does not advocate a purely subjective approach to history. Religion, even in its most abstract and universal form, cannot be completely segregated from its concrete social milieu. Religion—there is nothing irreligious in accepting this—is an ideological expression of certain moral imperatives which are acceptable to the people in a certain spatio-temporal context and some of these imperatives may well transcend this spatio-temporal frame. It would, therefore, be wrong to treat religion as a mere mental abstraction unconnected with the social reality within a particular socio-temporal frame and thus consider religious conflict as a substitute for historical forces and class conflict.

The parallel goes much further. Maududi, like the Marxists, wants to develop a comprehensive theory of social sciences in the light of Islam. He, therefore, talks of Islamic economics, Islamic sociology, Islamic politics and so on. Islam, for Maududi, as pointed out before, is a revealed religion which has no concrete roots in a social structure but is based only

[19]*Ibid.*, pp. 63-64.

on Gods' will. These sciences also, therefore, would remain purely idealistic without any concrete social content. Maududi clearly states that the main characteristic of Islamic society is that its whole structure is based on the concept of the sovereignty of God. No person, class, nation or even entire humanity can have any claim to sovereignty. Everything is subject to Him and it is His right to rule and make laws.[20] All the social sciences, Maududi tells us, must be interpreted in the light of these laws given by God. No other approach will be admissible. Thus in Maududi's scheme of things, laws define the social structure rather than social structure determining the laws. He thus tries to stand philosophy on its head.

Needless to say, the chief of Jama'at is irreconciliably opposed to the concept of secularism. In fact the Jama'at believes that the two staunch enemies of Islam in the contemporary world are secularism and communism. Maududi says that a secular state is opposed to an ideological state based on Islam root and branch. It does not have anything in common even in smallest possible detail.[21] Maududi, again like the communists, believes that an Islamic state can be run only by a specially trained cadre as it demands special aptitude, discipline, commitment and integrity of character. Its army, its police, its judiciary, its finances, its revenues, its administrative policies, its foreign policy, its war and peace, in fact everything is different from a secular state[22] and to handle these matters require proper appreciation of Islam and its religious philosophy.

Maududi, not uncharacteristically of him of course, maintains that a chief justice of a secular state is not even fit to become a peon in the court of an Islamic state. The inspector general of police from a secular state would not deserve appointment even as a constable in the Islamic state. In short, all the officials and others associated with a secular state are totally unfit to run an Islamic state.[23] It is obvious that the Maulana has a deep hatred towards secularism and makes such statements which show his fanaticism and hatred rather than his understanding and analytical power. Whatever his merit as a political theoretician, as a sociologist and economist (he delves in these subjects also while attempting a critique of modern secular or socialist states) is, at best, second rate.

The Maulana considers participation in a secular state as nothing less than a rebellion against God and his Messenger. While departing to

[20]*Ibid.*, p. 692.
[21]*Ibid.*, p. 693.
[22]*Ibid.*
[23]*Ibid.*

Pakistan, he addressed Muslims remaining in India and told them: "So far as the Muslims are concerned, I want to tell them that present irreligiousness (secularism) and the concept of national democracy are out and out opposed to your religion. If you bow your head before them, you will be going against the teachings of Quran. If you participate in its establishment and sustenance, then you will be raising the banner of revolt against God."24 Thus according to Maududi all those Muslims in India and elsewhere who are participating in the secular governments are rebels against God and His Prophet and are leading a life of sin and are worthy of being put to death as in Islam the punishment for apostacy or rebellion is death. Maududi is of the firm opinion that the Muslims in a non-Islamic government *ought* to keep away from the process of governance for, as good Muslims, they cannot take part in any activity which is ungodly in character and a non-Islamic government certainly has that character. In other words, Muslims should prefer to live as second class citizens, enjoying no political rights, or rather voluntarily renouncing them than becoming part of secular state and risk God's wrath. It is for this reason that the committed members of the Jama'at in India do not take part in election nor do they aspire for any political office. However, they do so in Kashmir where Muslims are in majority though Kashmir is also a part of secular state. They see no contradiction in this. Of course, Maududi would not like them to be the part of administrative machinery either as the same is controlled by secular politicians. (It is not known whether any members of Jama'at in India are serving as civil servants or not but I do know of some Jama'at sympathizers who were working in Bombay Municipal Corporation). If Maududi's point of view is accepted then the Indian Muslims cannot serve in military, police or any other civil service. They can only pursue independent professions or business. How disastrous such an advice would be for the Indian Muslims need not be commented upon.

Nature of Islamic Government

Western democracy or secular democracy is totally unacceptable to Maulana Maududi. People cannot become sovereign and make laws. It is God who alone deserves sovereignty.[25] Maududi does not accept theocracy in the western sense either. Islamic theocracy, he maintains, is

[24]See Nafis Ahmad, "Reactionary Politics of Jama'at-e-Islami" *Mainstream*, June 21, 1969. Cf. Asghar Ali Engineer *Islam-Muslims-India*, Lok Vangmaya Griha, Bombay, 1975, pp. 83-84.

[25]Abu'l A'la Maududi, *op. cit.*, p. 129.

quite different from the theocracy as understood in Europe. In the European sense a priestly-class rules in the name of God and enforces its own laws thus perpetuating its own rule in the name of God. Maududi says in his characteristic way that such a government should be called a "Satanic government" rather than theocracy. As against this, Maududi says, the Islamic theocracy does not mean a rule by any priestly class but it means common Muslims wielding reigns of power. But the Muslims have to wield this power in keeping with the Book of God and Sunna of His Prophet. Maududi prefers to call the Islamic form of government as "theo-democracy." In this form of government Muslims have been allowed a limited popular sovereignty under the paramountcy of God.[26]

The legislative and executive in this form of government would be constituted by the Muslims and only Muslims will be empowered to dissolve these bodies (non-Muslims, of course, will have no voting rights in such an Islamic state). All those matters about which there is no categorical or definite rule in *Shari'ah* will be decided by this elected assembly and God's laws, wherever in need of interpretation, would be properly interpreted not by any particular class of priests or race but anyone who, by way of his Islamic learning, has achieved that capacity (it must be noted here that Maududi does not accept the principle of *ijtihād* i.e. interpretation in general but only in cases where there is no clearly stated law). As common Muslims, without necessarily belonging to the priestly class (in fact there is no priesthood in Islam) can participate in the process of interpretation and implementation of laws, this form of government can be construed as democracy (though franchise will not be universal but would be restricted to Muslims only). But again, Maududi says, since wherever there is clearly stated laws given by God and His Messenger no one is allowed to deviate from them even by a hair's breadth, not even if all the Muslims of the world combine, this government can be called theocracy. Hence the Islamic form of government is neither democracy in the sense of accepting the sovereignty of people nor a theocracy in the sense of only priestly class wielding power and making laws, it is combination of both i.e. theo-democracy.[27]

Maududi, without being apologetic, says that an Islamic state will have, so very comprehensive role that man's private affairs cannot be left alone. In this respect Maududi's Islamic state will have resemblance (this is

[26] *Ibid.*, pp. 129-30.
[27] *Ibid.*, p. 130.

Maududi's own confession) with a fascist state but then he hastens to add that it will not be totalitarian or authoritarian like modern (fascist or communist) states. In this form of government personal freedom is not taken away (one fails to understand how personal freedom can be guaranteed when one will not be allowed to deviate even by a hair's breadth from the Islamic laws as understood and interpreted by the 'ulama in the medieval period). In Maududi's Islamic state one will have no other freedom but to conform to the *Shari'ah* as applied by his party which he calls the party of God. It is nothing but totalitarianism as in this state no one will be allowed to advocate not only non-Islamic law but not even creative reinterpretation of *Shari'ah* in keeping with the comtemporary conditions.

Let us take certain examples. For theft there is Quranic injunction, and all the authorities in the medieval period have held, that theft be punished by chopping off thief's hand or that a murderer be put to death. These are categorical laws for which there have not been much differences in various schools of Islamic jurisprudence. And, in such cases, Maududi maintains that no Muslim will be allowed to deviate even by a hair's breadth. Well, many learned Muslims, as much qualified as Maulana Maududi himself, if not more, have held that there is great deal of scope, in keeping with the Islamic spirit, to reinterpret and modify many provisions of Islamic *Shari'ah* both in personal matters (*ahwal-i-shakhshiyah*) and penal matters (*'uqubat*). These matters, these thinkers argue, must be seen in the spatio-temporal frame and concrete historical conditions. The penal measures cannot be end in themselves, they are only means to an end. The aim is to create a just social order and to ensure its stability. If the modified and more humane penal measures can ensure this end (of course, the degree of stringency can be a matter of debate) the *Shāri's* (i.e. law- giver) motive is fulfilled. The *Shari' (law-giver), they argue, keeps the national characteristics, habits and customary behaviour of the people in view while prescribing laws for them. It is for this reason that different prophets who were sent among different peoples had given different Shari'ahs* some of which were superseded by the succeeding *Shari'ahs*. Thus if some changes are warranted in view of the changed circumstances, it would not amount to violation of the Islamic *Shari'ah*, if its spirit is kept in view while permitting these changes.

Muhammad 'Abduh, some of whose views on Islamic polity we have discussed in the last chapter, permitted many such changes. 'Abduh issued a *fatwa* (religious opinion) legitimizing interest on saving accounts. What was condemned by Islam was highly exploitative usury and not every possible form of interest which might become necessary to perform certain regulatory functions in economy. Muhammad 'Abduh even says that reason should have precedence over tradition. "Abduh recognised independence of thought for every Muslim" says Mahmudul Haq, "and allowed him to hold what his own reason derived from the Qur'an and the tradition. 'Abduh would have it that the right to differ with the highest of men in religion is secured to every Muslim by the Qur'an. The supposed superiority of the ancients, according to him, was a mere pretext to keep intact the absurdities of the past, and such a pretext of infallibility must necessarily mean the thwarting of human intellect."[28]

But for Maulana Maududi no such position is acceptable. He wants to strictly adhere to all the medieval practices what 'Abduh describes as "absurdities" and does not admit of any deviation from them. The elected assembly would also not be permitted, in his scheme of things, to innovate and permit what is in keeping with reason, if opposed to tradition. Human conscience, in such a society, would be naturally totally subjugated to the enforced orthodoxy. No other parties would be allowed to function as only one party-Hizbullah—totally committed to the kind of programme evolved by Maududi would exist. Is it not totalitarianism? Then what is it? For him to legislate in minor unclarified matters amounts to freedom.

Bhutto, the former Prime-Minister of Pakistan, was hanged for conspiracy to murder one of his political opponents. The Maulana's party lent full support to the military dictator Zia-ul-Haq for hanging Bhutto on the ground that it was being done according to Islamic law which prescribes death for murder. Jama'at's support for hanging Bhutto raises several questions. The most important question from our point of view is that of political morality. The Jama'at is a religio-political organization and declares its commitment to strict morality and, in fact, condemns other parties, specially the communists, for their amoral or immoral approach to politics. But their support to Bhutto's hanging (in fact they campaigned for his hanging and celebrated the occasion by distributting sweets) has exposed the hollowness of their claim.

Firstly, Bhutto was not tried in an Islamic court, nor was he put on trial before a qualified qādī well-versed in Islamic law as it should happen in an orthodox Islamic system so fervently advocated by Maulana Maududi. Bhutto, in fact, was tried under the penal code which was enforced by the

[28]Mahmudul Haq *Muhammad 'Abduh,* op. cit., p. 90.

British in undivided India and which is still followed both in India and Pakistan with amendments from time to time. Moreover, the Islamic law of evidence is much different from the Roman law followed in Pakistani courts. In Islamic law there is no provision for an approver, i.e. evidence tendered by one who himself is party to the crime. Also, Islamic law prescribes death for the murderer and there is no clear provision for conspirator to murder and Bhutto was accused of conspiracy. Many other prominent Muslim 'ulama of Pakistan had also opined that the death sentence given to Bhutto was not in keeping with the Islamic law. This clearly shows that for political vendetta against Bhutto, the Jama'at even did not hesitate to violate Islamic law and its self-professed commitment to morality.

The Munir Commission's Reprort on anti-Qadiyani riots of Lahore in 1953 is also an indictment of Maulana Maududi and his Jama'at. The Report regrets that in the moment of crisis it appeared that there was no major force in society to give outspoken leadership to the conviction that Islam teaches not loot, arson and murder nor even narrow formalism, but democracy, freedom, equality, tolerance and social justice.[29] W. C. Smith remarks, "The riots were finally put down in the name not of Islam but of governmental stability, and may be common sense. Religiously they seem to elicit no rejoinder, beyond discouragement."[30] In view of such dismal records, how Maulana Maududi and his Jama'at can boast of any moral commitment and condemn other parties for their immoral political behaviour?

There are other more sordid records. What happended in Bangla Desh is a hair raising story. Mr Khalid says, "During the final days of military rule the then province of East Pakistan was turned into a slaughter house. Manifestly, it was not so much the Pakistani army which committed the atrocities but the para-military units of the firmly entrenched Jama'at-e-Islami. The notorious storm-troopers called Al-Badr particularly excelled in mass executions of Hindu and Muslim secularists alike."[31] Jama'at's Saudi Arabian connection is also well-know. The anti-Bhutto agitation of 1977 spearheaded by the rightist alliance called PNA of which the Jama'at was also a partner at that time involved massive expenditure. Where did the money come from? Conservative estimates speak of several

[29] W.C.Smith, *Islam in Modern History, op. cit.*, p. 238.
[30] *Ibid.*
[31] Detlev H. Khalid, "Phenomenon of Re-Islamisation," *op. cit.*, p. 24.

million dollars having been poured into the country. Bhutto alleged that the USA interfered directly because of his nuclear deal with France and bold Third World policies, his non-alignment and anti-Israeli stance, but he did not substantiate this.[32] He was caught in his own snare and could not indict the Saudis. The rightist press in Pakistan was extolling the Saudis for their role as saviour and the Saudis showed anything but embarrassment. One cannot, therefore, rule out Saudi Arabia also as a possible source of finance mainly through the Jama'at. The Jama'at was also vigorously supporting the counter-revolutionaries in Afghanistan and was involved, not only in looking after the refugees, but also in equipping and training the rightist cadres opposed to the then regime of Afghanistan. All this speaks volumes for the political ethis of the Maulana and his party.

The Maulana no doubt attacks capitalism as it leads to exploitation and creation of imbalances in the society. He even concedes that the rich, through their short-sightedness, refuse to give their due to weaker sections of society. They thought it quite legitimate to allow the poor to starve and rot in misery and their short-sighted policy did not enable them to see that such a course has forced many people to take to crimes, remain ignorant and contract variety of diseases on account of lack of proper food. The rich, he says, have developed many artificial needs and in order to satisfy their carnal desires and whimsical needs, deprive other members of the society of their legitimate right and thus deny them opportunity to develop into useful members of the society.[33]

But one need not be taken in by this radical rhetoric of the Maulana. He does not advocate any radical change in society in order to right its wrongs. His solution of the problem is what has been suggested by many before him i.e. change of heart through moral imperative. He is totally opposed to curbing the institution of private property. If only the rich could be persuaded to restrain their greed and treat their property as *amanah* (trust) reposed in them by God, everything will fall in order. He thinks that private property is in keeping with human nature and by itself there is nothing wrong with it. It is human lust and weakness of the flesh which leads to its misuse.[34] Hence instead of tempering with the institution of private property one should set about exhorting the rich and mending their ways.

[32]*Ibid.*, p. 23.

[33]Maududi, "Ma'ashi Mas'lah aur uska Islami Hal," *Islam ke Ma'ashi Tasawwurat* ed. Ghulam Dastagir Rashid, India Book House, Hyderabad, 1945, pp. 16-17.

[34]*Ibid.*, p. 16.

Communism, needless to say, is strongly opposed by Maududi. For his knowledge of communism, not surprisingly, Maududi mainly relies on common hostile propoganda literature. It is highly improbable that he ever read the original works of Marx, Lenin and other prominent Marxist writers. He hardly understands the true nature of capitalist society and its dynamics. Maududi thinks that it is immoral practices of capitalists and their failure to distinguish between what is *halal* (i.e. permissible, good) and what is *haram* (i.e. forbidden, evil) that is the root cause of all the problems of a capitalist society. Among other evils of the capitalist society he lists bribery, theft, gambling, speculation, fraud, hoarding, monopolistic practices, etc.[35] This itself shows that the Maulana is confused about what are common evils found in many societies, capitalist or not, and certain practices of capitalist society.

It is common knowledge that the Marxists do not condemn capitalism on such grounds only; even if all the capitalists become scrupulously honest and do not resort to fraud or other dishonest practices, it would not be able to produce a just and humane society. Joan Robinson says, "Marx does not indict capitalism in the manner of the naive idealists who treat exploitation as robbery. On the contrary, with a kind of logical sarcasm, he defends capitalism. There is no swindle—everything exchanges for its *value*, as is right and just. It is not the *value* he produces, but the *value* that he costs which is the worker's due.... The system is not unjust within its own rules. For that very reason reform is impossible; there is nothing for it but to overthrow the system itself."[36]

Nowhere in the writings of Maulana Maududi do we find a proper grasp of the critique of capitalism by Marx. He has not been even able to attempt a criticism of his theory of surplus value which, according to Marx forms the very basis of exploitation of labour in the capitalist system. Neither does Maududi mention anywhere in his writings on communism Marx's forecast about the diminishing return of profit with the change in the organic composition of capital. Maududi does not seem to be aware of Marx's denunciation of the bourgeois concept of equality in his critique of the Gotha programme. Now without carefully studying these fundamental aspects of Marxist critique of bourgeois political economy, no one can honestly claim to refute the Marxist concepts of economics. But this is what Maulana Maududi does. His criticism of communism is mainly based on superficial propoganda literature and his attack on it is from the following

[35] *Ibid.*, p. 27.
[36] Joan Robinson, *Economic Philosophy*, Penguin Books, 1966, pp. 38-39.

angles :

(1) Communism does not believe in God and hence rulers in such a society will have no sense of being answerable to any such power who can punish or reward them.

(2) State control over economy results in curbing individual initiative and thus ultimately results in inefficiency.

(3) Under communism the state becomes all powerful, in fact totalitarian. It functions as the worst form of collective power and in its oppressive measures proves worse than Nimrod and Pharoah. Maududi feels that under this system a few men sit together and adopt a collective philosophy which then they set out to forcibly impose on the entire country. What kind of democratic justic is this? he indignantly asks.

From what Maududi has to say against communism one can see that his criticism is common place and he hardly has the grasp of the basic issues involved. Firstly, he is unable to understand the fact that a humanistic ethical system can be evolved independently of the concept of God or revealed religious morality. It is not only so in the case of secular philosophy like communism; it is equally true of Buddhism which is legitimately bracketed with other religions. Buddha had adopted an empirical approach and never claimed his authority from any supernatural source. In fact he did not confess existence of God. But that does not, nevertheless, reduce his importance as a great spiritual leader and founder of the ethical system. It is wrong to assume that an ethical system can be derived only from a supernatural source or that man's honesty and integrity is dependent only on acknowledgement of a supernatural authority. Such a view of human morality is not only narrow but is based on wrong understanding of human psychology and deeper sources of spiritual behaviour and character structure. If only the fear of God could induce man to behave morally, the entire history of mankind would have been different. Even the Islamic morality and undoubted honesty and integrity of the eminent companions of the Prophet could not avert the bloody civil war within thirty years of the death of the Prophet in what has been called the period of the rightly guided caliphs in the Islamic history. One can hardly ignore the complex socio-economic factors while trying to understand a social phenomenon. Any concept of morality not rooted in the social complex of which man is an integral part cannot be sustained. At best it would be a glorified ideal put on pedestal but without any living and dynamic interaction with the social reality around.

Secondly, Maududi's contention, like that of other opponents of Marxism, that the state control over economy curbs individual initiative, is based on very simplistic and primitive view of capitalist society. This is essentially a petty bourgeois view which confines capitalism to an era when free competition and individual initiative played an important role. The capitalist society has developed far beyond that state and in the modern era it is characterised by large monopolies and multinational corporations. Some of these corporations command resources which are far greater than those of some of the African states. The authors of *Unity or Poverty*? in the chapter "Small Countries, Large Firms" point out "The divided states of Africa cannot achieve economic independence....The resources of the large firms dominating the export sectors of most states in Africa—like the Uniliver—United Africa Company, Shell-B.P., Societe Generale-Union Miniere, the 'Mauritanian' iron consortium, ENI, Bethlehem Steel—are far larger than those controlled by the single African state. Shel-BP.'s £130 million-odd stake in Nigeria is significant but not vital to the company; the development of the delta oil fields is vital to Nigeria. The inability of individual African states to negotiate on an equal basis with the giant foreign combines is accentuated by the close links and harmony of interest which often—though not always—exists among such firms.[37]

Maududi's criticism of economic aspects of capitalist or socialist societies is ill-informed and is not based on rigorous understanding of the modern science of economics. Let alone Maududi, who is a traditional scholar of Islam and is hardly expected to know much about the modern social sciences, even those members or supporters of the Jama'at who have acquired modern qualifications in these sciences, do not give much evidence of the thorough grasp of modern economics and, none of them, like Marx, has attempted any thorough analysis of modern capitalism or critoique of Marxist socialism in order to establish, what they claim to be a superior Islamic economic system. At the most they repeat certain cliches about the moral imperatives without its proper sociological concept.

Even Max Weber, who feels that the Protestant work-ethics played a decisive role in the development of capitalism in Europe does not take totally one-sided view as Maududi and his followers do while trying to super-impose "Islamic ethics" on the early 19th century concept of capitalism. About Weber's concept Raymond Aron says: "It has been often said that Weber tried to refute Marx and to explain economic behaviour

[37]Reginald H. Green and Ann Seidman, Unity or Poverty?, Penguin Books, 1968, p. 129.

by religion instead of presupposing religion as the superstructure of a society whose infrastructure consisted of the relations of production. Stated thus simply, I do not think that this is Weber's idea. It seems to me that his intention was to establish two propositions. (a) The behaviour of men in various societies is intelligible only in the context of their general conception of existence; but religious dogmas and their interpretation are an integral part of the world views that render the behaviour of individuals and groups, including their economic behaviour, intelligible. (b) Religious conceptions are actually a determinant of economic behaviour and consequently *one of the causes* of economic change" (emphasis supplied)[38]

Max Weber has made very significant observation :

> The various great ways of leading a rational and methodical life have been characterized by irrational presuppositions, which have been accepted simply as 'given' and which have been incorporated into such ways of life. What these presuppositions have been is *historically and socially determined*, at least to a very large extent, through the peculiarity of those strata that have been the carriers of the ways of life during its formative and decisive period. The *interest* situation of these strata, as determined socially and psychologically, has made for their peculiarity, as we understand it[39] (emphasis added).

I have quoted Raymond Aron and Max Weber at length in order to show that even the great sociologist like Weber who gives due importance to the religious factor as the determinant of economic behaviour does not ignore other important factors and gives due emphasis on the other factors also which are historically and socially determined (and hence peculiarity of every society) but Maulana Maududi (although he himself accuses Marx, wrongly of course, of considering economic factor as the only determinant of every social phenomenon) keeps on arguing, with all the force at his command, that the divinely revealed laws in their most abstract form, are the determinant of social and political structure, whatever the historical, social and economic conditions. From the Hausa tribes of Africa to the Bali tribes of Indonesia and whatever the historical period, Islamic laws, as codified by the 'ulama in the Middle Ages according to their light and

[38]Raymond Aron, *Main Currents in Sociological Thought-2*, Penguin Books, 1970, pp. 217-18.

[39]Max Weber, "Major Features of World Religions," *Sociology of Religion*, ed., by Ronald Robertson,Penguin Books, 1971, p. 35.

interpretation of the Quran and *Sunnah*, can be uniformly applied and that too, with the same result. All that is needed to achieve this result is the establishment of an Islamic state under the hegemony of a party like the *Jama'at-e-Islami*. Maulana, in his sectarian zeal, was not preparerd to learn from his own experience in Pakistan during several decades of its existence. The Maulana puts the cart before the horse and keeps on arguing that an ideal Islamic state does not exist in the world today not because efforts have not been seriously made to reinterpret the Islamic laws in keeping with the changed conditions but because no one has taken it as a serious project to apply Islamic laws *as they are*. The Maulana feels that those born in Muslim families but have been influenced by European social sciences are incapable of grasping the significance of the concept of Islamic state.[40]

Thus it is very clear that Maulana Maududi's entire approach is idealistic. He refuses to take into account the decisive part which the socio-economic factors play in shaping the political superstructure. According to him the divinely revealed laws have no roots whatsoever in the social conditions but are expression of the Divine Will which is essentially indeterminate. Divine sovereignty, the Maulana maintains, is the basis of Islamic state. It's God's country and it is for Him to govern it in whatever way he deems fit. The whole humanity put together cannot claim any sovereign rights. Human beings have no other choice but to surrender to this Divine Will expressed Through His Messenger.[41]

It is not very difficult to understand for any serious student of political science that through these authoritarian pronouncements the Maulana wants to establish his own sovereignty although this is sought to be done behind the religious mask. It is not unknown to a student of Islamic law that in the Quran and the *shari'ah* there are number of ambiguities which can be differently interpreted depending on the issue involved and also the situational context. It is for this reason that the same Quranic verses have been radically differently interpreted by different authorities and since Maududi argues that in his scheme of Islamic state only one party i.e. hizbullah (in Pakistan only the Jama'at aspires to fulfil this role) would be allowed to function, no other organized political group will have any say and ultimately it would be the Jama'at e-Islami which would be decisive in the interpretation of the Quran and *Shari'ah*. As far as the communists are concerned the Maulana strongly attacks them for their totalitarian rule

[40]Maududi, *Islami Riyasat*, *op. cit.*, p. 691.
[41]*Ibid.*, p. 692.

and suppression of freedom by imposing Marxist philosophy. But is not Maududi wanting to perpetrate the Jama'at's totalitarianism although in the name of Islam? Or does he believe that totalitarianism is to be condemned if perpetrated in the name of secular ideology and is to be wholeheartedly welcomed if imposed in the name of divinely inspired religion? Will it make any difference for the victims whether they are being persecuted, tortured, or killed in the name of religion or secular philosophy? Perhaps it does as far as Maulana Maududi is concerned. Totalitarianism in the name of religion passes off as true freedom. After all for Maududi true freedom lies in the total submission to the divine will and divine will is to be determined by Maulana Maududi and his followers in Pakistan.

Thus we see that Maulana Maududi, in order to establish his political Islam, tries to combine the medieval religious thought of Islam with the modern totalitarian political philosophy (his concept of one-party system and total submission to the 'divine law' bears close resemblance to the Fascist philosophy) and tries to pass off this amalgam as "unalterable divine will." His criticism of modern social sciences, especially of Marxism, is based on half-truths or total ignorance. The rhetorical qualities of his writings, devoid of serious thought content, has great appeal for the petty-bourgeois intelligentsia which is more in search of certainty and security than truth.

The totalitarian character of Maududi's Islamic state is also indicated by the status which he proposes to give to non-Muslims. It is undoubtedly true that the classical Islam does not give dhimmis (non-Muslim protected communities) the governing rights and while guranteeing them security of life and property, does not permit them to become an integral part of the ruling class. The Maulana wants to uncompromisingly follow this provision for the non-Muslim communities in his modern Islamic state also. Maulana Maududi, as pointed out earlier, is votary of medieval Islam and hardly approves of any creative interpretation of its provisions in keeping with the modern conditions and hence, in this matter too, is not prepared to understand the provision for *dhimmis* in the light of the then historical situation. In those days the vanquished were hardly given any rights, civil or political. The Islamic provision for the treatment of *dhimmis*, who more often than not, happened to be the conquered peoples, was thus much more humane and must be seen as such. Taken in that spirit, it would be wrong to insist that Islam is totally opposed to giving equal political rights to the non-Muslims under all conditions. Even during the later period of Muslim rule (under the Abbasids and Fatimids) the *dhimmis* (specially the peoples of Book Like the Jews and Christians) rose to eminent positions and even held key policy-making positions.

But Maulana Maududi maintains that the *dhimmis* can enjoy neither equal political rights nor can hold key policy making positions in his Islamic state. In reply to a question by a Hindu Mahasabha worker the Maulana clearly says that only those who accept the Islamic principles can be permitted to sharing the burden of running Islamic administration and holding key policy-making positions. Those who do not accept these principles cannot be allowed to do so. They can only expect to be allowed to live in peace and security.[42] They will be given such a gurantee in return for the payment of a tax called *jaziya*. It will thus be seen that Maududi wants to follow the letter of the Islamic law as it was formulated in the early Islamic period under certain historical conditions rather than its spirit.

Islam, even as interpreted in the medieval period, did not deprive other religious groups of their right to follow their faith. How can then it be interpreted in the modern age to deprive non-Muslims of their political rights in a Muslim country? It is more important to respect the spirit of Islam than the historical form it assumed in a particular period. The Prophet, when he established the first skeletal structure of state in Medina through the document he drew up which we have discussed in the first chapter, he allowed the different religious groups to follow their respective faiths and still accepted them as co-partners in the political community. If all the practices of the Prophet are part of his *Sunnah*, there is no reason why this act of the Prophet be overlooked specially when there is nothing to categorically contradict it. It was from this document, as already indicated earlier, that the equally knowledgeable leaders of the *Jami'at al-'Ulama-i-Hind* constructed their theory of composite nationalism and lent their support to the Indian National Congress. But Maulana Maududi's unrelieved orthodoxy (in this author's opinion it is his conservative political compulsions rather than mere religious orthodoxy) does not permit him to look at this problem in the right spirit of Islam.

In fact what Maulana Maududi preaches in the name of Islam would not have found unanimous acceptance even in the medieval period, much less in the modern period. Right from the early history of Islam, there have been radical currents whether led by Abu Dhar Ghifari or Khawarij or the Isma'ilis or their sub-sect the Qaramitah who have rejected the property

[42]*Ibid.*, pp. 522-23.

relations of their time in order to follow more faithfully the ideal of equality in Islam. What Maududi preaches is more in keeping with the historical form of Islam it assumed during the medieval ages under the Byzantine and Sassanid influences rather than its true spirit of equality as embodied in the earliest period of Islam. But then the Jama'at in Pakistan upholds the statusquo and not the true spirit of Islam which, through its historical praxis in the medieval period, stood completely transformed.

6. The Resurgence of Islam and Islamic State

What has happened in the last few years in the Islamic world, especially after the escalation of oil prices in 1973 has aroused interest of the entire world. Moreover, the developmens in Iran and Pakistan have further added to the significance of these events. The militancy of some of the Islamic regimes especially that of Saudi Arabia, Iran and Pakistan, has raised many questions which need to be answered. The liberals—both Muslim as well as non-Muslim—the world over are deeply concerned about these developments. The world press has also taken deep interest in the goings-on in the Muslim countries in view of their increased weightage in the world affairs, especially due to boom in the oil market. In short, the people of the world are concerned in one way or the other about the future of the peoples of these Muslim countries as they are as much an integral part of the world political community as any other people are.

The phenomenon of Islamic resurgence is not as simple and reducible to, as is often thought, religious fanaticism only although it also plays an important role. The march of militant Islam is not motivated by divine will alone as is often believed by the faithfuls but the mundane matters like the motive for power, economic interests, etc. play a very decisive role in determining the strategies and policies of those rulers who are riding the crest of the wave of Islamic resurgence. More often than not—and I wish to say this with all the emphasis at my command—religion is used only as an ideological cover to hide these mundane interests. In order, therefore, to understand this phenomenon, we will have to take economic and political factors also into account. Also, we will have to examine, in the light of these factors, the claims made by the ideologies and the rulers and the concrete results achieved as a result of the enforcement of the Islamic laws.

Since ideological claims and facts are involved, it would be quite in order here to say a few words about ideology and beliefs. Erikson, for example, says that "an ideology is an unconscious tendency underlying religion and scientific as well as political thought: the tendency at a given time to make facts amenable to ideas, and ideas to facts, in order to create a world image convincing enough to support the collective and individual sense of identity."[1] Engels defines ideology as "a process accomplished by the so-called thinker consciously indeed but with a false consciousness. The real motives impelling him remain unknown to him, otherwise it would not be an ideological process at all. Hence he imagines false or apparent motives. Because it is a process of thought he derives both its form and its content from pure thought, either his own or that of his predecessors."[2] Mihailo Markovic, a Yugoslavian philosopher, gives a short and more precise definition of ideology. According to him, "Ideology is, then, the ensemble of ideas and theories with which a class expresses its interests, its aims and the norms of its activity."[3]

We have tried to define ideology here at length precisely because the Muslim rulers, in order to achieve their aims, are projecting Islam as an ideology of re-building society on moral and healthier lines and, in this respect, they rightly take communism as a serious competitor. Once an ideological discussion is involved, confusion and differences are bound to arise. It is clear from the above definitions that ideology expresses that which ought to be, that which man desires and that which is in the interest of a particular class. In ideological discussions, therefore, as pointed out by Erikson above, the tendency at a given time is to make facts ameanable to ideas and ideas to facts. Again, as Engels maintains, in this process, although thinking is conscious but with a false consciousness. It is, therefore, not very difficult to see that in any such discussion confusion is bound to prevail. Marxism, as rightly emphasized by Markovic,[4] is a unity of two different moments: the scientific moment and the ideological. Whereas science establishes what *is*, ideology establishes what *ought to be*. In the case of Marxism at least there is the possibility of methodological unity as the scientific element in it is as important as the ideological element. But in the case of religious ideology like Islam, it is all the more difficult as only the divine (i.e. ideological) has recognition and not the scientific element. The application of social sciences, if found to contravene any of the injunctions of *Shari'ah*, is totally rejected as irrelevant by the 'ulama.

[1]Erikson E.H. *Young Man Luther—A Study in Psychoanalysis and History*, Norton, London, 1958, p. 22.

[2]Engel's Letter to Franz Mehring, 14 July 1893, quoted by Mihailo Markovic in *The Contemporary Marx*, Spokesman Books, 1974, p. 59.

[3]Mihailo Markovic, *The Contemporary Marx, Ibid.*, p. 74.

[4]*Ibid.*, p. 75.

The divine determination (although the divine is not so pure as it always has human interpretative element which cannot be treated as immutable) ultimately prevails.

Islam, although the latest of all the divinely revealed religions, is more than fourteen hundred-year old and has passed through several historical epochs. Islam, moreover, spread through several continents having their own socio- religious traditions. These temporal and spatial changes have brought about many changes in the Islamic institutions originally evolved in the comparatively less complex society of Arabia of the seventh century A.D., both in content and form. The first great crisis in the ideological system of Islam developed during the early Abbasid period when the Greek philosophy and thought spread among the Muslims. The Quranic approach was basically inductive in orientation with more emphasis on observation of external phenomenon. The Greek thought, on the other hand, was speculative and did not lay much emphasis on what was external and concrete. Dr Iqbal, in fact, thinks that the Greek influence over the thought system of Islam changed the entire course of Islamic intellectual history. He says:

> ...A careful study of the Quran and the various schools of scholastic theology that arose under the inspiration of Greek thought disclose the remarkable fact that while Greek philosophy very much broadened the outlook of Muslim thinkers, it, on the whole, obscured their vision of the Quran. Socrates concentrated his attention on the human world alone. To him the proper study of man was man and not the world of plants, insects, and stars. How unlike the spirit of the Quran, which sees in the humble bee a recipient of Divine inspiration and constantly calls upon the reader to observe the perpetual change of the winds, the alteration of day and night, the clouds, the starry heavens, and the planets swimming through infinite space! As a true disciple of Socrates, Plato despised sense-perception which, in his view, yielded mere opinion and no real knowledge.[5]

The Greek thought was so closely assimilated that ever since, despite great efforts, the Islamic theology could not be completely purged of it. This is not to deny the fact that despite these vicissitudes an orthodox core always remained intact, and even active. Dr Fazlur Rahman thinks:

[5]Dr Sir Muhammad Iqbal, *The Reonstruction of Religious Thought in Islam*, Lahore, 1960, pp.3-4.

It is, a curious and striking fact about the religious history of Islam that at each critical points of its career the force that comes to the forefront and takes over the situation is not the then formalized established 'orthodoxy' but rather something that presents itself at every juncture as the 'raw material' of the orthodoxy subsequently to be formed...To some extent, of course, this happens with all developing religions. But whereas in Christianity, or even in as little 'reified' a religion as Hinduism, there is something that runs through it like a wave with new elements riding on its crest, Islamic orthodoxy seems to develop in recreated formations of quanta that issue from time to time from the very heart of Islam. It is characterised by an indistinguishable blend of reinvigorated fundamentalism and progressivism; it develops not by self-propulsion, so to say, but by watching, adjusting and absorbing within itself that which moves within it.[6]

Much of the codification of the Islamic laws took place over a century after the death of the Prophet under the complex influences of Roman law and Greek logic and philosophy on the one hand, and, under Persian feudal institutions, on the other. The democratic and egalitarian ideals of early Islam, which were product of a society still rather primitive and uninfluenced by the complex institution of an advanced civilized society, were thus relegated to a secondary position and, instead, Islam as a religion found expression in casuistic exercises and juristic concepts. The *Shari'ah*, itself a result of elaborate intellectual exercise and speculative and analogical reasoning, became the most predominant ingredient, naturally at the cost of Islam's true religious genius embodied into its value-system. Islam was thus reduced to mere legalism. It was no mere accident of history, although one can call it its ironies. This casuistic expression of Islam, relegating its fundamental values, was in keeping with the interests of the ruling classes which had organically grown from the new socio-economic set-up and ever since this institutionalized form of Islam has continued to serve them. It does so even today of which we shall talk later in more detail.

In view of its cardinal importance, we would like to throw some light on the value-system of Islam. I have discussed in more detail the origin of what I call the cardinal values of Islam in my article "Islam and Socialism—An Interpretative Approach." What follows is a brief

[6] Fazlur Rahman, *Islam*, Islamic Research Institute, Karachi, p. 111, (n.d.).

summary of the earlier part of this article.[7]

The values emphasized in a particular religion or an ideology depend on the immediate material circumstances in which it originates. Of course, certain values are universal. We are referring to fundamental and not instrumental values. Brotherhood, equality, truthfulness, goodness, justice, peace, honesty, etc. are such values. Besides these, some values are negatively expressed such as avoidance of killing, negation of evil, renunciation of lust etc.

These values are universal as no religion (here we will have to exclude certain primitive or tribal cults and political idologies such as Nazism or Fascism etc.) rejects them. However, it must be noted in the context of our subject that it does not imply equal emphasis on these values by different religions. The emphasis will vary according to the socio-economic conditions prevailing at the time of their origin or the later crucial period of growth. Let us illustrate with some examples. In Buddhism and Jainism there is great emphasis on renunciation of and detachment from the world, denial of carnal pleasures, denunciation of unnecessary killings as well as individual salvation (nirvana in the case of Buddhism). Later on these became the general characteristics of Hinduism too. Buddhism and Jainism were almost contemporaneous and both these religions emerged as a reaction against the Brahmanic rituals.

Why this revolt? These rituals were performed with great pomp and show entailing huge expenditure as well as slaughter of a large number of animals. These rituals were evolved during the Vedic period with its pastoral economy. The pastoral economy was being transformed into an agricultural one when Buddhism and Jainism emerged on the scene. The Vedic rituals became a great burden in an agricultural economy with their wasteful expenditure and unnecessary slaughter of animals which were useful in agricultural operations. Also, this transformation from one mode of production to another higher mode created pressure for many social changes, thus disrupting established practices and causing suffering to many people. This social situation, by and large, is reflected in the value system of Buddhism and Jainism. Buddha saw suffering all around and hence he came to the conclusion that life is suffering (*dukh*) and desire being its cause, renunciation of desire alone can lead to salvation which he calls *nirvana*. Thus we see it was this social situation which gave birth to

[7] Asghar Ali Engineer, "Islam and Socialism : An Interpretative Approach," Islam and the Modern Age, Zakir Husain Institute of Islamic Studies, vol. ix, No. 4, November 1978 and vol. x, no. 1 February 1979.

Buddhism with its emphasis on *nirvana*, non-killing, negation of the Vedic rituals which had lost their relevance in the new situation and renunciation of all desires to mitigate suffering. Whereas Buddhism adopted a middle-course, Jainism went to another extreme as it emphasized absolute renunciation—even justified self-inflicted torture on the body—of all desires, absolute non-killing including non-killing of invisible bacteria.

The Islamic value-system developed in a different social-complex which was emerging as a result of transformation of tribal society into a mercantile society. However, the emergence of mercantile relations did not go well with the prevailing socio-ethical norms and tribal way of life. The tribal way of life in Arabia was characterized by equality of status for all, equal distribution of booty obtained in inter-tribal raids (thus no economic disparities arose), production for immediate consumption (not for market), higher status for women of one's own tribe (the slave-girls or women captured in battles did not enjoy such a status), etc. But the developing trade in Mecca brought to the fore some enterprising men whose sole motivation was profit, and not honouring the prevailing tribal norms. These enterprising men who came from different tribes their sub-sections joined hands to pursue trade and they became rich. They did not distribute their profits equally among the members of their tribes as the tribal norms required of them, appropriating the same partly to plough back into trade and partly for personal consumption.

Thus economic disparities arose which other members of these tribes resented. Not only this, the economic power enhanced the status of the rich merchants which militated against the concept of equality which was jealously guarded by the Bedouins. Apart from this there were a large number of slaves and persons of foreign origin who were employed by these merchants to do manual jobs on probably low wages thus condemning them to a life of poverty and indigence. The Prophet who himself had spent his childhood among the Bedouins (his wet-nurse Halimah, belonged to one such tribe) knew the value the Arabs attached to equality in social status. But, in his young age in Mecca, he saw the clearly marked tendency towards accumulation of wealth and widening gap between the rich and the poor. He, theefore, laid great emphasis on equality of status of all men (before God) and by implication materially as well (The Quran advises the faithfuls to give away what is more than needed i.e. '*afw*). Due to historical circumstances explained above whereas non-killing and renunciation became the central values of the religions like Buddhism and Jainism, equality and brotherhood acquired primacy in the value system of Islam.

The basic character of Islam, so to say, is defined by these values.

However, in the interest of the clarity of thought, something needs to be said about the much misunderstood word "equality" here. When we talk of equality it should be seen in the historical perspective. In the context of early Islam it would be futile to maintain that the Prophet meant to establish complete equality. Such a view can be based only on naivete, not on social reality which is much more complex than it is often understood to be. Moreover, such a view would be ahistorical. Equality has often been misunderstood even in the context of communism. Marx had severely criticised the programme of the German Workers' party for its wrong concept of equality. It would be quite relevant to quote an important passage from the Critique of the Gotha Programme here since it removes misunderstanding about the concept of equality. Marx says :

> But one man is superior to another physically or mentally and so supplies more labour in the same time, or can labour for a longer time; and labour, to serve as a measure, must be defined by its duration or intensity, otherwise it ceases to be a standard of measurement. This *equal* right is an unequal right for labour. It recognises no class differences, because everyone is only a worker like everyone else; but it tacitly recognises unequal individual endowment and thus productive capacity as natural privileges. *It is, therefore, a right of inequality, in its content, like every other right.* Right by its very nature can consist only in the application of an equal standard; but unequal individuals (and they would not be different individuals if they were not unequal) are measurable only by an equal standard in so far as they are brought under an equal point of view, are taken from one definite side only, for instance, in the present case, are regarded *only as workers* and nothing more is seen in them, everything else being ignored. Further, one worker is married, another not; one has more children than another, and so on and so forth. Thus, with an equal performance of labour, and hence an equal share in the social consumption fund, one will in fact receive more than another, one will be richer than another, and so on. To avoid all these defects, right instead of being equal would have to be unequal (emphasis in the original).[8]

Even Marx's concept of equality, it can be seen, was not what is generally

[8]Marx Engels Selected Works, vol. ii, Foreign Languages Publishing House, Moscow, 1962, p. 24.

thought of—an equal share in the consumption fund. It was rather "to each according to his need" which essentially implies an unequal distribution. Equality thus interpreted means equal social status for all human beings without any differences of class, caste and race or nationality. Of course, it also clearly implies that no one should draw, from the social consumption fund, more than he needs i.e. the traditional concept of ownership, without any consideration of the personal and social needs of a person and without relating it to other individuals in the same society, is challenged.

The Quran, as the verse from the second chapter quoted above (give away what is more than needed), shows, is not opposed to taking away, in the interest of social justice, what is surplus with a person; in other words, the right to property in Islam, as is often thought, is not an unrestricted right. The concept of social justice is undeniably supreme and what is important is its realization (although the instruments of realization or the institutional form may change from time to time depending on the development of the forces of production) and not the right to property. But the conservative 'ulama have, for the reasons we shall examine, reversed the emphasis. The right to property, in their scheme of priorities, has acquired real sanctity, even if it injures the spirit of social justice.

As we have seen in the earlier chapters (see chapters one to three) Islam was born in a mercantile society which was emerging from the womb of a tribal society. But within a few decades after the death of the Prophet it entered into a feudal era and the office of caliphate which was essentially elective became hereditary. The 'ulama codified the Islamic laws during this period. It is not difficult to understand that any concept or doctrine (divine or mundane) has to be interpreted and this interpretation always gets influenced (whatever the degree of honesty and integrity of interpreter) by the institutions and concepts prevalent at that time. Islamic doctrines were no exception. Thus during the Middle Ages the Islamic concept of social justice was concretised in and through medieval institutions which were essentially feudal. The enactment of social justice, in a feudal age, wherein land is the main source of production and hence land-ownership a sacred right, can be conceived of only through charitable institutions. Thus the main instrument of social justice in Islam became charity. The right to property came to be accepted as inviolable even if it militated against the concept of equality of social status which was jealously guarded by the tribal Arabs.

Looking from the sociological angle this was quite a natural development. The concept of unequal social status and absolute obedience to authority are natural outgrowth of a feudal society and as Islamic civilization also flowered in this age, these concepts came to be integrally associated with the teachings of Islam. The Quranic verses were interpreted in this light and many traditions approving of unequal social status, unequal distribution of wealth etc., came to be ascribed to the Prophet. Through the ages these institutions and concepts which were essentially feudal and through which in that period the Islamic teachings found concrete expression, became so sacred that anyone opposing them was denounced as opponent of Islam. These institutions for the 'ulama and the conservative Muslims under their influence are more important than the spirit of social justice.

However, there are a few exceptions too. But on account of the great influence the conservative 'ulama wield, it has not been possible for those who dissent to create much impact. Al-Qayyim, a learned theologian, clearly chides those who treat the provisions of *Shari'ah* as fixed and final thus making them incapable of guarding the interests of people. Those who treat *Shari'ah* in this way, according to al-Qayyim, force people to turn to the sources other than it (i.e. *Shari'ah*).[9] Al-Qayyim clearly maintains that in (emphasis mine) *whichever way* a just rule is established, it is in accordance with *Din* (i.e. religion), not against it. He emphasized that only where there is justice (in whatever way it may be realised), there is God's *Shari'ah* and religion.[10] As for al-Qayyim the most important thing is social justice (and this naturally includes economic justice) it should not militate against the spirit of God's religion and His *Shari'ah* if, to realise this social justice, the modern principles of socialism and its well-known instruments like nationalization are used. Because he maintains that *whichever* the means, what is important is social justice. Private property, according to this view, is not fundamental to the teachings of Islam. Qayyim even goes to the extent of saying quoting Ibn 'Aqil from *Funun*, that any act, process or project which ensures social justice must be accepted even if it has not been clearly laid down by the Prophet or by the holy Quran.[11]

It would also be interesting to note the comments of Ustadh Ahmad Muhammad Jamal of Cairo on the views of al-Qayyim. He says: What has been quoted from al-Qayyim about his views on the Islamic rule...it

[9]Ahmad Muhammad Jamal "Fikr al-Dawlah fi al-Islam," International Islamic Colloquium papers, Punjab University, Lahore, 1960, pp. 1-3.

[10]Ibid.
[11]*Ibid.*

becomes clear that Islam came to consolidate freedom, justice and welfare and to safeguard the interests of people whether the specific rules for (ensuring justice) are revealed by God, laid down by the Prophet or derived from the *Shari'ah* and its principles by the jurists. Thus we can say that it is obligatory for the Islamic rule to establish a just society, to ensure particiapation of all the people in social welfare and to reconciliate the interests of all the classes among them without depriving anyone of his rights so that no one is aggrieved. This is real Islamic government. We call people towards such government....Those who establish government in the name of Islam and God but rule in a way that satisfies their lust for power or serves their interests are liars and such an Islamic government is only in name and not in reality as for the Islamic government interests of the people come first.[12] (My translation from the Arabic text).

Similarly Dr S'ad al-Din Fawzi of Khartum in his paper presented in an international Islamic Colloquium held in Pakistan in 1958 says: I would like to emphasize here that equality is of fundamental importance in Islam. There cannot be any doubt as to its importance as a fundamental principle for a constitutional rule. Islam has laid great emphasis on certain (principles) and equality is one of them as all are equal before God for He says, "Men, We have created you from a male and a female and divided you into nations and tribes that you might get to know one another. The noblest of you in Allah's sight is he who fears Him most." (49:13). Islam strictly enjoins upon its followers not to discriminate between man and man on the basis of origin or race. It has been reported in a tradition that people are like the spokes of a comb; there is no superiority for the Arabs over non-Arabs, for the whites over non-whites except by their good deeds. All of you have descended from Adam and Adam has been created from clay[13] (translation from Arabic mine).

Dr. A.H. Siddiqi, clarifying the concept of equality in Islam says, "What is the concept of equality in Islam? It means equality before law and in matters of civic rights and obligations to the state. Above all, it means affording of equal opportunities to all, irrespective of caste, colour, race, sex or birth. It also connotes social equality, a principle which even some of the most progressive and democratic states in the world have not been able to enthrone even in the present age. Only merit, character and devotion to the cause of Islam should enable a person to occupy the highest position

[12] *Ibid.*
[13] S'ad al-Din Fawzi "Fikrah al-Islam 'an al-Dawlah", Colloquium papers, *op. cit.*, p. 32.

in the state. A person's worth should not be judged by birth, but by efficiency, character and service to the cause of Islam."[14]

We have examined above some of the opinions on the Islamic rule, its nature and essence, expressed by the learned authorities. In the light of this we should examine how far the Islamic states, proclaimed in some of the Islamic countries, are implementing these principles. Before we embark upon this discussion, it must be emphasized here again that the Quran or the Prophetic *Sunnah* has not prescribed any specific form of government nor can it be maintained on the basis of Islamic principles either revealed by God or enshrined in *Shari'ah* that it is incumbent upon Muslims to follow whatever pattern of government was established during the rule of the first four rightly guided caliphs or later. Ustadh Ahamad Muhammad Jamal also clearly states that Islam has not prescribed any specific form of government, neither has it laid down any details about it. It has only prescribed universal principles and laws which do not change with time and place and which are in keeping with the interests of people.[15]

The Quran, as pointed out in an earlier chapter, does not aim to create a state but a society. Hence whatever the form and shape of the state, if the principles of social justice and equality are realised in it, it may be deemed to be an Islamic state. Prof. Jamal Khwaja points out that "out of about 6,200 verses of the Quran only about 250 are prescriptive in character, and out of these only about 10 deal with politico-economic issues."[16] Giving further analysis of this in a footnote, Prof. Jamal says "Even these contain some repetitions, so that in the final analysis, only four or five verses may be said to deal specifically with politico-economic issues in the structural or institutional sense....Apart from these the Quran contains numerous exhortations for decent public or economic behaviour as well as specific rules from which other rules can be deduced. Indeed this was done by the Prophet, his immediate sucessors and later jurists."[17]

It can thus be seen that institutional forms are not as important as the substantial applications of the cardinal principles prescribed by Islam if Islamic state has to have any concrete meaning for the people. However, what has been given importance for the ages is not these cardinal principles but the institutions developed during the Middle Ages. Any religion can

[14]Dr A.H. Siddiqi, "Concept of State in Islam," Colloquium papers, *op. cit.*, p. 32.

[15]Ustadh Ahmad Muhammad Jamal, Colloquium papers, *op. cit.*, pp. 1-3.
[16]Jamal Khwaja *Quest for Islam*, Allied Publishers, Delhi, 1977.
[17]*Ibid.*, p. 269 foot-note 34.

be subdivided into the following categories: (*1*) Institutional system, (*2*) Thought system, (*3*) Value system and (*4*) Ritual system. While we are not immediately concerned here with the ritual system of Islam which would include praying, fasting etc., we shall have to briefly say something about the three other categories.

The institutional system and thought system have direct bearing on the value system. Although in an ideal case the value system would directly influence the institutional and thought system of a religion. However, as we have seen, the institutional and thought system get greatly influenced by the space-time frame within which they are worked out even though they might injure the value system. In the socio-political complex within which the institutions and thought processes of Islam developed, its value system itself got influenced, insead of influencing the institutional and thought pattern of Islam. What is worse, ever since these categories have remained not only stagnant but have been thought to be immutable, many eminent Muslim thinkers have attacked this concept of immutability of Islamic institutions and its thought complex.

Iqbal, an eminent poet and thinker, though tends to be conservative on the whole, says: "The claim of the present generation of Muslim liberals to reinterpret the foundational legal principles, in the light of their own experience and the altered conditions of modern life is, in my opinion, perfectly justified. The teaching of the Quran that life is a process of progressive creation necessitates that each generation, guided but *unhampered* by the work of its predecessors, should be permitted to solve its own problems"[18] (emphasis mine). He also says, "No wonder then that the younger generation of Islam in Asia and Africa demand a fresh orientation of their faith, with the re-awakening of Islam, therefore, it is necessary to examine, in an independent spirit, what Europe has thought and how far the conclusion reached by her can help us in the revisions and, if necessary, reconstruction, of theological thought in Islam."

The thological thought and institutions thus need not be treated as sacred and immutable as often thought; they must be worked out afresh by every new generation in keeping with their requirements. In this process of re-fashioning, change and growth of thought and institutions, values, naturally, would remain intact. Let us now, with the help of concrete examples, try to examine as to whether there has been any serious attempt

[18]Dr Sir Muhammad Iqbal, *op. cit.* p. 168.

at re-fashioning the institutions or theological thought worked out during the medieval period.

Almost all the Islamic countries are situated in what has come to be called the third world. Most of these countries are underdeveloped and still retain, by and large, fuedal or semi-fuedal social structure. The economies of these countries depend, more or less, not without exceptions of course, either on sale of oil or export of raw materials and agricultural products, primarily to the advanced industrialized nations. Some of these countries like Saudia Arabia, Kuwait etc. have become quite rich with high per capita income due to many-fold increase in oil prices after the Arab-Israeli war of 1973. But other Islamic countries continue to be poor and backward. Even the oil-rich countries are, scientifically, technologically, industrially and socially speaking, quite backward. But, of late, and specially after the oil revolution of 1973, the Islamic world is in the throes of change. The present crisis—and the concomitant social turmoil—in the Islamic countries of the Middle-East, which we propose to critically examine here, is a result of this process of change which is gathering momentum.

The phenomenon in the countries of the Middle-East described as the resurgence of Islam has been widely discussed and rightly so. Many leading papers and magazines, especially of the Western countries have taken great interest in this phenomenon and have published articles under the banner lines "Militant Islam on the March" or "The Soldiers of Allah Advance." Such screaming lines relate to only a few countries and not, as mistakenly thought, to the entire Islamic world. The impression somehow has gone round by what has happened in a few Islamic countries that the entire Islamic world is under the spell of Islamic fundamentalism. The fact is that the Fundamentalist movement has been able to acquire serious proportion only in a few countries like Pakistan, Iran, Libya and Saudi Arabia. As against this there are several other Muslim countries like Afghanistan (till recently highly conservative and continues to be so as far as its people are concerned), Iraq, South Yemen, Syria, Algeria etc. where either Marxist or some sort of left of the centre regimes are well established. The people in these latter countries follow Islam as ardently as in any other country but in matters of state policies, traditional religion does not play a direct role. Also, there are countries like Malaysia and Indonesia where though the governments are not based on *Shari'ah* but some militant Islamic parties raise slogans for reviving traditional Islam and give impression of Islamic resurgence. It is, therefore, necessary, in the interest of an objective assessment, to refrain from sweeping generalizations and take a balanced view.[18a]

The countries where the Islamic militancy is surging forward can be divided into two categories: (*1*) Those countries which are poor and backward like Pakistan, Indonesia etc. and (*2*) Those countries which are oil-rich but backward that is industrially and technologically. In the second category we can include countries like Saudi Arabia, Libya etc. The ruling classes in the countries belonging to both these categories are threatened although the causes of social turmoil are qualitatively different in the countries belonging to different categories. Again Iran is little different as it is both oil-rich as well as poor and backward. As the problems faced by each of these categories are different we would deal with each category separately so as to achieve greater degree of clarity in the analysis.

Let us first try to analyze the causes of social turmoil and the consequent rise of Islamic militancy in poor and backward countries like Pakistan. As we know Pakistan came into existence as a result of the Muslim League's demand for partition of the Indian sub-continent on the basis of the famous two nation theory. The demand for Pakistan was voiced by a party which was dominated by the Jagirdars of north India an area which had been the cradle of Muslim power. The merchants of western India were, at best, junior partners in the power-structure of the Muslim League and, of course, there were no industrial bourgeois families among Muslims worth the name which could influence its policies. After partition Pakistan was ruled by an alliance of landlords, bureaucrates and the military.

As the movement for Pakistan was led by big landlords who dreaded democracy, there was no question of even parliamentary democracy striking roots in Pakistan. The down-trodden Muslim masses like the poor peasantry, semi-starving urban artisans and weavers had never participated in the agitation for Pakistan and so there was no question of Muslim League acquiring a mass character or committing itself to a truely democratic form of government. Thus Pakistan remained predominantly feudal. Tariq Ali says: "Pakistan was a largely agricultural country at the time of partition, and inherited from the British a feudal, colonial economy...A large proportion of the population lived on the land, where agriculture was dominated by feudal property relations. The land was tilled in the most primitive manner by peasants who were exploited by cruel and tyrannical landlords.

[18a]Some significant changes have taken place in the countries like Afghanistan, South Yemen, Algeria etc. since this book was first published. We will throw some light on this in the post script.

Six thousand landlords in West Pakistan owned more land than the 3.3 million peasant households."[19]

The big landlords were not seriously interested in industrialization and social transformation. What A. Abdel-Malek says in the context of Egypt is equally true of Pakistan after independence. Abdel-Malek sees as being formed in Egypt between the last years of Mohammad Ali (who died in 1849) and the revolution of 1952 a "capitalism of a colonial type, backward, predominantly agrarian, heavily tinged with practices inherited from the feudal past."[20] Pakistan until today has not been able to create a sound base for industrialization. It is for this reason that no serious pressure could develop for social change in the Pakistani society. In a backward society like Pakistan only a few belonging to the upper classes draw benefits of modern technological change. Only they have access to modern education and are initiated into the realm of modern thought. The large masses of people remain untouched by this process. The concept of new morality cannot, therefore, appeal to them. James Joll writing about Gramsci says, "When we succeed in introducing a new morality in conformity with a new conception of the world, we end up by introducing that conception of the world too, so that an entire reform of philosophy is brought about."[21] However, the Pakistani ruling elite is far from introducing a new conception of the world. Anything new has to be on a new social base, in a mundane history, not merely in the form of an idea. To use Bakunin's words we have to create "not only the ideas but also the facts of the future."

Any change has to be rooted in the social base and its movement. No analysis ignoring the concrete historical base of the society can lead to proper conclusions. Marx has pointed out that the real movement of society is a movement *in* its base and not merely *on* its base. In Pakistani society there has hardly been real movement in the base of the society since independence. As the feudal class has dominated it all along in collusion with the military and bureaucracy, one could hardly expect any meaningful change in its base. Even for meaningful democracy to strike roots it is necessary that a strong and determined bourgeois class should emerge in the society. But until today the bourgeois class is a weak and junior partner in the Pakistani power structure. How can such a weak class initiate bold

[19]Tariq Ali *Pakistan—Military Rule or People's Power*, Jonathan Cape, 1970, p. 37.

[20]See Maxime Rodinson, *Islam and Capitalism*, Allen Lane, 1974 p. 131.

[21]James Joll *Gramsci*, Fontana Modern Masters, ed. Frank Kermode, 1977, p. 99.

modern reforms? A senior journalist from Pakistan told me that no industrial house in Pakistan so much as owns a major daily. Unless rapid industrialization takes place it will be very difficult to create pressure from below for modern changes to become acceptable. Feudal outlook and values reign supreme in Pakistan for lack of such a viable base.

Gramsci has made an interesting distinction between the traditional intellectuals and organic intellectuals. According to him the Christian priests are traditional intellectuals and those who are the product of the new revolutionary society and are in turn leading it can be called organic intellectuals as they have organically grown from it. As the process or change in Pakistan is painfully slow, '*ulama*, the traditional intellectuals, dominate the social scene. The organic intellectuals i.e. those who are the product of the new society are numerically weak and consequently subdued. They have not been able to provide a bold leadership to liberate the nation from the archaic leadership of the 'ulama who are, as if, breathing down the neck of the Pakistani nation.

Industrialization in Pakistan, as pointed out earlier, has been painfully slow. This retarded process has kept the old feudal social structure more or less intact. The powerful landlord lobby did not permit the Pakistani government even to carry out meaningful land-reforms. It was only during Ayub's regime that some half-hearted measures were taken in that direction when it was found that without such reforms it was not possible to introduce new agricultural technology based on capitalist farming to improve the dismally low agricultural production. However, these measures did not go very far as the landlord lobby was far too powerful. Even Bhutto who was modern in outlook and wanted to sincerely bring about structural changes in Pakistani economy in order to strengthen the bourgeois class found it extremely difficult to carry out the land reforms. It was reported in the Pakistani press that even during the Bhutto regime there were private prisons maintained by the big landlords of Sindh and Baluchistan.

In such a society it is not surprising that past-oriented 'ulama and medievalistic religion play a dominant role. Islam's fundamental value-structure heavily weighted in favour of equality was the product of re-feudal partly tribal and partly mercantile society. In Pakistan which is yet to emerge out of feudal era these values do not count for much. What passes for Islam is nothing but archaic, superstitious and irrational religious practices perpetrated by the traditional 'ulama. The vested interests in the Pakistani society collaborate with these elements and thus become a powerful force. This powerful combine militate against any meaningful social change. It is difficult even for a bourgeois *weltanschauung* to develop in such a society.

Jama'at-e-Islami has been systematically propagating its medieval beliefs as the only acceptable form of Islam for over three decades in Pakistan. During this period it has succeeded in creating a well-disciplined cadre which has been strongly conditioned to accepting Maulana Maududi's teachings (as discussed in the last chapter) without questioning his assumptions. For the followers of the Jama'at, the Maulana's teachings are as sacred as the holy Quran itself. A section of Pakistani intelligentsia has also been lured by the Jama'at. In a backward society like Pakistan it is not very difficult to convince at least a section of people especially the petit-bourgeois which suffers most in a backward economy that all their ills are due to westernization and the only solution lies in re-introducing the Islamic teachings. They are made to believe that the present moral degeneration has come about as a result of materialism of the west and its corrupting influences. Introduce, rigorously of course, the Islamic teachings and impose the Islamic *shari'ah* and lo and behold all the evils have disappeared.

Maulana Maududi's teachings are full of such naiveties. Although he has been acclaimed as the greatest thinker of Islam in Pakistan he totally lacks any sociological perspetive. He does not believe in searching for the roots of moral degeneration and corruption in the present socio-economic base and iniquitous distribution of the economic resources. He thinks that human behaviour can be controlled by imposing *ḥudūd allah* i.e. the divine limits and that the human character is autonomous and can be moulded in any desired direction without controlling or re-structuring the socio-economic base. He says "...These (divine) limits take the form of some regulations, some rules and some principles in every department of life which are necessary to maintain the equilibrium of the system in that department. The purpose of these (rules) is to impose limits on your freedom. Only within these limits you are permitted to make some subsidiary rules but you are not allowed to transgress these limits. If you transgress these limits the whole system of your life will be disrupted."[22] (Tr. from Urdu mine.)

It would be interesting to note the examples of this cited by Maududi in order to illustrate his point. He says: "Take man's economic life for

[22]Maududi *Islami Riyasat*, Islamic Publications, Lahore, 1974, pp. 132-33.

example. As far as this is concerned God has given right to personal property, has made *zakāt* obligatory, has prohibited interest, and also gambling and speculation, and has put restrictions on earning, accumulation and spending wealth and has thus imposed His limits on this sphere of man's activity. If a man organizes his economic activities within these limits then his personal liberty will be ensured on one hand and, on the other, there will be no class war and domination of one class over the other which begins with the tyrannical capitalism and ends with the dictatorship of the working class."[23] (Tr. mine). Thus one can very well see the naive understanding of socio-economic formations which Maududi displays in the above passage. He fails to understand the whole dynamics of the modern capitalist system and its fundamental structure. He thinks that 2.5 per cent *zakat* and imposition of the rules of inheritance will be a sufficient check for the concentration of wealth without tempering with the sacred right of private property which, according to the Maulana, is inviolable. The whole history of Islam has been negation of this. As we have seen in the second chapter some of the companions of the Prophet accumulated phenomenal wealth and this led to an explosive situation which ultimately erupted into a bloody civil war. By the end of the third caliph 'Uthman's period, the wealthy landlords had started indulging in all sorts of luxuries unknown in the Prophet's time. Right in Medina, the holy city of the Prophet, there sprang up number of centres where the wealthy patrons were entertained with music, wines and dancing belles. (See Chapter 2 for details. The value- system of Islam had suffered a severe set-back with the war of conquests which flooded Medina with wealth. Soon the pressures from the neo-rich built up for more concessions and 'Uthman, the third caliph, had to give in. With acquisition of the riches the classes began to form and the haves and have-nots—whether Maulana Maududi likes it or not—began to fight. We have already quoted from Dr Taha Husain of Egypt in this respect. In fact Dr Husain who considers the Islamic government during 'Umar's reign as a unique form of government which was most judicious and democratic had to admit that the excess of wealth brought about degeneration and corruption and gave rise to violent conflict during the reign of the third caliph 'Uthman.[24]

It amply proves that the root of social malaise and moral degeneration lies in mal-distribution of economic resources. If the right to personal or

[23] *Ibid.*, p. 133.
[24] Taha Husain F*itnat al-Kubrah*, vol.I. *op.cit.* The excerpts quoted in the second chapter prove this point and for this reason I have avoided repeating them here.

private property is upheld as inviolable it invariably results in the high degree of concentration of wealth—whatever the moral exhortations to the contrary even through the world of God—and this concentration leads to moral degeneration and corruption. It was on account of this high degree of concentration of wealth that the Prophet's own companions like Talhah, Zubayr, Mu-'awiyah and others who should have known his teachings better as they had lived with him, fell victims to bitter struggle for power and to preserve their personal possessions and privileges. It would only amount to rationalization and offering apologia on their behalf to maintain that they erred in their interpretation (*ijtihād*) of the events and thus got embroiled in the ensuing conflict. An objective historian who considers various aspects of a complex situation before arriving at any tenable conclusion would not be satisfied by any such simplistic explanation.

When the moral teachings of Islam failed to influence some of the highly reverred companions of the Prophet (there were some exceptions like 'Ali, 'Abd allah bin 'Umar, etc.) when the material conditions changed (as they could not resist temptation to possess more) and they were flooded with wealth, how others, centuries later and in greatly changed conditions, can be expected to mould their characters in keeping with the moral teachings of Islam? In fact without taking the relevant socio-economic factors into account one cannot successfully eliminate corruption or arrest the tendency to moral degeneration in the society. The history of Islam through Umayyad and Abbasid period does not present any inspiring and scintillating picture of truly moral society. Even the 30-year period of the rightly guided caliphs hailed as the truly Islamic period is not free of violent conflict and protest against corruption, nepotism and favouritism as already pointed out above. Mere moral teachings and exhortations, without introducing measures to ensure economic justice and equitable distribution of national resources, cannot bring about the desired change in the moral standards.

The orthodox proponents of Islamic state today be he Maududi, General-Zia-ul-Haq of Pakistan, King Khaled of Saudi Arabia or Ayatollah Khomeini of Iran, knowingly or unknowingly—more probably knowingly, try to assume deceptively simple position that it is the western materialism which has brought about moral degeneration and the things can be set right only if the provisions of Islamic *Shari'ah* are strictly enforced and religion and spiritualism become dominant in our life. A perceptive observer of human society can never agree with such naive assertions. While in any society integrity of human character and scrupulousness of conduct is a must, the same cannot be ensured without establishing an egalitarian and a just society. Vast differentials in income as they exist today in almost all the Islamic countries, are bound to lead to violent conflicts. Mere introduction of Islamic *Shari'ah* cannot eliminate class conflict as Maulana Maududi wants us to believe.

The orthodox 'Ulama throughout the Islamic world have taken the position that private property is sacrosanct in Islam and government cannot violate the Islamic right to property without violating the Islamic *Shari'ah*. In an Islamic conference held at Mecca in March 1976, the participants which included many prominent 'Ulama disapproved of nationalization. The *Times of India* reporter covering the conference wrote: "Islam, according to several speakers, did not approve of nationalization.[24A] It emphasized man's trusteeship of natural resources and of social and economic institutions. State intervention in their view should not extend beyond supervising the economic growth for realization of ideological objectives." (*Times of India*, 15 March 1976) The prejudice of the 'Ulama against tempering with the institution of private property is obvious. Mere government supervision, even control, as the experience of many underdeveloped countries show, cannot lead to distributive justice.

While the participants in the conference agreed that Islam emphasized the concept of welfare state with a democratic form, most of them, it is important to note, considered the matter too sensitive in view of the diversity of forms of governments in the contemporary Muslim societies. *The Times of India* correspondent M. Shamim, therefore, wrote that "the conference showed a great deal of political tact by refraining from making direct recommendations on this issue."[25] This is an eloquent comment on the sincerity of those who are advocating Islamic laws as the remedy for the ills of western materialism. In fact the so-called Islamic governments range from kingship to military dictatorship. The fact is that the rulers and ruling classes in these countries are using Islam as a convenient cover to perpetuate their family or personal rule which serves the interests of the rich in their respective countries. It is, therefore, not surprising that in none of these countries there is any trace of democracy. As we have seen in earlier chapters that although the Quran does not prescribe any particular form of govenment, the first Islamic government after the death of the

[24A]Though nationalization is not the panacea for all economic problems, it might become necessary in certain situations.

[25]*The Times of India*, Bombay, 15 March 1976, M. Shamim "Updating Islamic Economics."

Prophet was established on a democratic pattern and consultation with the people or at least with the important companions of the Prophet (*Shūra'*). *Shūra'* was considered as a fundamental obligation of the elected caliph. This was written in 1980 when Zia-al-Haq had usurped power through a military coup. Neither Pakistan nor Saudi Arabia today have any trace of democratic process although they claim to be Islamic governments. None of these governments are ready to adopt a radical type of democratic rule (except perhaps Libya, the only country in the contemporary Islamic world which has initiated an experiment for some form of people's participation on a restricted scale) which will be more in keeping with the Islamic form of government.

Saudi Arabia which is encouraging Islamic fundamentalism throughout the Islamic world and is spending millions of dollars on re-enforcing Islamic orthodoxy is anachronistic monarchy for which there is no sanction in Islam. It is for this reason that instead of welcoming the Islamic revolution in Iran which was taking place with the massive involvement of people, it was in a state of fear, even panic. In other circumstances one could even have expected Saudi support for such a movement. What lay behind the Saudi anxiety then was, of course, not the Islamic idology of Khomeini's movement but its purported revolutionary chacter (Khomeini's revolution has already turned sour as we shall see later) and its explosive potential. The Saudis were disturbed by its call for the spread of Khomeini's brand of "Islamic radicalism" (it did not turn out to be radical, of course) along with its rejection of the institution of monarchy, and its hostility to the West and to Western-oriented regimes. In the beginning the radical nature of the Iranian revolution had afforded it the ability to unite the extreme left and right. The Saudis feared that such a force could take root in Saudi Arabia where some factors at least can throw up similar challenges as the Shah of Iran was faced with. Corruption is stated to be wide-spread in Saudi Arabia, both in the upper- echelons of the regime and in the royal family. The scandal around 'Adnan Khashugi, who is alleged to have received bribes from the Lockheed aircraft company was widely talked about. It is also alleged that Khashugi was not the only one to benefit from these funds and that he had accomplices within the royal family.

Saudi Arabi too, like Iran during the Shah's regime, suffers from gross inequality, and immense wealth alongside poverty among a section of the Saudi people although, unlike Iran, the relatively small Saudi population, benefits relatively well as a whole from the oil wealth. The enormous amount of money flowing into Saudi Arabia lines the pockets of a very small percentage of the overall population. This enormous disparity, ostensibly perpetrated under the pretext of Islamic right to property, to say the least, is against the spirit of the Islamic value-system as discussed in the earlier part of this chapter. This has not only led to imbalances in the economy but has also encouraged corruption and moral deparavity among the wealthy Saudi families. Despite imposition of rigorous *Shari'ah* laws these wealthy families indulge in all conceivable luxuries including drinking and womanizing. Moreover, the Saudi rich go holidaying in Europe and freely indulge in what has been totally banned in Islam and, for which, the poorer sections of the Saudi population pay with life.

Saudi monarchy does not encourage people to involve themselves in the business of governing. Participation in the political process is limited to a privileged few who enjoy the benefits of office thanks to their family origin and ties and not through any form of election. Nothing has been done to change this in recent years. Crown Prince Fahd's promise to form a nominated consultative council (majlis-i-shura) is hardly a revolutionary gesture. This promise to set-up the Majlis, with limited powers, is yet to be fulfilled. Steps are still being taken in that direction. This picture of relative stagnation in the structure of the Saudi regime may very well already have aroused wide-spread, but unspoken oppostion....Thus we see that Saudi Arabia may talk of Islamic fundamentalism but cannot accept any radical form of Islamic government which would be more democratic in form and work for cleaner and healthier society by re-distributing more justly (this is rightly claimed to be in keeping with the Islamic spirit) the national resources. The present Saudi regime is feudal rather than Islamic in spirit. In order to preserve statusquo the Saudi rulers are busy reinforcing the medieval Islamic orthodoxy (which is completely divested of its early revolutionary character) throughout the Islamic world.

In Pakistan too, General Zia-ul-Haq, in order to perpetuate his dictatorship, tried to use the cover of Islam. The Jama'at-e-Islami, for its own political reasons, chose to support the military dictator, again under the cover of Islam. Zia-ul-Haq and the Jama'at had the backing of powerful vested interests who did not want to bring about any change in the social structure. Although various punishments prescribed by Islam are not the essence of Islam, Zia-ul-Haq, while declaring the beginning of Islamic era in Pakistan, chose these punishments like cutting off the hands of thieves, stoning adulturer or adulteress to death, flogging those found drinking etc. as the starting point as if, not equality and socio-economic justice, but these punishments (*'uqūbāt*) have top priority in Islam. As per this declaration hoarders, profiteers and speculators, who are real culprits would escape with light punishments but petty thieves and robbers will have their hands chopped off. Under the Islamic regime of Zia not only those who drink wine but journalists and workers have also been publicly flogged and humiliated. A common man in Pakistan knew then that the Islamic regime meant public flogging of those who upheld the right to freedom of expression and struggled for the betterment of workers' plight through trade-unions.

The introduction of the Islamic era did not mean better quality of life for the common people or re-distribution of the national resources in favour of the weaker sections of the society. It did not even mean end of corruption in administrative and law and order enforcement machinery. Salamat Ali[26] wrote in *Far Eastern Economic Review* after introduction of these punitive measures: "President Zia's collaborators in the government, the leaders of the six right-wing constituting the Pakistan National Alliance, have hailed the move as the beginning of a glorious era. Parties outside the government have not yet reacted officially, but the Tehrik-e- Istiqlal's Air Marshal Asghar Khan articulated mass reaction more explicitly by declaring that, irrespective of the proclamation by the government of an Islamic order, police stations were being auctioned off to the highest bidders among competing corrupt police officials. Although alchohol was banned in the bazars, it was being consumed in police stations." He also declared; "We shall not permit the fooling of the people through slogans, for we want something done about a situation where out of an abysmally low per capita income of $160 per annum, $ 40 is taken away by the government through taxes."[27]

General Zia and the rulers of his ilk in other Islamic countries were doing greatest disservice to the cause of Islam—if at all Islam meant more equitable and a just social order—by enforcing the punishments and relegating the Islamic values to the background. All, including the orthodox 'Ulama, tell us above all Islam stands for equality and justice. Then why an Islamic state is sought to be proclaimed by enforcing rules like cutting off hands for theft and publicly lashing for other petty offences

[26]Salamat Ali, for writing an honest account of the situation in Baluchistan in the Hong Kong based magazine, have been sentenced for one year's rigorous imprisonment by the military court. Zia's 'Islamic regime' is notorious for the suppression of basic freedoms.

[27]Salamat Ali, "Islamic Era in Pakistan," Far Eastern Economic Review, reproduced in *Times of India,* 9 March, 1979.

while maintaining complete silence about the most fundamental economic problems facing the exploited and downtrodden masses? Are these punishments the real essence or embodiment of Islam? Or are these punishments more central to the teachings of Islam than say its values like equality and social justice? If not, then why so much emphasis on enforcing these punishments at the cost of socio-economic justice? Does it not mean that the rulers of these countries are using Islam for their own political motives i.e. to perpetuate themselves in power, to maintain status quo, to defuse political crisis developing on account of inability to solve basic economic problems or some similar reason? Certainly a dictator like Zia had no moral right to enforce Islamic punishments when he himself had most blatantly violated the Islamic spirit of democracy by refusing to hold general elections on one or the other flimsy pretext. He was afraid of facing the masses precisely because he knew it well that the people of Pakistan had seen through his game and could no longer be fooled in the name of Islam.

General Zia did little to solve the people's problems. The Pakistani economy was then in a shambles with the rate of inflation running very high. The rate of inflation had touched a high of 50 per cent by the end of 1979. There was little progress on the industrial front and the number of unemployed was jumping up. In fact to achieve breakthrough on the industrial front structural changes in the form of radical land reforms was highly necessary which the status quoist ruler like Zia was not willing to carry out. In fact all the reports emanating from Pakistan and also personal interviews with those who came across the border to India unmistakably showed that Gen. Zia's 'Islamic socialism and his slogan *"Roti, Kapda aur Makan"* had aroused much more popular enthusiasm and he continued to be popular with the wokers and toiling masses until he was hanged and even after his death his popularity did not wane. Gerard Viratelle wrote in the *Guardian,* "Despite his 'feudal' origins and 'oriental' authoritarianism, the former premier was a politician with modern ideas and aware of contemporary political movements. He tried to introduce reforms and tone down some of the more crying inequalities. But Zia was *maintaining the status quo,* strengthening ownership rights and turning Islam into a state 'ideology'. Religion comes handy for providing the regime with a political content"emphasis supplied).[28] As Gerard Viratelle points out Bhutto became so popular only because he was the first politician in Pakistan to

[28]Gerard Viratelle, "Islamisation of Pakistan Repressive Measures" First Guardian, April 22, 1979.

have thought of the dire poverty of the people of Pakistan and to have initiated at least partial measures—if not far reaching—to reduce crying inequalities. That is why he became so popular with the people that Zia had to first eliminate him before thinking of holding elections. But he did not dare to hold elections even after that since it was widely known that the People's Party would win the elections, if held impartially. Gen. Zia, therefore, had to choose between rigging and reneging and he chose the latter course.

The fact that Bhutto's not very far reaching measures to give some social and economic justice to the poorest in Pakistan became so tremendously popular shows that the people are greatly suffering and are really thirsting for a change for the betterment of their lot. Though the people of Pakistan are highly orthodox and deeply religious Zia's Islamization did not arouse much enthusiasm. This is because the people knew that it is a fraud being pepetrated and that they will only get lashes in Zia's "Islamic regime." According to Viratelle on the economic front Gen. Zia had announced only two symbolic measures: "the elimination of interest on salary advances given to public service workers to buy a bicycle and on loans to minor civil servants to build their homes."[29] What a step to dispense Islamic justice! Let alone anything else the "Islamic regime" of Zia could not even take serious measures to relieve the poor peasant from the clutches of userers in the rural areas. The rate of lending was said to be as high as 100 per cent a year.[30] Interest in Islam, as everyone knows, is strictly prohibited. In fact some Islamic authorities maintain that it is not so much as commercial interest as usury which is banned by Islam as usury amounts to a crassest form of exploitation. It was for this reason that Muhammad 'Abduh, the liberal Grand Mufti of al-Azhar (d. 1905) allowed interest on postal savings deposits. While there was talk of eliminating interest from the banking system in the Islamic regime of Gen. Zia nothing worthwhile was done to save the poor peasants from the usurious extortions of the rural money-lenders who also in many cases happened to be landlords. This spoke volumes about the intentions of Zia.

Those who are bent upon giving priority to punitive measures in an Islamic state and those 'Ulama who back them ought not to be unaware of the fact that when the Prophet started preaching in Mecca, he began by denouncing the rich for accumulating wealth and neglecting the poor, the

[29] *Ibid.*
[30] *Ibid.*

orphans and the widows. In none of these verses of early Meccan period there is any prescription of penal measures for various crimes. Not that crimes were not being committed in Mecca at the time; but it was a question of priority. The Prophet of Islam was more disturbed by the sufferings of the poor and needy in his town than the crimes being committed in a society wherein the old tribal structure was fast crumbling and the new economic forces were engendering great disparities in income.

In a way an analogous situation exists in most of the Muslim countries as the feudal structure is making way for capitalist mode of production. But the ruling classes in these countries, unlike the Prophet in the early Meccan period, for the reasons explained above, do not accord priority to removing the economic disparities and are using Islam by proclaiming its penal measures to serve their own interests. These ruling classes are responsible, for their own reprehensible vested interests, for projecting a brutal image of Islam. Unless these priorities are completely reversed and distributive justice is given the priority it deserves, such an impression would persist. Those Muslim countries where emphasis is on distributive justice and where left of the centre policies are followed so as to correct imbalances in income, like Iraq, Syria, Algeria, South Yemen et. al. these penal measures have either been modified or are not accorded such priority.

Not that the peoples in these countries are in any sense less concerned with Islam. For example there were riots in Homs and Hama (Syria) in 1973 because the constitution adopted in 1973 did not single out Islam as the state religion (although it recognizes Islamic jurisprudence as a principal source of legislation).[31] Similarly in another left-wing state, Algeria, the popular strength of Islam was reflected in a letter—in 1976, during a period of intense public debate on the contents of the National Charter—from metal workers in which they complained that "Islam upto now has been distorted by the bourgeoisie, who have interpreted the sacred text, deforming both its contents and very essence on the pretext that religion supported their actions. The working masses have been duped. That is why we ask for the broadening of the teaching of the true, austere and militant Islam."[32] Islam in all these countries too is a great force to be recokoned with. Seen in a sociological perspective, it is not difficult to understand that in all backward countries religion, on the level of the masses, continues

[31]Anthony McDermott, "Islam's Revival: the tests ahead," Financial Times, 17-2-79.

[32]*Ibid.*

to hold sway. As such, it can become a vehicle of both—i.e. reactionaery or progressive policies. What form it assumes depends on who wields power—those who want to perpetuate the status quo or those who desire revolutionary change. In countries like Iran, Pakistan and Saudi Arabia the forces whose interest lay in preventing any change in socio- economic structure are in power and hence they suppress those teachings of Islam which have revolutionary potential and emphasize those which have lost their historical relevance.

There is another vital question which the protagonists of the Islamic state will have to answer in the light of Islamic teachings. Islam, like communism, believes in the world community of faithfuls and treats all faithfuls as equal. Islam, in other words, does not believe in modern nation states. If the Islamic teachings are to be strictly enforced, as the protagonists of Islamic state insist, geographical boundaries between various Islamic countries become meaningless. All the Muslims, seen from this point of view, should be allowed, subject of course to some reasonable restrictions, to freely settle in any Islamic country of his or her choice and be entitled to the citizenship of that country. Moreover, the affluent Islamic nations should not confine their wealth to their countries alone and should share it with the less fortunate ones if Islamic teachings have to have any meaning in this respect.

But, however, the reality in the contemporary Islamic world is just the opposite. The Islamic countries are not only divided into nation states but many of them are involved in bitter border disputes. What is worse, in some cases even a single country like Yemen, was divided into two i.e. North Yemen and South Yemen. No Muslim country allows the fellow-religionists from other Muslim countries to settle. Even the Palestinian refugees for whom the Arabs are justly fighting against Israel have not been accepted by other Arab countries as their full-fledged citizens. In most of the Arab countries, the Palestinian refugees are treated as aliens or non-citizens. For example in Kuwait there were 300,000 Palestinians constituting an important segment of its work force. But these palestinian Arabs were treated as foreigners by the government of Kuwait. They were thrown out of the country after the Gulf war in early 1991 and still cannot enter its territory, let alone living and earning livelyhood there. While the foreigners enjoy free medical care and other social services in Kuwait, they could not own land or share significantly in the wealth of this country. Kuwait citizenship is nearly impossible to obtain. Without it, the migrants are locked out of the economic benefits.[33] Even Saudi Arabia takes elaborate

[33]Youssef M. Ibrahim, "Kuwaiti race to build real economy," *The New York Times News Service, The Times of India*, 8 October 1979.

precautions to see that no pilgrim from any other country settles down after performing haj.

This clearly shows that no Islamic country—even as fundamentalist and militantly Islamic country as Saudi Arabia—is prepared to practice what is most proudly referred to as Islamic internationalism or brotherhood. Similarly no oil-rich Arab country is prepared to render substantial help to other poor Muslim countries. Whatever help has been rendered is extremely limited and with political strings. It will be interesting to cite here the instance of the fifth Islamic conference held in Kaula Lumpur in June 1974. Opening the conference, Prime Minister Abdul Razak bin Hussein urged the foreign ministers of the Muslim countries "to come out with concrete proposals that can be implemented rather than merely propounding grandiose plans that look impressive on paper but that will not get off the ground."[34] Commenting on the proceedings of the conference Sydney Schanberg of *New York Times* wrote, "...so far this gathering of 37 nations plus the Palestine Liberation Organisation, representing about 700 million Moslems, has been characterized by the loftiness of its rhetoric and the fuziness of its actual programme. Major projects--creation of an Islamic development bank, for one—have either been deferred to future meetings or have simply been lost in committees. That was what happened to the proposal for a compensation fund to be set-up by the Arab oil nations to aid poor countries suffering from the drastic increase in oil prices."[35]

The conference did not show much enthusiasm even for investing the surplus capital in the poorer Muslim countries. Thus a special correspondent of *New York Times* wrote from Kaula Lumpur, "The appeal made to them (i.e. the oil-rich countries) by Malaysia to invest in the Moslem world was duly incorporated in the final communique issued from Kaula Lumpur, but discussion in committees left no one in doubt that the bulk of the capital surplus will gravitate towards traditionl investments centres (i.e. European countries and America) for reasons of security. Whatever is left over may be used in the first instance within the Arab world, with the other Moslem countries coming last in the queue. Viewed against this background, it is scarcely surprising that the idea of an Islamic Economic Adjustment Fund to provide immediate succour to member states faced with grave balance of payments problems never got off the ground..."[36]

[34]Sydney Schanberg, "fifth Islamic Conference," *New York Times*, 25 June 1979.
[35]*Ibid.*
[36]*New York Times*, "Business before Solidarity," 19 July 1974.

Thus the richest Arab country like Saudi Arabia which otherwise advocates Islamic fundamentalism and solidarity of Muslim ummah (community) become quite cool when it comes to rendering substantial economic assistance to the poorer co-religionists in other Muslim countries. Again, it is for the protagonists of Islamic fundamentalism to explain what practical use is the Islamic brotherhood if it does not find expression in rendering assistance to the less fortunate Muslim brothers in other countries? If, according to the Prophet the whole earth belongs to God and hence equally to all the faithfuls why such bitter disputes for boundaries between various Muslim countries and why monopolization of natural resources like oil by a few Islamic countries only? Why, one may ask, the repeated efforts on the part of some Arab countries like Egypt and Syria and Iraq to unite could not succeed so far? In view of these concrete experiences one should not hesitate to come out of the ivory tower of theoretical teachings and accept the fact that socio-economic factors and political considerations play decisive part in shaping the operative policies. Theory and practice are closely inter-related and one cannot be isolated from the other. Theory undoubtedly influences policies but not without taking cognizance of objective conditions. Throughout Islamic history theory and practice have co-existed rather as autonomous spheres, the 'ulama and the rulers adopting permissive attitude towards each other. There has never been a serious attempt (except for a brief period at the beginning which resulted in failure as we have seen in the second chapter) to develop an Islamic praxis. The result was that the pivotal Islamic values like equality, brotherhood and justice remained confined to the spiritual domain and could not be concretely realized in the material domain.

It is unfortunate but true that the 'Ulama who are supposed to be the custodians of Islam have generally played reactionary role throughout the history of Islam. Anyone who tried to give a direction to the teachings of Islam which was more in keeping with its spirit (of equality and justice) found himself staunchly opposed by them. From M'utazalites in the Middle Ages down to the modernists in our own time, they have faced the same fate. Although sociologically this phenomenon can be explained (in a backward society dominated by peasantry, petty traders and artisans religion tends to be past oriented and stagnant) but the 'Ulama can hardly be exonerated from this charge and it does little credit to them that they adhere to the letter of Islamic teachings even if it injures its spirit. The most glaring example of it is their upholding the system of slavery until the end of last century. Slavery was abolished in the Muslim countries despite them and not because of them. The inspiration to abolish slavery came from the western countries and its cause was championed by the modernist Muslims. No 'Ulama are known to have launched crusade against it. They, at the most, tacitly approved its abolition. Although slavery was permitted by Islam it was not encouraged. It also tended to militate against the spirit of equality. But since it was permitted by Islam (abolition of slavery was probably thought to be an impractical measure at that time by the Prophet) the 'Ulama stuck to the letter of law and never showed courage of conviction to campaign for its abolition. Same is the case with other domains of Islamic law. The Muslim personal law (*Ahwal-i-shakhshiyyah*) was changed or various restrictions put over it in most of the Muslim countries despite opposition from 'ulama. Similarly the rulers in Islamic countries find ready support from the 'Ulama today for imposing Islamic penal code without any regards to the Islamic value-system. Throughout the twentieth century there has not been a single case of a prominent Muslim theologian devoting himself to the cause of social justice. In my opinion it is hardly enough to condemn the role of the Muslim clergy in our time. The role of clergy in Iran recently has been no different. We now propose to examine the developments in Iran.

The case of Iran

Though the clergy in Iran headed by Ayatollah Khomeini was leading a popular uprising against the Shah of Iran, its role, after the ouster of the Shah, has not been much different from that of othr 'Ulama in other Muslim countries. It would be quite interesting to examine in little detail the recent happenings in Iran.

Before we examine the developments in Iran a few general observations about the developments in the Middle-East after the boom in oil prices will not be out of place. It is a well-known fact that since the beginning of the nineteenth century the Muslim countries, after a prolonged period of stagnation and decay, came under the subjugation of western countries in one way or the other. For a people who had a glorious imperial past, this was nothing less than humiliation. What was worse the scheming western powers divided the Arab world in different countries and thus destroyed forever the semblance of unity between the Arabs in general. The Arab people were forced to accept the artificial divisions which were primarily in the interest of the Western powers like Britain, France, etc. Creation of the state of Israel, with the help of the western powers further embittered the feelings of the common people towards these western countries. The

Arab people also strongly resented arming to the teeth of Israel by the United States of America although the ruling classes of the countries like Saudi Arabia continued to depend upon the American support.

It is against this background that the emergence of Nasser should be viewed on the Arabian scene. The reactionary and feudal rulers of various Arabian countries had thoroughly discredited themselves in the eyes of the Arab masses due to their total subservience to the Western imperialist powers. Nasser, with his emphasis on Arab nationalism and his bold step of nationalizing the Suez Canal in the teeth of opposition from the Western powers gave a sense of pride to the Arabs. Nasser thus emerged as their hero and became symbol of their aspirations. Nasser's political vision was dreaded by the feudal rulers of Arabia as it aimed at demolishing the feudal social structure. The *Ikhwan al-Muslimin*, on the other hand, using the Islamic rhetoric, was trying to frustrate Nasser's progressive policies. *Ikhwan al-Muslimin* supported feudal interests in the garb of Islam whereas Nasser became the symbol of progress and dynamism. Despite its religious rhetorics *Ikhwan al-Muslimin's* following remained confined to a few whereas Nasser came to acquire tremendous popularity. As opposed to the slogan of Islamic unity raised by the Ikhwan, he talked of Arab unity and Arab nationalism which appealed more to the Arab masses and he emerged as the champion of their liberation from the yoke of western imperialism.

It would thus be seen that the people of Middle-East deeply resented their subjugation to western imperialism. Although Nasser, through some of his bold steps like nationalization of Suez Canal, aroused the aspirations of Arab masses, he could not successfully lead them against Israel which has been considered as the outpost of American imperialism by them. The defeat in 1967 Arab-Israel war caused great humiliation to the Arab world. The developments after the 1973 Arab-Israel war in which Israel for the first time suffered a partial defeat should be seen in this background. This war brought various oil producing countries together and, again, for the first time oil was used as a weapon by the Arabs in their struggle against the western countries. The realization that the countries of the west on whom they had been subjugated for long depend on their oil gave the Arab masses a new sense of pride. That the western countries can dance to their tune caused great jubiliation among them. This new sense of pride also reflected itself through Islam which, as far as the Arabs are concerned, is their national religion. The phenomenon of resurgence of Islam cannot be properly understood unless seen in this context.

The flow of oil revenues of the Middle-East has thrown up many complex problems for the ruling classes. What is happening in Iran cannot be properly understood without taking cognizance of this important aspect of the situation. Almost all the Islamic countries in this region are industrially and technologically quite backward. In fact industrial revolution has yet to take place in these countries. The state of backwardness of these countries can be gauged from the fact that Pakistan—itself industrially a backward country—is considered as industrially most advanced compared to them. Most of these countries, therefore, have feudal or semi-feudal social structure. The increased oil revenues in such societies get concentrated in a few hands and thus aggravate social tensions. Also, with ever increasing resources at their command, the ruling classes tend to import more and more western technology which brings about progressive change in the outlook of the people and creates a class of intelligentsia. This class develops greater social and political awareness and begins to assert its rights. Such democratic consciousness threatens the feudal or semi-feudal interests. And these interests, in order to perpetuate the status quo, reinforce the religious orthodoxy. This is possible to do so in backward societies. This syndrome can very well be observed today in the Islamic world.

The case of Iran happens to be specially illustrative in this respect. The increased oil revenues created unprecedented social pressures which ultimately led to the great turmoil thus destabilizing and overthrowing the Shah's rule. The income derieved from oil was extremely unevenly distributed and thus led to concentration of wealth in a few hands. This *nouveau riche* class indulged in ostentation and adopted western style of life. This vulgar ostentation of the super-rich was sought to be legitimized as modernism. A part of the oil revenue was also spent on industrialization by the Shah. The oil revenue was channeled through credit institutions fully controlled by the Shah's administration to the private enterpreneurs who established industries. Thus the new class of entrepreneurs remained totally subservient to the Shah. It could not become so independent as to put pressure on the regime to loosen the shackles of monarchy and create a modern bourgeois democratic state apparatus.

In order to meet the demands of industries and modern administration the governement had to provide facilities for modern education. Number of modern educational institutions were opened which led to creation of liberal intelligentsia with ever increasing degree of political awareness. Also, due to inadequacy of educational facilities within the country, a large number of students were sent abroad for higher education thus exposing them to the western democratic ideas and institutions. The students and liberal intelligentsia ultimately became instrumental in leading the massive movement against the highly repressive regime of the Shah. Thus we see that out of necessity the Shah's regime had to encourage industrialization on the one hand (in the long run the oil revenues would be exhausted and hence it was thought necessary to create an industrial base so as to make the economy independent of oil revenues within thirty years by which time the Iranian oil deposits were estimated to run out), and, modern education, on the other. This process created pressures for democratization and Shah resorted to more and more brutal repression (The Amnesty International Report on Iran had cited several cases of inhuman torture by the SAVAK i.e. the Shah's secret police organization). As we have seen that despite several setbacks the democratic movement could not be suppressed.

Now the question arises why the Shah, like the other Arab rulers, did not reinforce the religious orthodoxy in order to perpetuate status quo? One can as well argue that the Shah voluntarily and consciously chose a modern course as he wanted to modernize his country and thus did not resort to the easier course of strengthening the obscurantist forces in Iran.

Well, such a probability cannot be ruled out but it looks unlikely. There are other strong reasons which could better explain the Shah's compulsions and choices. Right from the beginning of the twentieth century there has been a long and tortuous history of conflict between the monarchy and the clergy. The clergy in Iran was in the forefront of many a struggle vis-a-vis monarchy in the past also. Fred Halliday writes, "A curious absence from official ideology (of the Shah's regime) is any substantial emphasis on Islam. The nationalist movement in the late nineteenth century was explicitly Islamic in content and was led by '*ulema*, but in the twentieth century the groups which espoused an outspoken Islamic policy have not been as important, and both Shahs have clashed with religious leaders by secularizing education and the law."[37] Both the Shahs thought of relegating the clergy to background by encouraging modernization and secularization. However, such a strategy cannot succeed in a backward country like Iran unless a comprehensive programme for industrialization, technological revolution, honest land reforms and thorough democratization is launched. In other words, as Marx put it, there should be movement *in* the base of history not only *on* its base.

[37] Fred Halliday, *Iran*—Dictatorship and Development, Penguin Books, 1979, pp. 60-61.

But this was far from the Shah's intention. His attempt at modernization was half-hearted and extremely superficial. The Shah was not at all prepared to take the process at its logical end. His programme or modernization was carefully controlled and guided. He did not want to run the risk of endangering the institution of monarchy. His programme of land reforms was hardly calculated to distribute land to the *khosh-nashin* (i.e. landless agricultural workers) but was aimed at weakening power of clergy by confiscating their landed estates on the one hand and one the other enabling the rich land-holders to go for capitalist farming by purchasing more and more agricultural land rendered surplus by the reforms. According to Halliday, "Hence, from the mid-1960s onwards there has been another trend in government policy, one designed to supersede individual ownership with large-scale farming. Phase three was, in part, a preparation for this new process which aimed above all to consolidate rural holdings. The new policy either encourages farmers to participate in the new state-run farming corporations, or displaces them through the private agricultural firms in which Iranian and foreign business interests are collaborating to apply capital-intensive techniques to the countryside."[38] Thus many who were earlier dependent on cultivation were thrown out of it and were forced to migrate to big cities and towns to swell the ranks of *lumpen proletariat* as inadequate industrialization could not absorb them all. Thus the land reforms created strong resentment both among the peasantry as well as the clergy.

Similarly industrialization too could not develop with full vigour as the Shah never allowed an independent bourgeois class to grow. Historically there was no strong bourgeoisie committed to industrialization in Iran; private capitalist activity was based on trade and centred in the bazar. The bourgeoisie brought in existence through the industrialization programme of the government remains dependent on state funds and state policies and so "it would be erroneous to see this bourgeoisie as analogous to those in India and Brazil since the latter have pursued dynamic industrialization policies."[39] Hudson Institute has very aptly described this situation. It says: "...the oil countries, Iran included, are actually fragile economies in the very earliest stages of national development. With their high new oil incomes they have the *opportunity* (emphasis in the original) to make great strides forward in developing their industries and carryin out social

[38] *Ibid.*, pp. 112-13.
[39] *Ibid.*, p. 151.

reforms. But even if they capitalize on this opportunity—and many, it is probable, will not—they are condemned to remain members of what the United Nations politely describes as the "less developed countries," for many years to come.[40]

Thus it can be seen that the so-called White Revolution launched by the Shah was far short of transforming the traditional economic base of Iran; it only succeeded in upsetting its balance causing untold hardships to the people of Iran except perhaps the top 10 per cent which had benefited from the oil boom. A Vanaik rightly points out, "the reality, however, is that the Shah's 'modernization' programme over two decades has created a deep-seated and long-term structural crisis in the economy. The current social and political upheaval in Iran has to be studied in that context in order to make sense."[41] What was worse, the Shah, as pointed out earlier, was not prepared to face the logical consequences of even the limited programme of modernization initiated by him. He sought to ruthlessly suppress the aspirations of the liberal intelligentsia which was the product of modernization. The Shah was not at all willing to transfer power to the popularly elected government.

The traditional bazar merchants were also adversely affected by the Shah's policies and the oil boom which triggered off inflationary pressures in the economy. Thus the peasantry, the clergy, the bazar community of merchants, the students and teachers and other sections of the liberal intelligentsia all raged against the Shah which ultimately led to his overthrow in the most ignominious way. Thus we see that the half-hearted measures for modernization without transforming the economic base of a backward society like that of Iran can create far more explosive problems than otherwise. In an industrially backward country like Iran the backward peasantry in the countryside and the petty-bourgeois traders and lumpen-proletariat in the urban areas are normally deeply conservative and can be more easily mobilized by the clergy. This is precisely what happened in Iran. The Shah's regime was identified with westernization and imposing measures opposed to the teachings of Islam. In fact the upper classes which had enjoyed the maximum benefits of the oil income indulged in highly ostentatious living and westernized life-style which included cabarets, movies full of sex and such other things which were repugnant to the

[40]Quoted by Fred Halliday, *Ibid*., p. 168 from *Iran, Oil Money and the Ambitions of a Nation*, Hudson Institute, Paris, 1974.

[41]A. Vanaik, " Behind the Crisis in Iran," *The Times of India*, 2 February 1979.

traditional morality. This, coupled with the economic hardships of the poor masses and gradual ruination of the petty bazar merchants, provided the right kind of setting for a revolt led by the clergy. Some sociologists have described such a situation as producing "authenticity-openness tension". Ayatollah Khomeini, like the Mahdi of Sudan led the revolt against the foreign cultural attack. Arnold Toynbee in his *Civilization on Trial* lists the Mahdi of Sudan among those in Islam who adopted "Zeolot" position when faced with the challenge of modern Western culture.[42] In this context Zeolotism is defined as "archaism evoked by foreign pressure" and the Zeolot is one who responds to foreign cultural attack by affirming his own tradition "with abnormally scrupulous exactitude."[43]

Ayatollah Khomeini, it can be said without the fear of being contradicted, is the recent version of the Mahdi of Sudan. He has adopted the Zeolot position as defined above as he has responded to the foreign cultural attack by resorting to his own traditions. When the Ayatollah had to lead struggle against the Shah he made a common cause with the liberals as well as the Marxist groups like the chirika-i-Fedayeen-i-Khalq and the Mojahidini-i-Khalq. The Tudeh Party (pro-Soviet Communist Party) also supported him. In view of the necessity of the support of the liberal and the leftists, the Ayatollah was projecting his image as rather moderate and the one who respected democracy and dissent. In those days when the massive revolt was shaping against the Shah in Iran Liz Thurgood, the Guardian Correspondent, had described Khomeini as a "reactionary—revolutionary" and not without justification. In those days he often said that an Iranian Islamic Republic would be based on "universal sufferage" with "the official shape and type of government being defined by the people." At that time he also maintained that women would be able to choose their activities, their destiny, as well as the kind of dress, provided they observe some guidelines. After the overthrow of the Shah, Khomeini became master of the situation and substantially changed his position on all these issues. We will throw some light on this little later.

It would not be out of place here to examine the political repercussions of the revolt led by the Ayatollah in other countries of the Middle-East. The Shah fully enjoyed American support and, like Israel, Iran had become

[42] Arnold Toynbee, *Civilization on Trial and the World and the West*, Bloom-ing-ton : Indiana University Press, 1964, p. 105.

[43] See International Journal of Middle East Studies, vol. 10, no. 2 May 1979, Cambridge University Press, "The Mahdi's Position in the Authenticity-Openness Tension."

an outpost of American imperialism in that region. The Shah had armed himself to the teeth with the help of the weapons supplied mainly by America and intended to play a role of *gendarme* in the area after the withdrawal of the British troops from that region. The conservative Arab states were happy and appreciated the role played by the Shah although his policies were pro-Israel. The Shah's troops even went into action to put down the Marxist rebellions of Dhofar—a region adjacent to the South Yemen. Thus the semi-feudal Sheikhdoms in the region looked upon the Shah as their protector. It was, therefore, quite natural that the overthrow of the Shah sent a shock-wave through the semi-feudal Arab world. Seen from the religious point of view the Arab countries should have welcomed the emergence of Khomeini as he stood for Islamic revivalism. However, whatever the abstract thinkers might say, in the world of concrete realities one finds it difficult to separate religion from political, social and economic considerations.

The fact is that the Arab Sheikhs and monarchs, depsite Khomeini's Islamic overtones, deeply resented his emergence. Ibrahim Yazdi, Iranian Deputy Prime Minister for Revolutionary Affairs said after the revolution, "I think a new era of Islamic struggle and a new Islamic awareness have been triggered by our revolution. From now on, all Islamic movements that were dormant or apologetic in their approach to change or action will come out in the open in the Muslim world."[44] It was this militant tone of the Iranian Islamic revolution which frightened the semi-feudal Arab rulers and monarchs. The Saudi regime which claims to be the most fundamentalist Islamic regime dreaded the Islamic revolution of Iran the most. Way back in 1971, Khomeini, in an interview to British magazine *Impact* given from his exile in Iraq had declared, the history of Islam is a history of struggle against the monarchy.[45] After the overthrow of the Shah one of the closest colleagues of Khomeini, Ayatollah Mahmoud Taleghani (he died a few months after the revolution) said in an interview with a Beirut magazine that a single family rules Saudi Arabia and "that cannot be considered as Islamic."[46]

The Khomeini regime, moreover, was welcomed by the Palestinians as it was anti-Israel and anti-America. In fact immediately after the Shah's overthrow andKhomeini's triumphant entry into Iran, Yaser Arafat visited

[44]See *Time's* Special issue "Islam—The Militant Revival," 16 April 1979, p. 29.

[45]Quoted by Dilip Mukerjee in his article, "Khomeini's Triumph in Iran," *The Times of India*, 21 February 1979.

[46]*Ibid.*

Iran to express his solidarity with his regime. The people of Iran accorded a rousing welcome to the Palestinian leader. However, it must also be said that according to the report carried by *Patriot* of Delhi, the Iranian papers ignored Arafat's statement that the Iranian revolution will pave the way for the liberation of this region. Despite his deep conservatism and religious fundamentalism, Khomeini has remained a staunch opponent of America and it is for this reason that the pro-Soviet Tudeh party continues to support him. The Soviet Union too, for this reason, has rather a soft corner for Khomeini. It is argued by those who take pro-Soviet line that Khomeini's religious orientation (despite its medieval and reactionary content) need not be subjected to harsh criticism as he is irreconciliably anti-American and anti-imperialist. It is argued by them that the Western media is overplaying Khomeini's religious fundamentalism while relegating equally strong fundamentalist tendencies of pro-American regimes like Saudi Arabia.

There is, no doubt, an element of truth in this. The Western media is not free of its political biases. That the religious fundamentalism of Saudi Arabia is being underplayed is also true. One cannot ignore the threat the Iranian mass movement led by Ayatollah Khomeini poses to the status quo in Middle-East countries. As already pointed out earlier, the Iranian revolution is still being dreaded by the ruling classes of many Arab countries. A comparison has also been sought to be drawn between Gandhi and Khomeini. It is argued that, like Ghandhi, Khomeini, although socially and religiously orthodox, is politically progressive as he is opposed to American imperialism and its subjugation of the various countries of the Middle-East. The analogy between Gandhi and Khomeini cannot be drawn too far. The situation in Iran immediately before and after the overthrow of the Shah was greatly different from the one prevailing then in India. It is pointed out that Mahatma Gandhi was deeply religious-- even obscurantist--but he most successfully fought the battle for Indian freedom and used religion as a weapon in this fight.

But, in my opinion, this analogy is being overdrawn. Gandhi was no doubt deeply religious and in view of its appeal to the masses he even used it in one way or the other in the struggle for Indian freedom but--and this must be emphasized—he did not aim at establishing a Hindu Rashtra. He had accepted in good faith the principle of secularism which was sheet-anchor of the Congress policy. He did talk of Ram Rajya but did not find it at variances with Nehru's socialism. Again, it must be noted that Gandhi not only accepted Nehru's socialism for building future India but also, realizing his irrelevance in running the business of government, stepped aside and asked Nehru to shoulder the responsibilities of running government and shaping state policies. But it is not so with Ayatollah Khomeini. Apparently the reins of government were entrusted to the Prime Minister Mahdi Bazargan and his cabinet but Bazargan and his cabinet did not exercise actual power. "Nominally!" wrote Nicholas Gage of *The New* York *Times* from Tehran, "there is one government in power, that of the premier, Mr Mehdi Bazargan. But the other central authority is the revolutionary committee—the advisers around Ayatollah Ruhollah Khomeini who seem to be making decision that often vary from those of Mr Bazargan's cabinet."[47]

Bazargan was a moderate man who agreed to run the government in Iran under the guidance of the Ayatollah and his revolutionary council. But soon he found it frustrating as, to his dismay, he discovered that he is virtually powerless even in running day to day administration. Naturally, therefore, he chose to resign. The revolutionary council headed by Khomeini took over the reigns of the government. In the history of Islam theologians have never wielded political power with the exception of the Fatimid and Zaidite Imams. The theologians were at best consulted by the caliphs in enforcing the religious decrees. It is the irony of history that in the technologically advanced age when it is becoming more and more specialized to run the complex affairs of government and administration the ʻulama in Iran led by ayatollah Khomeini could capture power. Iran continues to be in great turmoil and it would require considerable political skill to pull the country out of present chaos. The Ayatollah was still basking in the glory of having led successfully an anti-Shah movement and arousing passions in the name of religion.

Also, he could not formulate any blue-print for the future re- construction of Iranian economy and he remained discretely silent about the direction he wanted to give it. He did not open up beyond making some vague statements about Islamic justice and Islamic government. But this is not saying much. As we have seen in the first part of the book that Islamic government has no fixed and universal form unanimously accepted by all. It can mean anything to anyone. From monarchy to military dictatorship anything can go under its banner. In fact, in the Islamic world today it has become a favourite ploy of most of the rulers to declare their states as

[47]Nicholas Gage, "Power Vacuum in Tehran—too many authorities," *The New York Times News Service*, *Times of India*, 1 March 1979.

Islamic state by imposing the Islamic *shari'ah* which is easiest thing to do as it does not require unpalatable economic decisions nor does it necessitate to disturb the vested interests well entrenched in the society. After all publicly flogging a few drunkards from among the toiling masses and cutting off the palms of some thieves from among the poor classes lightens the burden of their Islamic conscience.

Ayatollah Khomeini, since he assumed power, could not make any far reaching declaration as far as the socio-economic goals are concerned. Immediately after assuming power, Khomeini had declared a 14-point political and social programme on 28 February 1979. This programme consisting of 14 points had only one point relating to economically weaker sections of the society. As per this point the country's under-privileged would be provided with free water and electricity. According to him the "measure would apply to all those who are destitute because of the former corrupted regime" and also hinted that it could later be extended to other social classes.[48] Well, such a measure could be termed as a welfare measure but certainly falls far short of any radical measure to ensure economic justice. The Ayatollah had told in an interview on French television that "there could be no other regime more just for the people than Islam."[49] But there has been no instance in the Muslim world today of concretizing the concept of Islamic justice. Khomeini's regime which insisted on calling itself a revolutionary Islamic regime took no concrete steps so far to justify this insistence. No revolutionary measures were announced. In this respect the so-called revolutionary regime of Khomeini was no different from other reactionary Islamic regimes.

The whole emphasis in the Islamic republic of Khomeini restricted to announcing traditional measures of Islamic *shari'ah.* Women have been asked to wear chador (traditional veil) whenever they appear publicly. Sexual crimes are also being punished by death. The more moderate Ayatollah Kazem Shariatmadari had assured Paul Lewis of the *New York Times* News Service that "Iran would not return to the Middle Ages if it became an Islamic republic." "Now take amputation, prescribed by the Quran for thieves," he continued briskly. "First, many conditions must be fulfilled. Then it is a more merciful punishment than the present Iranian law, which executes all armed robbers."[50] About the adulterers he said,

[48] *Times of India*, 2 March 1979.
[49] See *Times of India*, 7 April 1979.
[50] Paul Lewis, "A Moderate Ayatollah Speaks of New Iran," The *New York Times News Service*, *Times of India* 16 January 1979.

"Quranic law says adulterers should be stoned to death but then, Quranıc law also makes adultery hard to prove. You need four righteous witnesses."[51] But according to the newspaper reports number of persons have been shot dead for sexual crimes. Many prostitutes were also shot so much so that the son of Ayatollah Khomeini had to issue a public statement that shooting down prostitutes would not solve the probelem and that an attempt should be made to rehabilitate them. Thus there was potential danger of Iran relapsing into the medieval ages..

In his 14-point programme referred to above, Khomeini had said that free speech and freedom of press would be protected. But this assurance has been observed in breach. The freedom of press was suppressed. Even the liberal paper like *Ayendagan* was banned. The Islamic revolutionary guards have been attacking the offices belonging to the Tudeh Party and Mojahidin-i-Khalq (an Islamic left group) and other left groups. The newspapers belonging to these left groups were suppressed. He justified these measures by dubbing his opponents as American agents. To him even those young revolutionaries belonging to the two Marxist guerrilla groups were such agents, the people who made supreme sacrifies in their struggle against the Shah. Answering a question of an Italian journalist, Oriana Fallaci that the new Islamic government would guarantee freedom of thought and of expression for everyone, including communists and ethnic minorities, Khomeini said, "...You even presume that I should permit the plots of those who want to bring the country to anarchy and corruption--as though freedom of thought and of expression were freedom to plot and to corrupt. Therefore, in answer to your question, I say: For more than five months I tolerated—we tolerated—those *who did not think as we do*. They were free, absolutely free to do whatever they wanted. They fully enjoyed the freedom that was granted to them."

Continuing further Khomeini said, "I even invited the communists to have a dialogue with us. But in response they burned the wheat harvest, they burned the urns of the electoral offices and they reacted to our offer for a dialogue with fires and arms. In fact, they were the ones who stirred up the problems of the Kurds. Thus, we understood that they were taking advantage of our tolerance to sabotage us, that they did not want freedom but the licence to subvert, and we decided to stop them. And when we discovered that—urged on by the former regime and foreign forces—they were seeking out destruction with other plots and other means, we shut

[51]*Ibid.*

them up to avoid further problems."[52] In answering another question, the Ayatollah said that he banned the liberal daily *Ayandegan* because it "was part of the plot I mentioned. It had relations with the Zionists. It got ideas from them to do harm to the country. The same goes for all the newspapers that, through a phony opposition, tried to restore the old regime and to serve foreign interests. We shut them up because we know who they were and what they were after. And this is not contrary to freedom. This is done everywhere."[53]

From the answers he has given Khomeini's mind can be very well read. He is not only intolerant of opposition but he does not hesitate in the least to resort to the old trick of giving the dog a bad name and hanging him. He accuses his opponents of being plotters in collusion with the foreign powers specially the Zionists and American imperialists. He accuses them of wielding guns and burning electoral offices instead of responding to his invitations to talk. The rulers in power and specially the fascists have often used such flimsy accusations against their opponents to suppress them. If Khomeini had evidence of such plotting why did he not try them in the open court? I have myself gone through the several issues of *Ayandegan* published after the establishment of Khomeini's regime in Iran. It clearly gave, an impression of being a liberal paper and it was impossible to find in it the traces of what Khomeini was accusing them of. As for the communists replying with gun his invitation to talk was the gravest and most irresponsible charge being made by him. In fact the communists had made common cause with him not only before the overthrow of the Shah but continued to do so even after that. It is he who has been, a religious fanatic that he is, denouncing them as "sons of Satan," an epithet even the Saudi fundamentalists are not known to have used in their public statements against the communists. A careful study of the available literature and discussions with the supporters of the two Marxist guerrilla groups namely Mujahidin-i-Khalq and the Fedayeen-i-Khalq convincingly show that they were not sheer adventurists and were certainly not in a hurry to capture power. Though they were armed they showed considerable restraint in using them. Even when their offices were attacked and their rallies broken by the armed bands of the Islamic guards in Teheran and other places, they decided to lie low as they were fully aware of the

[52]Oriana Fallaci, "The Ayatollah Answers," The *New York Times*, reproduced in *The Times of India*, 18 November 1979.

[53]*Ibid.*

popularity Khomeini enjoyed with the large sections of the Iranian masses. It is sheer travesty of truth to accuse them of wielding guns. The fact is that the partisans of Khomeini, his Islamic guards were wielding guns and forcibly breaking up peaceful rallies of those belonging to opposition groups.

One of the pamphlets published by a group called *Puyan* which supports the Fedayeen-i-Khalq group says: 'The most glaring fact about the public declarations of Khomeini is that he does not use rational arguments to refute the theory of communism. He maintains that the "accursed" theory of communism needs no refutation. Khomeini, your only argument against communism is that the communists are the agents of Shah and agents of America. You also have said that one who does not have faith in *ghaib* (i.e. unseen) is not a human being at all. Khomeini, your false accusations against communists would not convince anyoene for a long time.'[54] It is thus clear that Khomeini was hurling accusations against his opponents for which he did not have any convincing evidence. By these accusations he was trying to provoke his followers against the leftists and minority nationalities like the Kurds by dubbing them as the enemies of religion, agents of Zionists, agents of the deposed Shah etc.

Khomeini's accusations against the communists appear to be quite hollow when one bears this fact in mind that despite his unrelieved orthodoxy, Russia was scrupulously avoiding to criticize him. Not only that the pro- Soviet Tudeh party was extending support to him and had taken the line that his anti-American stance was a blow to the world imperialism and that it would be tactically wrong to oppose his religious views, however orthodox they may be. Even the spokesman of the Iranian Socialist Workers Party—a Trotskyst group—Farhad Nouri in a CBC national radio interview when questioned if Khomeini will go the way Shah did, he maintained that "No. You have to understand that the present government came to power on the wave of the revolution. There are many advances made in Iran. It's not a regime like the Shah's that came to power as a result of a CIA coup supported by the United States government." He further maintained that "We don't want the image of the revolution damaged around the world and governments unfriendly to the Iranian revolution to use this to discredit the struggle the Iranian people have been involved in."[55] It is clear from these statements that the left in Iran had taken a pragmatic

[54] A cyclostyled pamphlet published by *Puyan* group in India.
[55] See Farhad Nouri's interview published in *Socialist Voice*, vol. 3, no. 13, 1 October 1979, Montreal.

line towards Khomeini and his Islamic regime. They were not plotting to overthrow him. The question then arises why Khomeini was trying to shut them up?

For the first five months after the overthrow of the Shah there was complete freedom in Iran. All the groups (barring the pro-Shah elements of course) were freely propagating their ideas irrespective of their political allegiance. The reports in the liberal daily *Ayandegan*[56] clearly show that even on radio and T.V. networks, leftist propaganda was permitted and some Marxist groups were well-entrenched among the employees of the Iranian Radio and T.V. These issues of *Ayandegan* also unmistakably point out how the aspirations of the Iranian masses were aroused by the revolution. The May-Day was celebrated with great fan-fare and lakhs of workers, students and others participated with great enthusiasm in the May-Day rallies. The people of Iran for the first time breathed free air and expected revolution to fulfill their aspirations. The left groups were propagating their ideas and programmes and thus putting pressure on the revolutionary government to take radical measures.

It was perhaps under pressure from the demonstrations of the aspiration of the common masses that even Khomeini was couching his declarations in rather radical terms. He was giving progressive interpretation to Islam. In one of his speeches in Qom as reported in *Ayandegan* he said, "In an Islamic government one should be afraid of oneself, not of the government. The God has promised that the weak will be triumphant over the powerful. The weak will assume the leadership over all. The God's promise will soon be fulfilled and the down-trodden will supplant the rich. In an Islamic republic there is no oppression and injustice, there are no poor and rich, everyone will have equal rights, in an Islamic republic all the layers of society, all religions, all races and communities will have equal rights..." (translation mine).

But as far as practical measures were concerned Khomeini did not go beyond his declarations. The left groups, on the other hand, were mounting propaganda pressure and egging him on to fulfill the aspirations of the people. The influence of left was increasing and Ayatollah Taleghani who was favourably disposed of towards left was becoming more and more

[56]The issues of *Ayendagan* for the first five months make a highly interesting reading. One gets a fairly good picture of what was going on in Iran immediately after the revolution and that how the masses of people were involved in the revolutionary upheaval and how their aspirations were aroused. I am thankful to the Iranian Students' Association in Poona for giving me the file of *Ayandegan*.

popular. When Taleghani left Tehran and went into hiding after his two sons who were members of the Mujahidin-i-Khalq group, there were massive demonstrations in his support. For Khomeini situation was taking a turn for the worse. The conservative patriarch decided to act. He issued decrees to strengthen his Islamic regime. Women were required to wear chador, music was banned and censorship clamped. The Ayatollah also decided to call a halt to the Kurdish movement. The Kurds became his target as, according to Farhad Nouri, "the revolution in Kurdistan had advanced more than in other places. There was democracy and freedom. The Kurds organised peasant councils to carry out the land distribution."[57] Peasant councils and workers' councils were not palatable to Khomeini as they gave more impetus to the revolutionary process.

Khomeini also began to assume more and more power. He also got the council of experts to pass the most controversial clause giving him authority to name armed forces' chiefs, declare war and veto candidates for the presidency. The council had earlier named him as Iran's supreme political and spiritual leader. The six-point constitutional article also empowered him to act as a head of the armed forces as well as to name the chiefs of the three services.[58] All this followed the death of Ayatollah Taleghani, who was highly popular and whose strength lay in spanning left and right. Dr Bazargan also greatly resented these amendments and according to Liz Thurgood of *Guardian* he accused the Moslem clergy of deceiving the country. According to the same report in *Guardian* Dr Bazargan stated bluntly that Islam was opposed to "imposed freedom, which is tantamount to slavery." He also said that a veil or scarf imposed on women by force (was) one hundred times worse than their wearing no veil at all.[59]

With the passage of time the process of Islamization assumed more and more serious proportions as the challenge of the left was increasing. So much so that Fred Haliday, in a report filed from Iran wrote, "One Azerbaijani poet I met went so far as to argue the daring thesis that events in Iran would mean 'the end of Islam', as popular revulsion against the akhunds (religious priests) led to a backlash in the months ahead."[60] For imposing curbs on women's liberation ridiculous propositions are being advanced. For example, Dr Ali Shariati, supposedly a theorist of a new

[57]See Farhad Nouri's interview, *op. cit.*
[58]See *Reuter's* report from Iran, 15 October, 1979.
[59]Liz Thurgood, *Guardian,* London, 17 September 1979.
[60]Fred Halliday, "Iran's Fascist Islam," *Sunday,* Calcutta, 7 October 1979.

enlightened Islam, argues in his *Ummat va Imamat* that woman's liberation is a plot by the western cosmetic monopolies to boost their exports to the third world.[61]

As for Khomeini's economic programme it was vague and resorts to rhetorics so as to appeal to the working class without scaring off the other allies of the Islamic movement. Fred Halliday wrote "...it would seem that despite the immense sums of money available from oil, the new regime has not brought tangible benefits to these people. Loans for housing of up to 12,000 (300,-000 Tomans) are available but only to those who can make a deposit of one-tenth this amount. The economic correspondent of one pro-Islamic paper told me that apart from providing electricity of under 100 Kilowatts free of charge nothing had been done to benefit the poor in the six months since Khomeini came to power. Meanwhile inflation runs at over 30 per cent."[62] Khomeini maintains in the interview with Oriana Fallaci that "Our revolution is only six months old. And it is a revolution that took place in a country that was eaten alive like a field of wheat infested with locusts. We are at the beginning of our road. What do you expect of a child that is six months old...."

It hardly needs to be said that revolutions, more often than not, occur in societies afflicted with poverty and misery as they occurred in Russia and China. Iran was comparatively better off at the time of revolutionary upheaval at the beginning of 1979. It has oil resorurces which puts it in a far more comfortable position. Khomeini by saying that our revolution is just six months old is evading the main issue. No one expects in such a short period that all problems would be solved. Even a left government cannot achieve such a miracle. But what is important is the direction in which the country was being led by Khomeini. The main emphasis of Khomeini's pronouncements was not economic justice and equitable distribution of the national wealth or establishing an egalitarian society. His Islamic rhetoric of working for the welfare of *mustad-'ifin* (the weak or deprived) was nothing but a confused amalgam of socialism and Islam and lacking any concrete programme. Such amalgam of religion and socialism or nationalism and socialism is often adopted by fascist parties or right wing populists. The main thrust of Khomeini, it is regrettable but true, is towards imposing, like other reactionary rulers in the Islamic world, conservative Islam with its emphasis on punitive measures rather than

[61] *Ibid.*
[62] *Ibid.*

social justice and democratic polity.

Thought the situation in Iran is highly explosive but it is difficult to predict what way the events would turn. Khomeini, it cannot be denied, still continues to enjoy great deal of popularity, specially among the conservative peasantry, petty traders, *lumpen proletariat* and a section of students. He has further sought to consolidate his position by playing up the issue of American hostages as anti-American feelings run high in Iran. Khomeini's anti-Americanism, it must be pointed out, is not directed so much against its capitalist enploitation as against its support to the Shah. Khomeini is taking advantage of these anti-American feelings of the crisis being faced by Iran is very acute indeed and Khomeini is as much responsible for precepitating it as any other agency. The traditional left represented by the Tudeh party, in keeping with the Soviet policy, has decided to support Khomeini and justifies this support on the grounds of his opposition to America. The new left as represented by the two guerrilla organizations, though not immature, is yet to acquire sufficient organizational experience and correct tactical line. The objective situation is as much ripe for socialist revolution as for fascist take-over or a military coup. Much will depend on human factor which cannot be underrated. The role of an individual is also quite important in history. In the current chaos in Iran what is certain is Khomeini's religious medievalism, whatever his rhetorical claims. Also, if he continues to remain in command, it will be restoration rather than revolution. No mistaking about Khomeini's choice.

Islamic State - A Postscript

The first edition of this book was published in 1980, much water has flown since down the ideplogical streams of the world. A reassessment of what was written specially in the last chapter i.e. "The Resurgence of Islam and Islamic State" is necessary. The other chapters i.e. from 1 to 5 are of historical nature and hence do not call for any revision or reassessment. Thus it was thought that after all that has happened since the book was published first, it would be necessary to write a post-script to the last chapter.

The major development in the late eighties was the collapse of the communist state in the former Soviet Union. It was, undoubtedly, an earth-shaking event. It, not only brought about disintegration of a great country which effectively countered the monopoly of power by America, another super-power, but also put question-mark on a great ideology which had given hopes to the millions of toiling poor throughout the world. Many people began to think whether a state machinery could be relied upon to control the greed for accmulation of wealth and dispence social justice. Also, it was found that ideological rhetoric was no guarantee for a clean state-machinery. The Soviet Government and bureaucracy was found as vulnarable to corruption as any other capitalist government. What was then the way out? Do we have to live with greed for private accumulation and corruption for ever or could any other form of ideological state like the Islamic state shows the way out? These are important questions. Whether they can be categorically answered or not is a different question. These questions are bothering a large number of people throughout the world accross ideological lines.

On political front too many changes have taken place in the Islamic world itself. The Afghanistan scene has totally changed. The left revolution has been defeated there too and the Islamic fundamentalists have taken over. Zia-ul-Haq who ushered in what he claimed to be an Islamic state is no more on the scene and in the recent elections the people of Pakistan have rejected the Jamaat-e-Islami and other fundamentalist parties clamouring to build a strong Islamic State. For them even Zia's efforts to consolidate the Islamic state were inadequate.

The West Asia or the near east, as the Americans prefer to call it, has also witnessed great changes. Ayatullah Khomeini is no more on the Iranian scene and there too many socio-political changes have taken place. There too the Islamic state of Khomeini's dream could not become a reality. In Algeria, on the other hand, the socialist revolution seems to have failed and the masses are flocking behind the Islamic militants having been disillusioned with socialism, they have turned supporters of Islam and feel the Islamic state is the panacea. In Egypt too, there is disillusionment with the present regime and the Islamic militants there have been able to win support at least of a section of the Egyptian people.

These developments need a deeper analysis. As pointed out before, mere ideological rhetoric, Islamic or otherwise, does not take us too far. It also does not enable us to grapple with the complex ground reality. An ideological formulation at best reflects our ideals and wishes. Morever, the reality is so complex that no ideological frame-work can hope to capture this complexity in its entirety. Whether is is a communist state or an Islamic state, it is essentially an ideological state. The ideologues try to sway the masses merely through their ideological rhetoric. They try to push all problems behind this rhetoric. But people's problems cannot be hidden too long. The hard realities of life have to be faced one day which defy all ideological frame-work.

Also, all ideological states tend to be authoritarian in essence. If ideological rigidity is shed and authoritarianism diluted, it cuts the very ground on which the authority stands and derives legitimacy from. The ideology is thus not allowed to be 'contaminated' with reality. However, this ideological purity does not help grapple with the complex reality and the result is further reinforcing the 'ideological authority'. Thus an ideological state tends to become more and more authoritarian. There is no escape from this viscious circle. Whenever the authority is relaxed it results in total ideological collapse as it happened in the case of Soviet Union. The Islamic states cannot be an exception.

Another dilemma of an ideological state also should be taken into account. Ideologies fear being rethought. If it is rethought the fear is that it would loose its authority and rigidity. The rigidity of an ideology empowers the ideologue. Any attempt to rethink erodes the authority of the ideologue. But the ideologue does not realise that in refusing to compromise he ultimately looses all the authority when the final collapse comes and the final collapse cannot be avoided indefinitely. The Muslim '*ulama*, the ideologues of Islam too, show this rigidity. They refuse to rethink the issues in Islamic *shari'ah* and many of these issues are closely related to enforcement of laws in an Islamic state. Thus the Islamic state too tends to become rigid on the one hand, and, authoritarian, on the other.

Here we would also try to throw some light on the causes of genesis of Islamic revival or reassertion. Firstly, the Islamic world, has been facing, like other third world countries, the challenge of western supremacy and imperialism. Various Islamic countries were humbled and they had to live with this humility in a state of helplessness. But things began to change after the second world war when many of these countries achieved independence. However, even then they could not completely break from their colonial past. It took a longer time for them to do so. However,with the oil revolution in early seventies they began to regain their religio- cultural pride and discover their pre-colonial past. There begins their Islamic assertion which, in certain cases, assumes militant form. Also, they become aware of their exploitation by the imperialist west. They intensely resent this exploitation. Politically this assertion is expressed either by turning to the left or to political Islam. Egypt under Nasser turned to the left and emphasised its Arab nationalism, rather than Islamic identity. South Yemen also turned to the left and Arab nationalism. However, the political scenario changed after a couple of decades. Egypt under Sadat gave up its left of the centre stance and drew close to America by following the open door (*infitah*) policy. Well, drawing close to America had its own risks for a Muslim country and soon Islamic opposition emerged which ultimately cost Sadat his life. The South Yemen also adopted a different course by merging with the North and compromising its left policies. Among the West Asian countries Libya and Iraq continue to confront America and have not compromised on this score. Iraq, of the two, has paid dearly for daring America. Iraq has also not fallen prey so far to Islamic extremism but of course Saddam Husain has ruthlessly suppressed the pro-Iranian Shi'ah opposition. President Gaddhafi has permitted what he calls basic democracy and successfully contained Islamic extremism. Saudi Arabia of course has continued to sustain monarchy in collusion with the orthodox '*ulama*. It has also not allowed Islamic militancy to emerge. When some militants captured Ka'aba, the holiest mosque in Mecca, they were killed inside by the commandoes, more than hundred of them grossly violating the shar'i provision not to shed blood inside Ka'aba. The Islamic extremists have not raised their head ever since in Saudi Arabia. Needless to say in Saudi Arabia too, no dissent is permitted at all. Any opposition to monarchy is ruthlessly put down. Saudis are politically aligned with America. The American army was allowed to invade Iraq from Saudi Arabia during the Gulf war. Though the Saudis follow extremely rigid Hanbali Islam - popularly known as Wahabi Islam - it finds no embarrasment in aligning itself with America and other countries of the west. The Islamic militants are totally opposed to any political alignment with the west. In fact they totally reject western political and cultural imperialism. They consider western culture as totally destructive of Islamic values. This is why the Saudi authorities suppress any signs of emergence of Islamic militancy. The Saudi Islam thus could be described as moderate but orthodox.

The developments in Iran are unique in their own way. We have already discussed in the preceeding chapter the developments in Iran. The Shah closely alinged himself with America. But unlike the monarchy in Saudi Arabia, it did not align itself with the '*ulama*' and also earned their wrath by forcibly imposing modernity from above. In fact the Shah took series of measures to displease the priesthood. Not only this he deprived them of their *wakf* properties. The lands attached to various religious establishments were confiscated to break the power of Shi'ah priesthood. It should be noted that the shi'ah priesthood is much more powerful than their Sunni counterparts. The Saudi monarchy has forged a strong alliance with the priesthood and has never done anything to break their power. It has maintained rigid orthodoxy, as explained above. Thus the Saudi monarchy remained safe and secure until today whereas the Iranian monarchy was pulverised by the angry priesthood. Thus it will be seen that earning displeasure of priesthood and imposing modernism from above has great political risks. The Shah could not survive wrath of Ayatullah Khomeini.

The Islamic revolution in Iran was certainly epoch making. It gave Muslims throughout the world a sense of pride and self-confidence. It was a systematic political revolution. It emphasised its sympathy with the weaker sections of the society. In fact Khomeini theorised that in the Quran there is constant confrontation between the *mustad'if in* (weaker sections) and the *mustakbirin* (the powerful and the arrogant) and that Allah is on the side of *mustad'if in*. He quoted, in his support, the verse (28:5) of the Quran which says, "And we desired to bestow a favour upon those who were deemed weak in the land, and to make them the leaders, and to make them the heirs, and to grant them power in the land..." Khomeini theorised that the third world countries were weak and they are being oppressed and exploited by America whom he described as "the Great Satan". Internally too, Khomeini's Islamic political discourse favoured the poor.

However, Khomeini either could not or did not do anything substantial to favour the poor after capturing political power except some symbolic acts like establishing Bunyad-i-Mustad'ifin (foundation for the weaker sections of the society) the capital for which came from the confiscated properties of the Shah who fled Iran. Except from formation of this Buniyad there were no signs of radical economic reforms favouring the poor. Khomeini's radical rhetoric did no translate itself into any concrete practical form. It did not go beyond words. Even formation of consumers' cooperatives did not meet with great succes. Ayatullah Mousavi who favoured land redistribution, greater government control of the economy, nationalisation of foreign trade, and fostering of cooperative sector, did not meet with any success. He was opposed by conservative parliamentarians and conservative clerics - as well as *bazar* leaders, who view the growth of consumer cooperatives (being set up at the government's behest in mosques, factories and other work places) as a threat to their own existence. They have the ear not only of the president Khamanei (the then president, A.E.) but of the decidedly conservative Guardians Council. (see Dilip Hero "Iran Today", *The Times of India*, 19th Feb..1986)

Khomeini was far more interested in the downfall of Saddam Husain of Iraq with whom he was at war than radical re-structuring of Iranian society. If at all, he took interest in the internal affairs, he talked of spread of Islam. He is reported to have said in a press interview, "The most important duty of high Iranian officials is to spread Islam, and the central task of the government is the *establishment of global Islamic state*." Addressing the Iranian people Khomeini also said that the high state officials' task is to continuously improve the manner of "conducting people's affairs" but they should not allow those affairs to take up so much of their time that they neglected the spread of Islam to the rest of the world. According to Khomeini the people of Iran had on numerous occasions shown they were ready to pay any price for the realisation of the "holy aim" so that the current economic difficulties should not worry Iran's officials. (*Times of India*, March 24, 1993).

This clearly shows the priorities of Khomeini. The holy Prophet of Islam never neglected economic difficulties of the poor, the widows, the orphans and the needy. He used to say that it is more meritorious to feed the poor, the orphans and widows than to pray whole night. For the Prophet the priority was removing hunger and for the Iranian leader it was "spread of Islam" even if it meant economic hardships for the people. The revolutionary movement during the Shah's time had produced fine intellectuals and Islamic theoreticians like Ayatullah Taleghani and Ali Shari'ati. They were extremely popular with the people of Iran. They envisioned a new Islamic Iran free of exploitation and oppression. However, they and their ideas were marginalised afer Khomeini successfully led the revolution. Khomeini was more interested in fighting with another Islamic country than radically restructuring the post-revolutionary Iranian economy. It is interesting to note that Khomeini's above statement came in the wake of serious economic problems in Iran. There was high rate of inflation and serious unemployment. The prices of some commodities had risen by 30 and 150 percent and unemployment rate was as high as 17 percent. Also, he was more interested in enforcing formal shari'ah measures than rethinking issues in the light of the contemporary experience. Thus their priority was to put women under *hijab* than according them their Islamic rights. Whenever the *Shari'ah* is enforced, it is women who suffer. And Khomeini's Iran proved to be no exception. Also, as long as Khomeini lived, there were no democratic freedoms. Perhaps it was more on account of extremely complex revolutionary situation and power-struggles between various groups of clergies than anything else. It is also true that Khomeini was not keen to introduce democratic freedoms in Iran.

Khomeini died in early June,1989. When Khomeini died there were several issues of urgent nature. These were, whether the effort to export the Islamic revolution should continue; should economic policy take a leftward tilt, leading to land reforms and the redistribution of the land to the tiller; with the nationalisation of the import-export trade, should economic assistance for Iran's post-war reconstruction be accepted from the West etc. These questions were being debated in Iran at the time. The clergy was divided into three groups: the radical, the pragmatic or moderate, and the conservative and traditionalists. In the last five years before the Imam Khomeini's death the pragmatists and the radicals together fought against the conservatives on economic, cultural and political issues, and won the ground. However, various economic issues like land reform, private ownership, foreign trade urban property and laws relating to workers. But there was no unanimity on these issues.

However, it should also be borne in mind that like other revolutionary leaders, Imam Khomeini also had a complex personality. When needed, he displayed radical postures too. For example, the radical children of the war had mobilised masses of people to fight at the front. Imam Khomeini favoured them. When the 'Ulama asked him for permission to preach in favour of the sanctity of private property as laid down in Islam, Imam Khomeini replied that by doing so they would discourage the young people, volunteering for martyrdom at the war front. He then said: I don't need you, the 'ulama, I need volunteers, who can go and fight. Imam Khomeini used the concept of *maslaha*, the best interests of the community, as the best principle for evaluating religious rulings. When the survival of the system is at stake, you can deviate from the Islamic principles and innovate. (See "Conflict between radicals and pragmatists", *Times of India,* 7th June, 1989).

As pointed out before there are no easy solutions for economic problems be it an Islamic state or a Marxist state. Economic logic often denies ideological logic. All states, ideological or otherwise, face serious economic problems in varying degrees. Naturally the Islamic revolution in Iran too failed to find easy solutions for its economic problems. Even one year after the death of Imam Khomeini, there were food riots in Tehran (in 1990). In one year the prices of basic commodities doubled. By then over half the work force was unemployed. Mr. Rafsanjani, a moderate, had then taken over as President (through direct elections based on adult franchise which goes to the credit of Iran) and he favoured market economy. But it was not easy for him to move in that direction as the radicals could veto his proposals.

The Islamic Republic of Iran today is hardly different from other Islamic countries. It is dogged with economic problems, it is riven with corruption and it can hardly be said to be morally superior to any other country. It is Islamic to the extent that there is prohibition there, there are some public performances of Islamic rituals and that women have to stick to certain dress code and of course there is interest-free banking. However, as pointed out before interest-free banking has hardly resolved economic problems Islam certainly provides a set of iedals to build upon but where can one find perfectly moral human beings to act upon these ideals. But the Islamic militants do not take human problem into account and feel that "Islam is the only solution". As pointed out earlier also,the ideology can certainly provide valuable guidelines and a frame-work of values, but *by itself* it can never become the "final solution".

Today Algeria is required to cope with the Islamic militancy. A few decades ago the people of Algeria had great hopes from the socialist system introduced there after independence from France in early sixties. However, it led only to authoritarianism, not to the promised goal of economic abundance and exploitation and corruption-free society. The ruling elite were seen by the masses as westernised and corrupt and completely alienated from the masses and their religious feelings. In Iran too, as we saw in the preceeding chapter, it was such feelings which led to overthrow of the Shah's regime. The only difference is that the Algerian rulers first permitted "democratic elections" and when they saw that the Islamic militants are winning, they backed out from their democratic commitment and enforced military rule.

It was not a sudden development in Algeria. Things were simmering below the surface for long. On 8th October, 1988 too, riots broke out in Algiers as well as elsewhere in the country. The army brought out tanks on the street and more than 170 persons were killed of which 115 people died in the capital and about 60 in other parts of the country. The interior minister El-Hadi Khediri had to say in his radio broadcaste, "Is this the answer to our problems? Is wrecking schools and buses and shops the answer to our problems"?, the minister said. (See *Times of India* October 9, 1988) The same report in *The Times of India* said, "Groups of Islamic militants ran through back streets shouting *Allahu Akbar* (god is great)... and troops fired automatic rifles to force the curfew violaters inside... Eyewitnesses reports sopke of protestors, thought to be Islamic fundamentalists, lying covered in blood in outdoor stairways near the central Didouche Mourad street." (*Ibid*). Algeria has been suffering from deeply entrenched corruption, censorship, and poverty. The country has been facing economic disaster and, due to absense of democracy, has no legitimate outlet for people's grievances. In fact, never before her independence from France in 1962, Algeria had witnessed uprising of such gravity as in October 1988. After twenty five years of its truimph over French imperialism, the great words of revolution seem to ring hollow and the FLN, the only political party in Algeria has run out of ideas. And of course, the October 1988 uprising was not the last one but begining of more violent upheavals. The militant Islam today enjoys much greater support than the so-called revolutionary regime. It is interesting to note that while the middle and upper-class elites support the military regime, the poorer masses support the Islamic militants. The poorer masses, sick of corruption think that Islam will provide the moral alternative. However, the Iranian experience speaks otherwise. Islamic regime cannot ensure cleaner and corruption-free politics. The Pakistani experience also has been no different. Zia-ul- Haq promised clean and accountable Islamic regime when he captured power after overthrowing Zulfiqar Ali Bhutto whom at that time Pakistani people perceived to be corrupt and authoritatrian. However, Zia's promise became a big joke as corruption increased by leaps and bounds during his regime. In fact there were serious accusations of involvement in the drug trafficking against some top military officials who also happened to be the close confidant of Zia. Zia, who hanged Mr. Bhutto for complicity in a murder, himself met with a violent death.

Egypt too, in recent years, has been facing the worst of the Islamic militancy. Egypt also is overpopulated and riddled with economic problems. These Islamic militants have been making violent attacks on foreign (read western) tourists. They think it is the contamination with the west which has brought about their woes and it is return to Islamic morality which will solve all the problems. In August, 1993 these militants even tried to kill the Egyptian interior minister. President Hosni Mubarak had appointed him (i.e. the interior minister) to tackle the Islamic militancy. The other fundamentalist organisation, The Ikhwan al-Muslimin looks quite moderate compared to these Islamic militants. Because of this extremist violence the Egyptian tourist industry has suffered serious set-back and its economic woes have increased.

In this connection it will be interesting to note that the Islamic militancy is assuming serious proportions only in those Islamic countries which are facing mass poverty, chronic shortages and breeding corruption. In other conservative Islamic countries which have small populations, rich petrolium resources, there is no such threat. We have already mentioned the Saudi Arabia in this connection. Other examples are Kuwait, Dubai and other Gulf countries. Same thing can be seen in Malaysia too. Initially the Malay population (generally known as *Bhumiputras*) also resorted to Islamic slogans but the Malaysian Government could successfully manage this problem by giving concessions to malays in government jobs, trade licenses etc. Thus for the present at least, there does not seem to be any immediate danger of Islamic militancy. Thus it will be seen that basically from Iran to Algeria and Pakistan to Malaysia Islamic fundamentalism has thrived on poverty and corruption not for love of Islam *per se*. Of course the Islamic militants would violently reject this proposition but it is clearly borne out by empirical observation.

MAIN INGREDIANTS OF ISLAMIC STATE

What are the basic constituents of Islamic state. It is claimed by the

Islamic theorists that once an Islamic state is established it would solve all economic problems and establish a moral and corruption-free society. They also maintain that the western influences have bred moral corruption in the Islamic societies and this moral corruption cannot be fought without posing serious challenge to the western cultural hegemony. For them western contamination has led to degenaration of Islamic countries. Their first attack therefore, is against the west and western culture. The Islamic fundamentalist also maintain that neither capitalism nor communism (or socialism) but Islamic economic prescriptions are the way out. But when it comes to concretely defining the Islamic economic prescriptions, all they are able to do is to talk about setting up interest-free banks and establishing the institution of *bait al-mal* on the basis of the Islamic system of *zakat*. These measure are undoubtedly fundamental to Islamic society but certainly they do not add up to solving modern economic problems which dog all the societies today. The modern economic problems are too complex to be solved only by setting up *bait al-mal* or interest- free banking.

There is no doubt that with the help of system of *zakat* and *bait al-mal* based on it, weaker sections of the society can be helped and the holy Quran has prescribed institution of *zakat* basically to help the weaker sections of the society but this system cannot help putting the whole economic system on a sound footing. It is one thing to set up a welfare state and something else to build a sound modern economy. Even interest- free banking cannot go too far in this regard. On the other hand, interest- free banking creates problems of its own in an inflationary economy. It is small depositors who would loose out and capitalist borrowers investing in high profit seeking areas who would gain tremendously thus leading to more intense exploitation. Also, a modern economy which has far reaching linkages with global economy, mainly based on interest, will find it difficult to transact business with other countries except on interest- based banking. But even if no such problems existed, interest-free banking by itself cannot solve other complex economic problems. The Islamic economists have yet to develop a comprehensive economic theory, concept of Islamic econometrics, areas of state interventions, and planning, avenues of employment creation and so on. In fact one has to develop the whole discipline of development economics in Islam. Few prescriptions would not do. Those who proclaim Islamic State have no such ideas. They merely feel satisfied by enforcing the *shari'ah* measures as evolved by the medieval jurists. In enforcing the *Shari'ah* also, emphasis is, more often than not, on *hudud* (punishment for certain crimes) and *ahwal-e-shakhsiyyah* (i.e. matters pertaining to personal laws) than anything else. And, if they go further, they abolish interest-based banking, apart from enforcing the system of *zakat.*

The Quran lays strong emphasis on social justice and equality both in social as well as economic sense. But the real problem is how to establish an economically just society that too on sound economic basis. Islam also exhorts Muslims to avoid consumerism and lead as simple a life as possible. In those days the Prophet proscribed gold and silk, symbols of consumerism then thus clearly condemning consumerism. The holy Quran also laid down that what is in excess of basic needs (*'afw*) should be given away for more needy in the society. The renowned Urdu poet Iqbal even saw traces of concept of Islamic communism in the Quranic doctrine of '*afw*'. However, no Islamic state that we know of in our times which lays emphasis on this Qiranic doctrine of '*afw*. The oil-rich states of the gulf are neck-deep in the quagmire of consumerism. There are hardly any signs of these states being liberated from such consumerism. In the Islamic world today either we have affluent societies like the Saudi Arabia and few other gulf countries or those dogged with problems of poverty like Egypt, the Sudan, the Yemen, Bangla Desh and others. These affluent societies cannot be strictly speaking true Islamic societies. They violate both the Quranic doctrine and the Prophet's *sunnah.* Thus there are no signs of Islamic economic theories having been evolved, let alone being practiced. Any Islamic economic theory will have to answer questions about permissible levels of consumption, rates of unemployment, removal of poverty, ways of controlling inflation in the absense of manipulation of rates of interest and other related questions. Whatever the economic theories, any Islamic state has to devote itself to create a just society wherein weaker sections of the society will be given top priority. The Quran repeatedly lays emphasis on taking care of weaker sections of the society which in those days included slaves, orphans, widows, needy and the poor. The Quranic concept of *ma'un* (commodities for the basic needs) also requires this. Unfortunately, no Islamic theorist, let alone the conservative *'ulama* are emphasising this.

Another important constituent of an Islamic state is the treatment of women. All conventional Islamic societies emphasise wearing of *hijab* and confining women either at home or in certain fields of activities. In fact conventional Islamic societies have been taking very constricted and paternalistic view of women and their rights. This is not in the true spirit of Islam. In fact Islam has accepted women as a legal entities and apart from certain biological functions, they are in no way different from men.

The Quran has also declared that their (i.e. women's) rights are equal to their duties (*wa lahunna mithlul ladhi 'alayhinna*). No Islamic society so far seems to be prepared to accept this revolutionary Quranic concept of sexual equality. The Islamic jurisprudence as evolved during the medieval period was weighted in favour of man though it is not strictly in keeping with the Quranic spirit. There is great deal of need, therefore, to rethink certain *ahkam* (injunctions) in order to bring closer to the spirit of the Quran. The great fourteenth century theologian Imam Ibn Taymiyyah has said that the *shar'i ahkam* should change in keeping with the time and time has come to review many shar'i ahkam in respect of women. This review has to be taken on the basis of the Quranic principles. The Islamic jurists (*fuqaha*) interpreted the Quranic injunctions in the light of ethos of their times and we have to interpret in the light of ethos of our times while the principles would remain intact. It is in this sense that Imam Taymiyyah says that the shar'i injunctions should change with the time. It is unfortunate that no jurist today campaigns for this reinterpretation for fear of being ignored or left out of the race. The great Islamic thinkers like Jamal al-Din Afghani, Muhammad 'Abduh, Rashid Rida and others who pleaded for change and rethinking have been totally ignored. The women's issues are of basic importance in modern society and no society can be meaningfully ordered without according proper place to women. Sexual justice in contemporary society is no less important than the social justice. The Islamic state will also have to cope up with this problem. The women will have to be given not only individual dignity but also equal opportunities in every field of life. No restrictions in this respect could be prescribed by the state. Such an approach would be quite in keeping with the Quranic doctrines. This has been summed up by the Quran in the words "For men is benifit of what they earn. And for women is the benefit of what they earn."(4:32). Here is the statement of the Quranic principle. The Quran does not restrict here field of activities for women. It only states a principle that she can earn and what she earns would belong to her and her only, not to anyone else, husband, brother or father. No specific field of earning has been specified. It is theologians and some other Islamic thinkers who prescribe certain restricted field of activities and then they are thought to be sacrosanct. It is not at all the Quranic prescription.

In the sphere of personal law too the Quranic intention is to accord women equal rights, be it marriage, divorce, property or custody of children. In fact in matters of inheritance too, she has been given half that of brother not because she has lesser right but because her maintenance is the duty of either her father or husband. In the event of her remaining unmarried, father can make special provision for her through will or *hibah*. Though some Islamic states have brought about changes in the *shar'i* laws, in no country she has earned equal rights. In my opinion a true Islamic state should accord equal status to women.

The third important constituent of the Islamic state is the treatment of non-Muslim minorities. It is often said that the non-Muslim minorities do not get equal treatment in Islamic state or Muslim countries. As far as the Quran and *sunnah* are concerned non-Muslim minorities are not to be treated as politically inferior. On the other hand, in those days when religious persecution was the norm, the holy Quran clearly stated that each community had its own rituals and they worship Allah accordingly and that the paradise is not the monopoly of any community. "And for every nation", the Quran states, "there is messenger. So when their messenger comes, the matter is decided between them with justice, and *they are not wronged.* (10:47) (emphasis added). Yet in another verse the holy book says, "And certainly we rtaised in every nation a messenger, saying: Serve Allah and shun the devil. Then of them was he whom Allah guided, and of them was he whose remaining in error was justly due." (16:36) Thus from these Quranic statements it would be seen that other religions are to be respected as Allah's messengers brought these religions to different nations and communities.

It was based on such Quranic statements and the Prophet's *sunnah* that the Islamic jurists - *fuqaha'* - developed the concept of *dhimmi* in respect of religious minorities. *Dhimmi* is derived from the Arabic word *dhimma* which means responsibility and *dhimmi* is one whose responsibility of well being is on the Muslim *ummah.* By any standard it was a revolutionary concept. Thus it was binding on the Islamic governments to protect the lives and properties of the *dhimmis.* No wonder than that the jews and Christians were appointed to the high office by the Islamic regimes. However, in those days there was no concept of democratic processes and electing the rulers through restricted or universal franchise and hence neither Muslims nor non-Muslims had such rights. A caliph was a religio-cum secular ruler and hence no non-Muslim could have aspired to that office. In those days even secular rulers could not be from other religious groups, let alone one discharging religious functions as well. Morever, we should not project our concepts and norms back into the past. It does not help in understanding those societies.

In the world of today democratic polity is the norm and we have to accordingly change our thinking in respect of religious minorities as well. Most of the governments today are elected on the basis of universal franchise and the elected rulers are not required to perform religious functions. The modern polity has separated the secular from religious. In no Islamic state today no elected ruler performs any religious functions. The non-Muslim minorities in Islamic State today should, therefore, be allowed to take part in the political processes without any discrimination at all in the political sphere. There is no need for the separate electorate too as provided for in pakistan during the Zia regime.

Also, the controversial *jaziyah* should no more be levied as the modern taxation system has no need for it. Even in those days *jaziyah* was not a symbol of discrimination or humiliation, but an alternate tax system as non-Muslims could not be expected to pay Islamic *Zakat*. Today such different tax systems are not needed for different religious groups at all.

We have laid down above three main constituents of an Islamic state. Any Muslim country which fulfills these criteria should be considered an Islamic state.

Conclusion

There is no fixed concept of an Islamic state—much less a divinely ordained one to be treated immutable. The Quran, as pointed out, elucidates a concept of society, not of a state. The theory of Islamic state, as we have seen in the preceding chapters, changed and conformed more to the concrete situations than to any *a priori* concept. In the matters of state the Prophet himself, as could be seen from the first two chapters, followed the most pragmatic course keeping in view the concrete situation, of course, often supported by revelations, but not always. The Prophet was head and shoulder above his companions in every respect. He was not only a law-giver but also a shrewd judge of events and persons. He successfully strove to unite various desperate groups and tribes of Arabs, nomadic as well as the sedentary—no mean achievement. As a great reformer he had to observe the time honoured policy of give and take. He gave more than he took but he did take.

There is deep imprint of the Arab traditions on many of his acts. A reformer and a prophet, however great, cannot completely transcend spatio- temporal frame within which he operates. His vision gets concretized through the norms and practices of his age. These norms and practices change with the process of development. But, for the faithfuls, these norms and practices acquire as much importance as the vision itself, quite often, even more. The immediate successors of the Prophet tried to follow, as scrupulously as they could, the norms and the practices of the Prophet—called *sunna—and with good reason as they lived in the same spatio- temporal frame. In the then contemporaneous situation the vision and the prophetic practices remained coterminous. The sunna* thus remained the only valid model.

The Prophet, inspired by his religious vision and within the limits of his situation, strove to establish a just society. W.C. Smith in his *Islam in Modern History* rightly maintains that "The Islamic enterprise has been the most serious and sustained endeavour ever put forward to implement justice among men; and until the rise of Marxism was also the largest and most ambitious. But within a few decades after the death of the Prophet, the events overwhelmed this ambitious endeavour. The vision was subordinated to the temporal events. Soon an Abu Dharr al-Ghifari had to protest--and stand persecution--to remind the Prophet's successors of the social justice the Prophet envisioned. A Husain had to court martyrdom to remind the '*ummah* (the Muslims community) of the Prophetic mission. But the logic of history is so convoluted that even Husain's martyrdom—although mourned to this day--could not restore the mission. The caliphate gave way to monarchy and the Islamic society to feudalism. Islam, which arose from the sands of Arabia as a religious vision and a politically revolutionary movement—providing a new concept of state in that world dominated by monarchy—soon, in fact within thirty years, got bogged down in feudalism. For almost over thirteen hundred years it stagnated with the exception of the part of the Abbasid period when, under the influence of the Greek thought, it produced number of brilliant scholars and philosophers. But with the decline of the Abbasid empire the orthodoxy gained the upper hand and ever since has remained supreme.

The confrontation with the west in the 19th century induced a sense of humiliation in the Muslims as they were politically subordinated and lost their hitherto unchallenged supremacy. Politically subjugated and technologically in the inferior position, they took pride in their past when they were masters of the world. This mainly took the form of apologetics and lost touch with the facts of life in the contemporary world. Of course, a few intellectuals did attempt a genuine synthesis but, surrounded by the backward Muslim masses all around, felt completely isolated. Though after the two world wars many Muslim countries got politically liberated they could not completely wrest themselves free from the economic clutches of imperialism. Like the other third world countries, these Muslim countries also remained predominantly raw-material producing countries and could not go much farther from the feudal era. In such a condition, when the economic base could not be thoroughly transformed, whatever changes took place remained superficial without organic roots in the society. Modernization meant nothing more than permissive western style of life for the upper classes numerically very weak whereas the masses of people, for lack of thorough industrialization, remained backward and extremely poor.

The oil revolution in the early seventies in such a situation created social tensions which in countries like Iran proved highly explosive. On the one hand it disturbed the traditional economic pattern of the society causing economic misery to such sections which hitherto had felt quite secure and, on the other hand, put great deal of material resources in the hands of a few who indulged in vulgar ostentation and imitated superficial western modernity. In an essentially backward society those who were immiserized were, naturally, driven to the fold of orthodoxy. Thus poverty, orthodoxy and backwardness on the one hand, and, superficial modernity which often assumes the form of vulgar ostentation of wealth on the other, has become the bane of the Islamic world today. The Islamic movement has been sought to be revived by the ruling classes in such conditions not as a revolutionary movement as often claimed but as a conservative movement to strengthen their position as such a revival reinforces loyalty to traditional authority. Such a revival also assumes the form of a strong reaction of the masses against superficial modernity which often takes the form of permissiveness and complete negation of traditional morality. This can be very well witnessed today in the countries in the Islamic world toeing the fundamentalist line, specially in Iran.

The situation in Iran was extremely complex. Ayatollah Khomeini was using Islam to reinforce his authority on one hand and to arouse anti-American feelings on the other in his struggle against the Shah. Some of his statements were so couched as to appear ideological in as much as he denounced American imperialism. But he was also wont to use highly loaded religious terms like the "Satanic power" for describing America. He also called the communists as "sons of Satan." It is certainly misnomer to call him a revolutionary if the word revolutionary is to be used in the modern political sense. On the whole he remains an arch conservative and his interpretation of Islam does not inspire any revolutionary overthrow of the present social order.

How does one explain the massive Islamic upheaval in Iran? Has it aroused the aspirations of the Muslim masses and is Islam going to play a really vital role in shaping their lives? It all depends how one looks at the problem. Ahmed Bahaeddin, who at present, edits a magazine in Kuwait and is one of the most influential political commentators in the Arab world feels that for the Arab world and Islamic peoples the Khomeini revolution was the most important happening of the century. It brought back to the Muslim masses, according to him, much of the trust in themselves which they had lost in recent decades. For him, it is a human and social revolution against repression and dictatorship, on the one hand, and against social abuse and corruption on the other.[1]

[1]See Peter Mansfield's article "Impact of Khomeini Revolution" published in *The Listener*, reproduced in *The Times of India*, 28 March 1979.

In a way what Ahmed Bahaeddin says is true. Not only that, to a great extent it also explains the enthusiastic participation of the people of Iran in the revolutionary upheaval against the Shah. But it is only one side of the story. Did the Iranian revolution led by Ayatullah Khomeini really liberated the people of Iran from dictatorship? And abuse of power and corruption? Well, the answer may not be simple. A revolutionary situation is usually extremely complex. One can hardly expect a truely democratic society when a society is facing upheaval. It takes long time after a revolutionary upheaval for democracy to strike roots. In Soviet Union it could not until the communist regime was overthrown. It has still not. Even Yeltsin is behaving like a dictator, though in the name of democracy. Khomeini also could not have been a democrat. In a revolutionary situation he had to function like a dictator and he did. He did not tolerate any opposition and ruthlessly crushed it. The new Islamic regime had to be absolutist in order to fight the remnants of the old society. Unfortunately, but not unusually, it also came with a heavy hand on the Mujahidin-e-Khalq, an Islamic revolutionary party. Also, though perhaps it was inevitable, it tried to impose conservative, rather than revolutionary Islam. The women too were put under *hijab* and strict dress code was enforced on them.

Though one should oppose western culture but one should not dub concepts like freedom of conscience, human and specially women's rights as western and hence denounced. This is what seems to have happened in Iran after the revolution. The Islamic societies today are not as primitive as they are thought to be by the proponents of this view although, admittedly, they are technologically backward. It is rigid interpretation rather than the true spirit of Islam which is responsible for the formal adherence to the provisions of *Shari'ah* as codified during the Middle Ages. Professor Badawi, Director of the Islamic Cultural Centre in London, also agrees that the divine law is not inflexible, it is the lawyers who are rigid.[2]

There have been more liberal interpretations which better conform to the spirit of our times. However traditional a society, loss of human life or limb for sexual crimes or theft would not be approved of. Neither are these measures thought to be essence of Islam. Only the apologists of orthodox Islam would talk of "different value-judgements" in order to justify such measures. A more rational and liberal interpreter of Islam would take psychological aspects of sexual diviations and socio-economic aspects of

[2] *Ibid.*, II part, The *Times of India*, 20 March 1979.

crimes like theft etc., into account. Even the Islamic scholars of Maulana Abul Kalam Azad's stature, as we have seen in an earlier chapter, maintain that it is *Dīn* (faith) which is immutable and not *Shari'ah* (jurisprudence) which, according to the Quranic verses, can vary as per spatio-temporal variations. Those who talk of "different value- judgements" prevailing in traditional Islamic societies should remember that what is strongly resented by the Muslim masses is total permissiveness and vulgar ostentation on the part of western elite and not human and rational values. When permissiveness and vulgar ostentation of wealth—which itself is direct result of unequal distribution of wealth—is equated with modernization, it causes strong revulsion among the people. The developments in Iran must also be seen in this light and also that the Iranian ruling classes were too closely integrated with America and hence the strong reaction against American imperialism.

What course of action is then to be followed? One thing is clear that religion has great potential and certainly cannot be ignored. What is needed is sincere commitment to the establishment of a just and egalitarian society free of exploitation and an interpretation of Islam conducive to the growth of such a society. The question is how and who will do it. Whether the ruling classes in the Muslim countries and the orthodox 'ulama who strictly follow formal legalism would permit such an interpretation of Islam. Are the Muslim rulers who are keen to proclaim an Islamic state sincerely committed to an Islamic vision of a just and egalitarian society? It is not so. It would be interesting to quote here what W.C. Smith says while comparing those committed to Islam with those committed to communism. He maintains that "...Marxism is theoretically materialist. The ensuing distinction from Islam is profound and crucial, that while communism may treat ideals as an instrument for attaining political power, Islam treats political power as an instruement for attaining ideals."[3] Also, commenting on communist leaders he says: "But the power in the massive movement has rested with men at the top who, apparently, have been not superficially but profoundly atheist, have actually repudiated truth and repudiated goodness. Except as instruments of power, these to them have been bourgeois delusions. These men, standing then at the top of a hierarchy rigidly controlling a party...They bow down to no higher authority."[4]

[3] W.C. Smith, *Islam in Modern History*, Mentor Book, 1957, p. 216, footnote-8.
[4] *Ibid.*, p. 187.

I am afraid, Prof. Smith is not entirely right. No doubt Marxism is theoretically materialist and philosophically rejects the concept of God. It is also true that the communists at times consider violence as a necessary means for achieving the right end. But it is not *always* true that (in some instances it may be) communism may treat ideals as an instrument for attaining political power nor is it necessarily true (though theoretically it may be so) that Islam has always been an instrument for attaining ideals. Whatever the ideals, and whatever the theoretical vision, power seeking men, finding their appeal among the people, can use them for their own ends. The history of Islam, I do not think, has been much different from the general pattern, in this respect. With few exceptions—and such exceptions would be found whatever the system, spiritual or materialist including communism--Islam, like any other religion or system of ideals, has been used by the ambitious rulers for their own ends. The history of Islam is an eloquent testimony, if any testimony is needed, to the fact that mere concept of submission to higher authority (i.e. God) does not ensure that the political power will be necessarily wielded for the attainment of ideals. Ultimately what counts is the sincerity of purpose of the persons wielding power. The communists or atheists do not necessarily disregard all ethical or moral considerations as they have no fear of any higher authority nor is it true that those who believe in higher authority necessarily put moral considerations before their own personal interests. Such a formulation is too simplistic and what is most surprising is that otherwise a profound scholar like W.C. Smith has accepted it.

Islam, the recent developments in the Islamic world, clearly point out, has great potential for enthusing a new sense of confidence among the Muslim masses to wage struggle against exploitation by the imperialist powers on the one hand and, against inequality, corruption and injustice perpetrated by the rulers at home, on the other. The massive upheaval in Iran was as much directed against American imperialism as against gross inequality corruption and permissiveness at home. Islam represents for the masses of people, it must be understood, the moral ideal and an instrument of righting the wrongs. But it must also be understood, by those who want to sincerely use Islam as an instrument of attaining ideals of equality and justice, and not mere power, as has been the case more often than not, that, in order to achieve this purpose, it is necessary to liberate Islam from the clutches of orthodoxy which has given it a medieval orientation and reinterpret its teachings so as to conform to its own fundamental values like equality and social justice.

To achieve this purpose Islam will also have to be liberated from strict legalism into which it has fallen and of which the power seeking Muslim rulers have been making maximum use as it suits them fine. It will have to be transformed into an instrument of struggle against imperialist domination and exploitation on the one hand, and, against pseudo-modernism which means nothing more than adopting unrestrained permissiveness and vulgar ostentation, on the other. Its teachings will have to be seen in deepr social context and interpreted so as to ensure economic justice (using any appropriate instrument like planning, nationalization, expropriation of unearned income through suitable taxation and even abolition, if necessary, of the untrammeled right to private property as it is not as fundamental to the teachings of Islam as social justice, whatever the 'ulama might say) and to conform to the facts of modern life. Revelation, as even the most orthodox 'ulama would agree, upholds the sanctity of truth and truth is as much temporal as transcendental and in its temporal aspect it is conformity to fact.

Islam, if it has to serve as a living faith, will have to emerge out of its medieval shell and conform to the facts of life today while at the same time serving as a transcendental truth and guide for future life. Islam is neither superstition nor mere legalism; practical rationalism and values are its basic constituents and it is these constituents which add great significance to this living faith. In this sense Islam is not against modernism. If interpreted in this broad frame, Islam can serve not only as an effective instrument of social justice in our era but can also provide a moral corrective to the purposeless growth and tendency to treat consumption as an end itself. What is required for such an interpretation is courage of conviction and a strong sense of commitment to human values. If it is Allah's will, and His command too, to create a healthy society here on earth by partaking of life, Muslims will have to take it as a serious project to build up such a society.

Islam has been, since the colonial days, a rallying point for the Muslims to fight against foreign domination and exploitation. Strong anti-Americanism of the Islamic revolution in Iran has proved this once again. The oil revolution in the Middle-East has created altogether a new situation. The oil-producing nations have formed their own organization and have acquired great deal of bargaining power vis-a-vis the western countries which has given a new sense of self-assurance to them. Islam now, therefore, needs to be used as a revolutionary force against internal enemies.[5] The Quran has repeatedly warned those who accumulate riches (at least in Meccan verses, if not in later period but 'Ulama do not consider these verses as having been superseded) that painful punishment awaits them and so there is every reason to treat those who do not heed these warnings as the enemies of Allah. The oil revolution brought torrent of wealth which has been concentrated in a few hands thus leading to explosive social tensions in those countries. Those who have monopolized this wealth should be declared as the enemies of Allah and Islamic revolution, with its moral vision of a just society, should inspire the soldiers of Allah to sieze their excess wealth and declare it as the property of *bait al-māl* (i.e. state treasury).

If the Islamic revolutionaries want to serve the Muslim masses and not the Muslim ruling classes they would have to "apply themselves," says Maxime Rodinson, "to drawing from the Quran and the Muslim tradition values that are applicable to the modern world, and in the first place to those strata of the modern world that call for the abolition of privilege and exploitation. This they would have to do not by seeking in the scriptures economic precepts and a social system that are not to be found there, and which could in any case only be unsuitable for modern conditions, but by drawing from them valid precepts of social morality, and accomplishing within the religious framework an organic synthesis (and not a juxtaposition) between traditional religious values and the humanist values which exalt (*inter alia*) economic construction the only way to ensure a worthwhile life for the members of the community."[6] What is happening in the Islamic world today is far from inspiring. Khomeini's Islamic revolution in Iran has proved as deceptive as that of Pakistan. It appears that the 'Ulama have thrown their lot with the perpetrators of status quo. Now it is for the Muslim intelligentsia to take lead. Will they prove any different? Though I am not very hopeful I wish I am proved wrong.

[5]Least I should be misunderstood let me explicitly state here that I am not maintaining that imperialism has lost its power or that exploitation by foreign powers has ceased. Far from it. I am only speaking in relative terms and trying to emphasize that the powerful vested interests nearer home also need to be attacked.

[6]Maxime Rodinson, *Islam and Capitalism*, Allen Lane, 1974, p.234.

Index